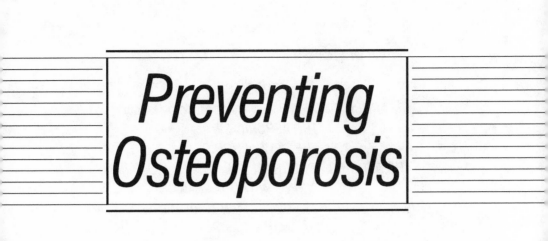

Preventing Osteoporosis

DR. KENNETH H. COOPER'S
PREVENTIVE MEDICINE PROGRAM

Preventing Osteoporosis

KENNETH H. COOPER, M.D., M.P.H.

BANTAM BOOKS
Toronto • New York • London • Sydney • Auckland

PREVENTING OSTEOPOROSIS
A Bantam Book / March 1989

NOTE
*Fitness, diet, and health are matters which
necessarily vary from individual to individual. Readers
should speak with their own doctor about their individual
needs before starting any diet program. Consulting one's
physician is especially important if one is on any
medication or is already under medical care for any illness.*

Library of Congress Cataloging-in-Publication Data

Cooper, Kenneth H.
  Preventing osteoporosis.   # 18463503

  Bibliography: p.
  Includes index.
  1. Osteoporosis—Prevention—Popular works.
I. Title.
RC931.073C66 1989   616.7'16   88-47826
  ISBN 0-553-05335-3

Published simultaneously in the United States and Canada

PRINTED IN THE UNITED STATES OF AMERICA

WAK   0 9 8 7 6 5 4 3 2 1

To my colleagues and staff at The Aerobics Center,
who faithfully and unselfishly work with our patients, diligently
conduct research, and always respond to my needs as
an author in an expedient, effective, and professional manner.

ACKNOWLEDGMENTS

In preparing a series of books on preventive medicine subjects as diverse as *Controlling Cholesterol* to *Preventing Osteoporosis*, it is necessary to utilize the knowledge and talents of many people.

Dr. Charles Pak, director of the Center for Mineral Metabolism and Clinical Research at the University of Texas Southwestern Medical Center, is one of the world's foremost authorities in the area of mineral metabolism and osteoporosis. His contributions, suggested reference material, and multiple reviews of the manuscript were essential to the preparation and publication of this book. His patience as well as his contributions were most appreciated in making this rather formidable project become a reality.

Again, William Proctor, my colleague in the preparation of this series on preventive medicine, contributed immensely to the manuscript. Bill has a unique ability to translate medical terminology into words and descriptions that are readily understandable. Coleen O'Shea, my editor at Bantam Books, continues to amaze me with her grasp of a multitude of subjects and her knowledge of what is necessary to ensure a readable and high-quality book. For over twenty years, Herbert Katz has reviewed and served as editorial consultant on all of my manuscripts, and *Preventing Osteoporosis* was no exception. Herb has become not only my literary agent and administrative and technical adviser, but also my patient and a trusted friend.

Cindy Kleckner, R.D., L.D., a highly trained and qualified member of the Cooper Clinic Nutrition Staff, designed all of the daily menus and recipes and provided the nutritional information included in the dietary section of this book. I am indebted not only to her but also to Brenda Reeves of the Nutrition Division and Cindy Savage of the Transcription Department for their preparation and typing of the recipes and menus.

Bill Grantham, director of The Aerobics Activity Center, developed the progressive age-adjusted weight training and calisthenics programs. He made his suggestions after carefully analyzing the needs and the capabilities of our Activity Center members, particularly those past 50 years of age. Karen Kaufman has provided some highly appropriate artwork for the exercise sections.

My secretary, Rachel Kahl-Meals, helped in a very supportive way with schedule adjustments, problem-solving, and organizing my time in a way that made authorship of this book a reality. Also, Cheri London, an occupational health consultant, has provided interesting and helpful information.

Finally, my wonderful family, including my wife, Millie, my daughter, Berkley, and my son, Tyler, have all been so very supportive, even though they know that another book means extensive traveling, long office hours, and time away from home. Even when I am at home, quality family time is limited. My hope and my prayer is that my family's sacrifice will eventually help tens of thousands, if not millions, of people to live longer, healthier, and more physically active lives. If that goal is reached, all of the Coopers will be pleased.

CONTENTS

Developing a Preventive Program

In the field of preventive medicine, concepts and ideas are in a state of perpetual change. During the past twenty years, I have found it necessary to change, modify, or correct some of my previous statements. For example, I used to say that exercise overcomes many if not all of the deleterious effects of diet. If a person exercised enough, I was less concerned about his or her excess body weight, cigarette smoking, or even diet. Now, however, I say that "there is nothing known to man totally protective against coronary artery disease, including medications, surgery, or marathon running." Exercise helps, but it is not a panacea for preventing medical problems including coronary artery disease or osteoporosis.

Just as we consider many coronary risk factors as precursors to heart disease, we must also consider the multiple risk factors associated with osteoporosis; and like heart disease, the problem begins early. Adequate calcium intake in the diet, sun exposure or vitamin D consumption, and weight-bearing exercise are most critical during the first thirty-five to forty years of a person's life.

This age issue is extremely important for women, since the bone density or peak bone mass they develop during the first thirty-five to forty years determines if osteoporosis or stress fractures will be a major problem. If strong, dense bones are developed early, the normal 8 to 10 percent loss in bone mass that occurs after thirty-five to forty years of age will not place them at a level close to their fracture threshold. This is why it is so important for young mothers, as well as postmenopausal women, to know the causes of osteoporosis and take corrective action before that first stress fracture occurs. Even with adequate calcium and vitamin D supplementation, weight-bearing exercise, and estrogen replacement therapy, the best that a postmenopausal woman can hope for is to stop further progression of the osteoporotic process. With some of the new medications now being studied, perhaps new and strong bone substance can be developed postmenopausally, but at this time that is not possible.

Another disturbing trend is the great interest in changing or restricting dairy products in the diet with the goal of lowering blood cholesterol levels. By controlling or eliminating one problem, though, we may be causing another. The elimination of milk and other dairy products may have a beneficial effect on reducing the problems associated with high cholesterol, but don't be guilty of "throwing the baby out with the bath water." As you will see in this book, 1,000 to 1,500 mg. of calcium daily is required for pre- and postmenopausal women, and 1,000 mg. is required for men. Studying the dietary intake of patients who come to our Cooper Clinic in Dallas, I've noticed that the average man or woman is consuming no more than 400 mg. of calcium per day! Unless this pattern changes or adequate supplementation is used, many people are destined for unnecessary osteoporotic problems in the future.

Even though 1,000 to 1,500 mg. of calcium daily seems excessive, it is not difficult to consume that amount. An 8 oz. glass of low-fat or skim milk contains 300 mg. of calcium and Hi-calcium or fortified milk contains 700 mg. per 8 oz. glass. A cup of plain low-fat yogurt contains about 400 mg. of calcium and if it is not possible to obtain adequate calcium in the diet, then supplementation in tablet form is available. Dietary calcium deficiencies should be rare since there are so many ways to increase the calcium intake in the diet.

Finally, it is not just postmenopausal women who are at risk. Admittedly, the instance of osteoporosis in men is considerably less than in women and occurs approximately ten years later. But men still have a problem in this area, and it gets worse as they grow older. So, as you can see, *Preventing Osteoporosis* is a subject that should interest both sexes and people of all ages. If the problem is to be controlled, prevention must begin early and continue throughout life—and it's my hope that the guidelines in this book will help the reader achieve that goal.

ONE

The Lifelong Battle in Your Bones

Although much has been written about osteoporosis, the pervasive bone-loss disease, a great deal remains unknown. The best way I know to start shedding more light on this problem, and also to introduce possible ways to prevent it, is to make these four basic points:

Point 1. Contrary to the public's perceptions, osteoporosis—a silent but potentially life-threatening disease that is now compromising the health of an estimated 24 million Americans—is *not* just a disease of the elderly. Nor is it a disease limited to women.

Who is at risk? Men, women, and children, at every age, including:

- Cigarette smokers

- Heavy users of alcohol

- Users of a variety of drugs, such as those in the steroid family

- Female runners, ballet dancers, and other endurance athletes

- Male marathoners who fail to consume sufficient calories

- Young people with eating disorders such as bulimia and anorexia nervosa

- Teenagers on junk food diets

- People who are allergic to dairy products

- Fair and slim women

- Postmenopausal women

- All men and women over age 65

Clearly, there is a wide range of individuals who are at risk for osteoporosis, and any comprehensive prevention program must take the needs of *all* these groups into account. That is one of the major objectives of this book.

Point 2. Even the most healthy and health-conscious Americans have trouble finding and maintaining a palatable or acceptable diet that is also rich in calcium—despite the fact that calcium is crucial to proper bone development and maintenance.

In the first place, some just fail to pursue a balanced nutrition program. Also, millions of people are "lactose intolerant"—that is, their systems react poorly to the sugars in dairy products. For them, eating a calcium-rich, high-lactose diet may result in extreme stomach and intestinal distress.

The good nutritional news here is that it's possible to formulate menus and put together tasty food combinations that will satisfy almost every dietary need—and build tough bones. Again, that's one of my objectives in this book.

Point 3. Calcium supplements and calcium-fortified foods and drinks have always been regarded with some suspicion because many feared that what the body took in would mostly get flushed out. But major breakthroughs in the research into and manufacture of supplements have opened up new possibilities for absorbing adequate calcium through these extradietary means.

Point 4. Increasingly, medical research is revealing that weight-bearing exercise helps to develop and maintain tough bones. So I've designed a completely new set of exercises intended to help you develop and maintain a strong skeletal structure.

Through proper diet, supplements, exercise, hormone treatments, and other means you can expect to toughen your bones to the maximum—and protect yourself from the onset of osteoporosis. In fact, in a nutshell, achieving tough bones is what this book is all about.

What Is Meant by Tough Bones?

Contrary to many popular notions, bone is dynamic, living tissue that is constantly being built up, hardened, and then broken down, normally over a four-month cycle. This continuous process is usually referred to as "remodeling."

At the beginning of the cycle, "builder" cells called "osteoblasts" form the matrix of the bone, called the "collagen." Then, a mineralization and calcification of collagen occurs, during which the bone is toughened to its maximum potential. This process takes place through the depositing of calcium and phosphate. Finally, a "demolition squad" of cells called "osteoclasts" breaks down the bone for "resorption" into the body, and the cycle is ready to begin again.

In the early years of our lives, this bone-formation process usually works quite well. To a large extent, it's automatic. All we have to do is pay attention to our diets—especially our calcium intake—and to keeping active and exercising regularly. With this kind of healthy living, bones will get more and more *dense*, and this density is the key to making them as strong and tough as they can be.

Even in later years, although bone inevitably gets less dense with age, diet and exercise remain staples of tough bone maintenance. Proper prevention can help you stay "tough" enough and avoid the dangers of osteoporosis—or excessive bone loss that produces a porous and brittle skeleton highly susceptible to fractures.

The key to getting the toughest possible bones early in life—and being in the strongest position to avoid osteoporosis later—is the achievement of what's known as "peak bone mass."

What Is Peak Bone Mass?

Most people reach their peak bone mass when they are between 25 and 40 years of age. During this period, all the bones of the body reach their maximum density—or greatest strength and toughness. Those skeletal areas likely to be fractured later in life, including the hip, the wrist, and the spine, get as strong as they'll ever get.

After we pass this peak bone mass age, and especially after about age 45, all the bones in the body begin to lose density. For most people, it's at this point that the biggest danger of osteoporosis begins.

It's certainly true that after that peak bone mass has been attained, good nutrition, exercise, and other preventive measures can be extremely important in reducing the rate and amount of bone loss. But your bones won't get any tougher than they were between ages 25 and 40. So, the more bone you have to work with at a younger age, the less danger you'll face of losing too much later through the devastating action of osteoporosis.

Dr. Charles Pak, a nationally recognized bone researcher and my chief consultant for this book, emphasizes that it's extremely important for even small children to be placed on programs designed to start them on the road to maximum peak bone mass. Dr. Pak—who is director of the Center for Mineral Metabolism and Clinical Research at the University of Texas Southwestern Medical Center in Dallas—also recommends that all young men and women in their twenties and thirties develop high-calcium diets. Furthermore, he believes they should pursue regular weight-bearing-exercise programs. Principles like these have provided the foundation for many of my practical preventive programs on diet, exercise, and drug therapy throughout this book.

Does Youth Protect You— and Age Condemn You?

As far as bone loss is concerned, it certainly helps to be young. But youth is by no means an absolute protection against osteoporosis. Consider for a moment the wide range of ages at which serious bone-loss disease may strike:

• Children on strict vegetarian diets have been found to suffer from bone weakening and even rickets, which involves bone deformities such as bow legs, funneling or depressing of the chest, and beaded ribs. (*The New York Times*, March 25, 1987.)

• Children and adolescents suffering from anorexia nervosa, bulimia, and other "socially upscale" eating disorders have reduced bone mass as a result of osteoporosis. (*New England Journal of Medicine*, April 11, 1985.)

• Children who avoid milk and other dairy products, or who concentrate on junk food rather than good nutrition, tend to develop less dense bones than other children and are at greater risk of suffering from bone disorders later in life. (*The New York Times*, March 25, 1987.)

• A 22-year-old male marathon runner got too little food for the amount of exercise he was performing—to the extent that he was diagnosed as having anorexia nervosa. As a result, his bone mass decreased, and he suffered stress fractures of the pelvis and the vertebrae. (*Journal of the American Medical Association*, July 18, 1986.)

• Amenorrhea, or the failure to menstruate, can significantly lower women's bone density. Furthermore, amenorrhea affects up to 50 percent of all competitive runners; 44 percent of ballet dancers; 35 percent of noncompetitive runners; and 12 percent of swimmers and cyclists.

A report of the *American Journal of Clinical Nutrition* concludes that "amenorrhea in young athletes could place them at a higher risk for clinical osteoporosis in later life." (June 1986, p. 910.)

For a variety of such reasons, the groundwork for osteoporosis is laid in youth, and then the disease develops slowly but inexorably as a person gets older. Finally, we begin to see these results among those who have passed their peak bone mass:

• Osteoporosis is responsible for at least 1.2 million bone fractures in the United States each year, with the vertebrae, the hip, and the forearm near the wrist being the most common sites. (*New England Journal of Medicine*, June 26, 1986.) Also, one-third of women over age 65 will eventually suffer from fractures of the vertebrae.

• Osteoporosis affects an incredible 15 to 20 million women who have gone through menopause. That's one-third of all postmenopausal females in the United States!

• By the time they reach old age, one-third of all women and one-sixth of all men will have had a hip fracture. Even more disturbing, these hip fractures are fatal 12 to 20 percent of the time. (*New England Journal of Medicine*, June 26, 1986.)

Many people of all ages, then, are at risk from skeletal disorders that cause porous, brittle bones. To top it all off, the medical costs of osteoporosis and related bone ills have been estimated at $6 billion to $9 billion annually now, and that figure will rise to between $7 and $10 billion a year by 1990. There seems little doubt that we're facing a health problem of epidemic proportions.

Youth certainly doesn't give you any magic shield against bone disease. Far from providing absolute protection, the groundwork for debilitating bone loss usually begins during those early years. But even if you've failed to lay the best foundation and to achieve your maximum peak bone mass, there's still hope.

In fact, most people can protect themselves quite effectively from osteoporosis and other skeletal disorders. As we'll see in later chapters, it's essential to take certain preventive steps to avoid the problem before it occurs. Or it may be necessary to move decisively to contain the disease after it's already caused damage. One of the first of these steps is to evaluate your level of risk.

Your Bone-Loss
Risk Factors Evaluation

A number of publications have listed risk factors for osteoporosis, such as being calcium-deficient, slim, fair-skinned, or postmenopausal. But I've gone one step further. With the help of Dr. Charles Pak, I've formulated a Bone-Loss Risk Factors Evaluation point system, which is explained in detail in chapter 2. This evaluation, which focuses on thirty important risk factors, will help you determine, in light of the latest research, the extent to which you may be at risk for osteoporosis.

You'll see that as you get older, your risk level inevitably increases. Women who have gone through menopause, for example, are automatically at higher risk for developing dangerous bone loss that affects the spine and causes such problems as dowager's hump. Also, the risk levels of both men and women over 70 are higher than those of younger people, simply because of the steady loss in bone density that accompanies advancing age. These older men and women are especially susceptible to fractures of the "long bones," such as those of the forearm near the wrist and those around the hip.

If after taking this Bone-Loss Risk Factors Evaluation you find that you're in one of the higher risk categories, you should stay in close touch with your physician and embark on a serious prevention program to toughen up your bones and ward off further dangerous loss in density. Sometimes, the preventive answer may be an increase in calcium consumption and more weight-bearing exercise. Or it may be estrogen replacement therapy. Or perhaps you'll elect to make use of all these, as well as other preventive steps. Whatever your decision, knowing your personal risk category will provide you with important information about where you stand physically and which preventive measures are advisable.

Other than the Bone-Loss Risk Factors Evaluation, is there anything more you can do to determine your level of risk for osteoporosis? In particular, are there more precise scientific tests that can show you exactly what condition your bones are in?

Unfortunately, at this point the Bone-Loss Risk Factors Evaluation is the best tool we have to evaluate those without symptoms—mainly because osteoporosis remains an extremely silent, though highly destructive, disease.

Osteoporosis: The Silent Destroyer

At the present, there really is no alternative to the Bone-Loss Risk Factors Evaluation—primarily because of the insidious "undercover" nature of osteoporosis. In fact, the very *definition* of osteoporosis is that it's a reduction in bone density that results in a clinical manifestation such as a broken bone. In other words, you often have to experience a fracture of some sort before your doctor can begin to help you combat the serious health problem you're confronting.

If you do have clinical manifestations, like a broken bone, certain scientific tests such as dual-photon asborptiometry may be used to determine your level of bone density. But without clinical signs, physicians are wary of relying on these tests to determine risk levels. Instead, they prefer to emphasize risk factors, such as those I've detailed in the evaluation in chapter 2.

Applying the risk factors to your personal situation as a kind of early warning system is essential to your health because you probably won't have any other indications of what's happening to your skeletal tissues until disaster strikes. Osteoporosis and its bone-destroying "relative" diseases are among the most silent, subtle enemies to your health—difficult to detect until the most devastating damage has been done. Then, the results of bone loss will become all too obvious.

When you reach the advanced stages of osteoporosis, in which fractures become common, there are far fewer promising measures you can take to repair damaged bone. But no matter where you are in the process of fighting this sneaky and deceptive bone deterioration, it is within your power to maximize your protection and minimize your risk—*if* you embark on a systematic, proven program of prevention.

The key to your future good health is learning to change your lifestyle and personal habits *now* so that you enhance the development of tough bones in your body. To this end, in the following pages you'll find a series of practical plans, beginning in childhood and continuing into old age, for building up your bones and protecting yourself from skeletal deterioration. Among the most important of these is a lifetime dietary program that I call the Tough Bone Diet Program.

What Is a Tough Bone Diet— and Must You Be on It Forever?

Throughout your life, no matter what other preventive measures you may employ, a solid, well-balanced diet averaging 1,000 to 1,500 mg.

of calcium per day is essential to building up and maintaining your bones. Therefore, I'll provide you with my Tough Bone Diet Program, a set of flexible, personalized daily menus devised for both men and women with varying nutritional needs.

Specifically, you'll find that the calcium and other nutrients you need for your bones have been included in a way that makes them "bioavailable," or usable by the body at all ages. Various studies have shown, for instance, that calcium is absorbed best into your system for use in bone formation if you ingest it in divided portions several times a day. With this in mind, our nutritionists have included calcium-rich snacks and supplements intended to be eaten between hours.

Also, we've taken into account the typical behavioral and biological traits of those at different age levels—such as the lactose intolerance common among older people. So, one set of diets emphasizes milk and dairy foods, while another focuses on nondairy sources of calcium and on the most effective calcium supplements. With the variety of foods and the possibility of exchanging various dishes according to our easy-to-use food exchange system, these diets will be effective for a lifetime as the basis for your food plans.

The diets, however, are only the beginning. They represent only one of a number of important principles and practical preventive techniques that we'll consider in the following pages.

Among the Questions We'll Consider . . .

The lifelong battle for the health of your bones must be waged on many fronts—depending on your most significant risk factors, your age, and a variety of other considerations. To give you the most powerful weapons for your preventive program, here are a few of the important questions we'll be considering:

Q: What exercise program should I be on?

A: An appropriate exercise program to build up and preserve solid bones. To this end, I've designed a special two-part approach: (1) an "aerobics answer" to bone deterioration and (2) a high-rapidity weight-training and calisthenics regimen. Using this two-pronged technique, you'll be able to increase your chances to promote bone development before you reach the peak bone mass period, and to protect yourself against bone loss after you pass the peak.

Q: Can estrogen replacement therapy help me?

A: Estrogen and other hormones and drugs can be quite effective in retarding bone loss for postmenopausal women and others in high-risk categories. So I've included an extensive explanation of how these drug and hormone treatments work, and how you can make use of them in your bone-protection program.

Here are some other common questions that will be answered in the upcoming chapters;

• What does it mean for calcium and other nutrients to be "bioavailable"?

• Why may vegetarian diets be dangerous to my bones?

• What do I need to know to make the best use of calcium supplements and calcium-fortified foods?

• What, if any, impact will caffeine have on my bones?

• What's the problem with alcohol?

• How can fiber be a two-edged sword for my health?

• Why will smoking put me at significantly greater risk for osteoporosis?

• What is the possibility of inheriting a tendency toward osteoporosis—and what can I do to neutralize or minimize this tendency?

• What's the best way to deal with potential bone problems in children?

• Is there a connection between osteoporosis and other diseases, such as rheumatoid arthritis?

• What are some ways that I can change my lifestyle, including my approach to sleep, posture, and lifting things, so as to lower my risk and reduce any pain I may be experiencing from bone deterioration?

Throughout this book—as with all the other volumes in my Preventive Medicine Program series—I'll be emphasizing practical self-help programs to enable you to analyze and deal personally with your health problems. Of course, I'm *not* recommending that you pursue self-help plans exclusively and ignore professional advice. In fact, you should always be in close touch with your physician and any medical specialists you need to advise you, to prescribe medicines, and to guide you in more healthful directions.

At the same time, however, I'm a firm believer in the principle that each person should have a clear idea about what's going on in his or her body—and about what needs to be done to correct existing problems or head off future trouble. It's only by becoming informed and aware of your health situation that you can ask the right questions and be in a position to take the initiative to make the necessary changes.

Now, let's take the first important step in winning the lifelong battle in your bones—a step that involves evaluating your personal risk for osteoporosis.

TWO

Are You at Risk for Serious Bone Loss?

Every one of us is at risk for serious bone loss. The reason? Nature has arranged steady reduction in bone density as a natural part of our development as human beings. And the risk of bone-related health problems increases geometrically as we get older.

Ages 35 to 45 is when the trouble usually begins. After this point, you have passed your peak bone mass period, when your bones have reached their greatest density and strength. Once the peak has been attained, more bone tends to be lost than is gained.

For some, the reduction in bone strength after that peak may occur gradually and may not move into any danger level. For many others, however, the deterioration of bone mass—and the ensuing development of a porous, brittle, easily breakable skeletal structure—can be highly dangerous and even potentially fatal.

Unfortunately, because osteoporosis is such a silent enemy, you may not find out you have it until significant damage has already been done. A smashed vertebra, severe and chronic back pain, or a fractured wrist or broken hip may be the first clinical manifestation. These fractures may occur without much trauma. By the time any of these "spontaneous" fractures develop, you may find that you're limited in the preventive measures you can take.

Is there any way to find out earlier, before the onset of the advanced stages of bone disease, that something is wrong? Or to put this another way, is it possible to calculate your risk of developing osteoporosis and related bone problems?

As we'll see in chapter 11, there are a number of ways of testing your bone density with highly sophisticated diagnostic equipment. But often these procedures are quite expensive. Also, they may not be able to give you a definitive reading on the status of your skeletal structure. As a result, these methods are usually reserved either for those who already are showing clear symptoms of the disease, or for those suspected of having a high risk of developing osteoporosis.

A better approach, if you are not yet showing any clear symptoms, is to evaluate your risk level in light of a number of factors that have been scientifically identified through extensive medical research. To this end—with the help of Dr. Charles Pak—I've formulated the following Bone-Loss Risk Factors Evaluation. This evaluation includes thirty factors that are known to place a person at high or low risk for osteoporosis.

To find out how you stand, read the explanations of all of these risk factors and decide which ones describe or apply to you. As you'll see, this evaluation has been divided into three separate sections: (1) factors that you *can* control; (2) factors that you *can't* control; and (3) factors that, with your physician's help, you *may* be able to control. Although many of these issues will be discussed in much more detail in later chapters, the brief explanations should be sufficient at this point to enable you to understand the basic meaning of each risk factor.

Finally, after each set of risk factors is a risk-factor point figure that has been assigned to the question. On a separate sheet of paper, write down the number of risk points that you receive for each risk factor. Then, at the end of the evaluation, I'll show you how to calculate your relative risk profile. In rating these risk factors, I've perhaps given a little more weight to those you can control, because it's most important to be aware of the factors you can do something about.

The Bone-Loss Risk Factors Evaluation

I. Risk Factors That Can Be Controlled

1. Smoking cigarettes
   _____ No (0 risk points)
   _____ Yes (4 risk points)

Explanation: Research has clearly established that cigarette smoking lowers the estrogen levels in women. Furthermore, women with lower estrogen levels—especially those who are postmenopausal, or roughly over 50 years of age—are at higher risk for developing osteoporosis. Also, smokers tend to be leaner than nonsmokers, and leanness is a separate risk factor associated with bone loss.

2. Drinking alcoholic beverages
   _____ No (0 risk points)

_____ 1–2 ounces a day (2 risk points)

_____ 3 or more ounces a day (4 risk points)

Explanation: Alcohol reduces bone formation—or what's known as the "osteoblastic" activity of bones. Every ounce of alcohol you drink has a negative impact on those cells that build up your bone structure.

One study reported in the December 1983 issue of the *American Journal of Medicine* noted that alcohol consumption, along with cigarette smoking, was a major factor in promoting osteoporosis in the spines of 105 men ranging in age from 44 to 85 years.

3. Avoidance of milk, cheese, and other dairy products in your diet

_____ No (0 risk points)

_____ Yes (3 risk points)

Explanation: Many people of all ages neglect to drink milk or consume other dairy products, which are our best sources of calcium. Young people may drink carbonated beverages and otherwise concentrate on junk foods, rather than nutritious, high-calcium dishes and drinks. Older people may see milk as a "kid's drink," or may never have developed a taste for yogurt or other dairy products.

Unfortunately, the act of choosing not to drink or eat foods that are high in calcium will prevent young people from reaching their peak bone mass before they reach the crucial age range of 25 to 40 years. Moreover, the failure of older people to include these dairy products in their diets means they'll be less able to ward off the loss of bone in later years.

4. Exercise

_____ Regular exercise (0 risk points)

_____ Little or none (3 risk points)

Explanation: Most experts believe that regular exercise—and especially exercise that causes your body to work against weight resistance or the force of gravity—will help build up your bones and also help prevent the loss of bone density after you've reached peak bone mass.

In general, it's necessary to pursue an exercise program at least twenty minutes a day, three to four days a week. Also, the exercise program should be accompanied by good nutrition, including the consumption of 1,000 to 1,500 mg. of calcium a day.

5. A female who exercises a great deal, with irregular or no menstruation

_____ No (0 risk points)

_____ Yes (4 risk points)

Explanation: Although it's important to get plenty of exercise to ensure that your bone mass will be protected to the maximum degree, it's also possible to go too far with your workouts. As indicated in chapter 1, female marathoners, ballet dancers, and others who exercise to the point where they stop having their periods may increase their risk of bone loss.

6. Eating disorder, or consumption of too little nutritious food
_____ No (0 risk points)
_____ Yes (4 risk points)

Explanation: Again, as I mentioned in chapter 1, both men and women with eating disorders, such as anorexia nervosa, bulimia, or generally poor nutritional habits, may experience the symptoms of osteoporosis at a relatively young age. Even adolescents and young adults in their twenties and thirties, who have not passed their peak bone mass period, may suffer fractures because of brittle, porous bones.

7. Diet high in animal protein, such as red meats
_____ No (0 risk points)
_____ Yes (2 risk points)

Explanation: Any time the percent of protein content in your diet (including red meat) exceeds 20% of the daily total caloric intake, the consumption is too high. If your diet is high in animal proteins, such as those contained in red meats, there is evidence that too much calcium may be washed out of your system through your urine. This process may create a "negative calcium balance" in your body. These lower calcium levels could contribute to osteoporosis.

8. Adding salt to food at the table
_____ No (0 risk points)
_____ Yes (3 risk points)

Explanation: Almost all Americans, and many people in other Western countries, eat far too much salt. There's more than enough salt contained naturally in our foods. So, if you add salt to your food when you sit down at the dinner table, you're giving yourself more than you need. Furthermore, if you're a woman, and especially a *post*menopausal woman, you are putting yourself at a higher risk for osteoporosis.

With postmenopausal women, excessive consumption of salt in the diet washes out calcium from the body through the urine. And because women who have gone through menopause lack the estrogen necessary to make the active vitamin D that's required to process calcium from foods, they end up with too little calcium in their bodies—and a higher risk of developing porous bones.

With *pre*menopausal women, in contrast, extra salt also tends to wash out calcium in the urine, and salt may contribute to other health problems as well. But the estrogen present in their bodies allows them to make extra active vitamin D, which facilitates the absorption of calcium from their foods. As a result, as long as they're consuming an adequate amount of calcium in their diets, premenopausal women face less of a problem from salt than do postmenopausal women.

So, if you're a postmenopausal woman who adds salt to her food—or if you're a premenopausal salt eater who eats few dairy products or calcium supplements—give yourself 3 risk points.

9. Vegetarian, or diet heavily weighted toward vegetables
_____ No (0 risk points)
_____ Yes (2 risk points)
Explanation: Women vegetarians lose excessive estrogen through their feces. As a result, they have a decreased concentration of estrogen in their bloodstreams, and this lack reduces their ability to process calcium in their bones. Also, vegetarians have more fiber in their diets, which "binds" calcium, thus making it unavailable for the body's use.

10. High amounts of fiber in diet
_____ No (0 risk points)
_____ Yes (2 risk points)
Explanation: Many people who are not vegetarians still eat relatively high amounts of fiber, both as a natural laxative and as a protection against cancer of the intestines. Although fiber is certainly an important part of your diet, too much of it can work against you. More than 35 to 60 grams of fiber in the diet daily is considered excessive. For example, one-half cup of beans or high-fiber cereal (All-Bran, Fiber One, etc.) will provide nearly one-half of your daily fiber needs.

So, if you eat relatively large amounts of fiber—and if you didn't give yourself any risk points under question 9—award yourself 2 risk points at this time.

11. Three or more cups of coffee each day—or an equivalent amount of caffeine from other sources, such as cola-type beverages
_____ No (0 risk points)
_____ Yes (2 risk points)
Explanation: Research is still being done on the relationship between caffeine and osteoporosis, and though many experts assume there's a connection, the exact biological mechanisms haven't been identified. One explanation that's been offered is that caffeine stimulates loss of calcium in urine and thus increases the loss of calcium from the body.

The less calcium you have, the less your system has to work with in replacing lost bone. Also, caffeine is thought to cause demolition of bone.

II. Risk Factors That Can't Be Controlled

Clearly, in the preceding eleven areas, you can take steps to eliminate risk points and reduce your chances of getting osteoporosis. But, as with all aspects of health, there are some things you *can't* control. So now let's consider those risk factors that you'll probably just have to live with.

12. Family history of osteoporosis or other bone disease
_____ Yes (4 risk points)
_____ No (0 risk points)
Explanation: One of the most important things that can predispose you to osteoporosis or related bone diseases is the genetic factor. If a member of your immediate family—grandparents, parents, or siblings—has osteoporosis, then the chances are much greater that you too have inherited a tendency toward this problem.

13. White, northern European, or Asian ethnic background
_____ No (0 risk points)
_____ Yes (3 risk points)
Explanation: Closely related to the family factor is this ethnic risk factor. Studies have revealed that your risk of getting osteoporosis is higher if any of the following are characteristic of your background:

• You're a white person.

• Your ancestors come from northern Europe.

• Your ancestors come from China, Japan, or another area of the Far East.

14. Fair complexion
_____ No (0 risk points)
_____ Yes (2 risk points)
Explanation: People with fair skin and complexion tend to get osteoporosis more often than darker-skinned people. In fact, osteoporosis is a rarity among blacks.

15. Small-boned frame
_____ No (0 risk points)
_____ Yes (4 risk points)
Explanation: Small-boned people are more at risk for bone-loss dis-

eases than those who have larger bones. One reason for this may be that small-boned people have less bone to lose. So, when the inevitable process of bone loss begins after the peak bone mass period of ages 25 to 40, their bone density may reach critical levels, where fractures are common, sooner than those with larger skeletal structures.

16. Low percentage of body fat (less than 15 percent of total body weight)—or lean build

_____ No (0 risk points)

_____ Yes (4 risk points)

Explanation: Those whose bodies are relatively lean, or who have a low percentage of body fat in relation to their total weight, may be at lower risk for heart problems and other diseases. At the same time, however, the lower your body fat, the less weight you put on your bones—and the less dense they become to support your weight. Also, some estrogen is made in fat tissue. So you may have less of this important "bone-sparing" hormone if you are lean. So, ironically, even though extra fat may be a disadvantage for other diseases, it can be an advantage in protecting you from osteoporosis.

If you know your precise percentage of body fat, you can see clearly whether you fall above or below 15 percent, which is the cut-off point in evaluating your bone-loss risk. On the other hand, if you don't know your exact percentage of body fat, you can just make a subjective determination at this point as to whether you consider yourself "lean."

In designing risk-factor charts for heart disease in my other books, the cut-off point of 19 percent body fat for males ages 40 to 49 and 21 percent for females of the same age is used. In other words, you begin to accumulate risk points for heart disease if your body fat is above those cut-off figures, but you don't have any increased risk if the body fat is lower.

I'd recommend that for overall good health, the average middle-aged man should try to keep his percentage of body fat between 15 and 19 percent. Similarly, the average middle-aged woman should try to keep her weight between 15 and 21 percent.

17. Over 40 years of age

_____ No (0 risk points)

_____ Yes (2 risk points)

Explanation: If you're older than 40, you've passed your period of peak bone mass. That is, your bones have developed as much as they're going to, and from this point on, bone loss begins. The greatest danger from osteoporosis for both men and women begins after this point.

18. Over 70 years of age

_____ No (0 risk points)

_____ Yes (4 risk points)

Explanation: Although the groundwork for bone loss has usually been laid years before, the threat of osteoporosis accelerates further for both men and women after age 70. As we've already seen, one-third of all elderly women and one-sixth of elderly men will suffer from hip fractures.

19. Ovaries removed

_____ No (0 risk points)

_____ Yes (4 risk points)

Explanation: Women who have had their ovaries removed can no longer produce estrogen. But estrogen is necessary for maintaining bone health because it inhibits the bone-destroying cells (i.e., the osteoclasts). Also, estrogen is essential for the production of active vitamin D, which facilitates the absorption of calcium into the body for use by the bones.

20. Breast-feeding of one child

_____ No (0 risk points)

_____ Yes (1 risk point)

Explanation: If you've had one child and you've breast-fed that child, there is some evidence that this experience may put you at a greater risk for osteoporosis. One reason offered is that a considerable amount of calcium and other nutrients pass out of the mother's body during breast-feeding. Animal experiments have demonstrated that the mother's bones can become quite porous during the breast-feeding period.

On the other hand, if you've had several children, you may gain some extra protection against bone loss—even though you've breast-fed the youngsters. The reason? Probably the extra hormone production during multiple pregnancies offsets the loss of nutrients during breast-feeding.

21. Allergic to milk or other dairy products

_____ No (0 risk points)

_____ Yes (3 risk points)

Explanation: Many people are allergic to milk or other dairy products to some degree. Furthermore, this "lactose intolerance," as it's called, often increases with age, or may appear for the first time as a person gets older. The allergic reaction may emerge in the form of gastric problems, such as gas, diarrhea, and stomach cramps.

Obviously, if you can't drink milk or consume other dairy products without considerable discomfort, you won't be able to get an adequate amount of calcium through your diet. Unless you take calcium supplements, you'll probably become calcium-deficient—and this lack will increase your chances of accelerated bone loss.

22. No children
_____ No (0 risk points)
_____ Yes (2 risk points)

Explanation: Women who are childless, or in a state of "nulliparity," tend to be at a somewhat higher risk for osteoporosis. One explanation for this phenomenon, as I mentioned under question 20, is that the production of extra hormones, including estrogen, during pregnancy can enhance the body's utilization of calcium and the buildup of bone. Also, it's possible that the pregnant woman's greater body weight puts extra pressure on the bones and thus promotes denser bone development.

23. Early menopause
_____ No (0 risk points)
_____ Yes (3 risk points)

Explanation: Sometimes a woman goes through a relatively early menopause—say before about age 45—perhaps as a result of a smoking habit or leanness. When this happens, the estrogen production in her body ceases. As a result, her ability to maintain bone health and to process vitamin D and absorb calcium for bone use diminishes. These changes in her body will put her at greater risk for developing osteoporosis later in life.

III. Risk Factors You May Be Able to Control

This final set of risk factors relates directly to your health and to the medications—such as steroids or anticonvulsants—you may be taking to correct certain physical problems. Sometimes there may be nothing you can do to change a medication you're taking. On the other hand, your doctor may be able to suggest some alternatives that can deal effectively with your medical difficulty—but *without* putting you at a higher risk for bone loss.

In any case, you should be aware of the implications of the medications and conditions referred to below, and then consult your physician to see if there's any way to reduce your risk of osteoporosis.

24. Use of steroid drugs
_____ No (0 risk points)
_____ Yes (4 risk points)

Explanation: Patients who are on steroid drugs typically include those with rheumatoid arthritis or asthma. Also, those who have just had kidney transplants are often put on steroids.

The problem with these drugs is that they inhibit the formation of bone by acting negatively on the osteoblasts, or bone-forming cells. In addition, they could impair your ability to absorb calcium from food. Various studies have shown that those who take steroids for three years or longer may have as much as a 70 percent chance of getting osteoporosis. In fact, significant bone loss may occur after a person has been on these drugs only six months.

25. Thyrotoxicosis, or an overactive thyroid gland (with such symptoms as fast pulse and heart rate, loss of weight, and "hyped up" bodily metabolism)

_____ No (0 risk points)

_____ Yes (4 risk points)

Explanation: If you have an overactive thyroid gland, or what's called "thyrotoxicosis," you'll lose weight and experience an overactive bodily metabolism. As far as your bones are concerned, the thyroid hormone will directly stimulate the breakdown of bone—or the action of the bone-destroying cells called the "osteoclasts." One result of this thyroid problem is the promotion of osteoporosis.

Sometimes, people may take thyroid medication just to get "pepped up"; unfortunately, they may be taking these substances in high doses. Like an overactive gland, though, thyroid medication can promote bone loss. So it's wise to consult your physician and be certain that if you're taking this medication, it's absolutely necessary. If it's not necessary, you and your physician might work out a program to cut down or eliminate the medication.

26. Hyperparathyroidism, or an excessive secretion of the parathyroid glands (which causes loss of calcium from the bones, formation of cysts in the bones, and kidney stones)

_____ No (0 risk points)

_____ Yes (3 risk points)

Explanation: The parathyroid glands, which are located next to the throat near the thyroid gland, are essential in maintaining good health because they are instrumental in preventing blood calcium levels from falling below normal. Specifically, a carefully controlled secretion from these glands (called the "parathyroid hormone") regulates the amount of calcium being released by bones. This hormone also regulates the formation of active vitamin D, which stimulates calcium absorption from the intestines.

But excessive secretions of the parathyroid glands—which is called "hyperparathyroidism"—can have the opposite effect. In other words, too much parathyroid secretion can cause too much destruction of the bone and can raise blood calcium to high levels. Large amounts of this hormone tend to be more destructive to the long, hard bones of the body than to the "spongy" bones such as the vertebrae.

27. Biliary cirrhosis, or an inflammatory disease of the bile system connecting the liver and the intestines

_____ No (0 risk points)

_____ Yes (3 risk points)

Explanation: A problem with the liver may affect the way calcium and vitamin D are processed in the body. The result may be an inadequate supply of calcium to the bones and steady bone deterioration.

28. Chronic kidney disease

_____ No (0 risk points)

_____ Yes (3 risk points)

Explanation: Chronic kidney disease may affect the way that waste products are eliminated from the body. For example, the kidneys may be so diseased that they can't get rid of the body's acids through the urine. This state may cause a buildup of acid in the body and the blood. This condition, called "acidosis," isn't good for the bones and may actually cause bone loss. Also, failure of the kidneys to eliminate phosphate could result in phosphate accumulation in the blood. This process causes a condition called "hyperphosphatemia," which is not good for the bones. Another problem is that people with kidney failure often have trouble absorbing calcium from food because they lack active vitamin D. Consequently, those with serious renal or kidney difficulties may encounter accelerated osteoporosis.

29. Use of anticonvulsants, or medications designed to prevent convulsions or fits

_____ No (0 risk points)

_____ Yes (2 risk points)

Explanation: Anticonvulsants may also promote increased bone loss. An anticonvulsant like Dilantin can affect the liver's metabolism of vitamin D. If the vitamin D isn't metabolized properly, the body won't absorb calcium well, and bone loss may increase.

Another potential problem drug is Diamox, which goes by the generic name acetazolamide. This drug, which is prescribed to treat glaucoma, promotes acid retention in the body. If too much acid gets into the blood, the patient can lose excessive amounts of calcium in any wine that may be drunk and absorb calcium poorly from food.

30. History of stomach or small-bowel disease

_____ No (0 risk points)

_____ Yes (4 risk points)

Explanation: If you've had significant problems or disease with your stomach or intestines, it's likely that your ability to absorb and process important nutrients such as calcium is impaired. Such impairment can have a significant negative impact on your bone development and bone loss.

Now that you've tabulated your risk points, it is time to evaluate your level of risk. To find your appropriate risk category, move on to the next section.

How to Evaluate Your Level of Risk

First, add up the risk points you've accumulated. This will give you one raw score, which will serve as the basis of determining the risk category into which you fall.

There are four risk categories: low risk, moderate risk, high risk, and very high risk. In general, the more risk points you have, the higher your risk level will be. Specifically, the number of risk points correlates with the four risk categories in this way:

Low risk: 0–8 risk points
Moderate risk: 9–16 risk points
High risk: 17–24 risk points
Very high risk: 25 or more risk points

If you're in the low-risk range, you don't have to worry about making radical changes in your diet or lifestyle. But you should still pay close attention to good nutrition, exercise, and the other risk factors you can control. Inevitably, as you grow older, your risk will increase, so it behooves you to take steps now to minimize later threats to your bones.

If you're in the moderate-risk range, you must pay considerably more attention to changing those risk factors that can be changed. Among other things, you should consult the remaining chapters of this book to learn what practical action you can take to protect yourself from bone loss. Also, you may want to talk to your physician about changing drugs that may be causing bone loss. In addition, you may elect to embark on estrogen replacement therapy, if you've been through menopause and aren't already on this hormone treatment.

If you find yourself in the high- or very-high-risk categories, it's imperative that you take steps *immediately* to counteract the bone loss that is likely ravaging your skeletal structure. It is important to read the following pages carefully. Then, with the help of your physician, you can begin to formulate your personal bone-protection program. You may want to have the density of your bones measured by your physician to learn if any damage has already been done.

The precise program that you should choose is not something I can outline for you in just a few pages. Instead, you'll have to take into consideration such things as your age, your diet, your exercise habits, your medical history, and a variety of other factors. We'll deal with these and other issues in the upcoming pages.

But first, before we embark on these highly practical steps, it's necessary to get some more basic information to work with. So now let's take a closer, more detailed look at exactly how osteoporosis and other bone-loss diseases do their damaging work.

THREE

The Principle of Peak Bone Mass

Our bones are dynamic living tissues, constantly growing and changing.

The growth begins when you're in the womb and continues through childhood, adolescence, and young adulthood. Then, between ages 25 and 35, the growth of your bones reaches a peak—a key fact that underlies what I call the Principle of Peak Bone Mass. Simply stated, this principle says that it's absolutely essential for you to achieve the greatest possible density in your bones by the 25-to-40-year age range. Also, a corollary of the principle is that it's important for you to take preventive steps after you reach your peak to retard later loss in bone density.

As you get older, the mass of bone tissue you've built up in your younger years will inevitably decrease from its peak density. This gradual loss of bone is a natural part of the aging process. Even so, the bone tissue remains alive, always "dying" and then "coming to life" again through the ongoing process of bone turnover and growth.

What's the practical significance of the hidden mechanism of bone development in our bodies? The more you understand about the physical activities occurring in every part of your skeleton, the more effective you'll be in developing your own preventive program against bone loss. For example, it's important to know:

- How bones are formed in your body

- What the Principle of Peak Bone Mass really means

- What causes bone loss—and the most viable strategies to prevent it

Now, to put you on better "speaking terms" with your skeletal substructure, I want to consider each of these issues in somewhat greater detail. To this end, you might picture the bone-growth process as a project under construction by a kind of building company insid_ your body. The "workers" in the company include:

A *construction crew*, consisting of a demolition team, called osteo-*clasts*, and a building team, called osteo*blasts*.

An *executive steering committee*, consisting of the parathyroid glands, the thyroid gland, estrogen, and vitamin D.

A *supplies division*, which provides building materials such as "bone concrete" (collagen) and a superhardening agent, calcium phosphate.

Now, let's take a look at how these and other "employees" of your Bone Construction Company operate.

How Is Bone Formed in Your Body?

The "bone-construction crews," or bone-remodeling units, are first shipped in through the bloodstream to various bone surfaces that are ready for rebuilding.

Once a crew arrives on a skeletal construction site—let's say at your radius (thumb-side forearm bone) or your femur (the thighbone, which runs from your knee up to your hip)—the demolition cells, called "osteoclasts," are the first to go to work. These osteoclasts start destroying a minute section of the bone so that ditches or cavities are formed in the hard skeletal substance. The bone that's lost is said to be "resorbed" into the blood.

After this resorption occurs and the cavities have been created, the bone construction crew's builder cells, called "osteoblasts," get started on their assigned tasks. By the way, because the terms *osteoblast* and *osteoclast* are so similar, they may sometimes be hard to distinguish. So I find it helpful to remember the important letter *b* in the osteo*b*lasts, which are the *b*uilder cells. I focus on the *c* in osteo*c*lasts, and in the *c*avities they create in the bone.

As the first step in bone formation, the osteoblasts make a protein called "collagen." Collagen is a protein substance found in skin, tendon, bone, and cartilage. In some respects, you might think of collagen as a kind of bone concrete mix that hasn't yet hardened. The collagen is then wound and twisted around into a "matrix" or "osteoid," to fill up the cavities left by the demolition specialists, the osteoclasts. The matrix is bone by any definition. But it's not yet tough, calcified bone.

Bone eventually becomes hardened—a process that is also called "calcification" or "mineralization." This hardening occurs because of the action of calcium phosphate, which comes into the bloodstream through your diet and is deposited in the matrix.

Finally, the cycle begins again as another construction crew, consisting of osteoclasts and osteoblasts, arrives on the scene to begin demolishing the old bone and rebuilding it. Somehow, even though two different types of cells are involved, the demolition and building functions are closely linked. Perhaps there's some sort of chemical communication or even physical continuity between the osteoclasts and osteoblasts. So it's quite appropriate to regard them both as members of one on-site construction crew.

It's almost as though the osteoclasts, when they finish tearing up one section of the bone, raise a special signal flag. Or perhaps it's even more accurate to imagine that they pass the word to the osteoblasts through an intercellular intercom: "Hey, we're finished. Now it's your turn." The lines of communication between the destroyers and the builders are that immediate, and they constitute a relationship that scientists call "coupling."

How long does it take for one construction crew to finish its job? From the start of one bone-formation cycle to the start of the next usually takes about four months. In any event, it takes this amount of time in human bodies where bones are at their best and healthiest. The process may take longer or may not be completed at all as a person grows older or encounters internal obstacles in bone building.

If you examine a cross-section of bone through a high-powered microscope, you'll see that the process of bone demolition and formation is occurring at different stages throughout the skeleton. The construction crews, or bone-remodeling units, may be tearing things down in one part of your femur, spine, or wrist, while bone building is going on at another spot.

Looking at a segment of bone, you'll literally see little holes at some points, which are the cavities created by the bone resorption of the osteoclasts. At another location, you'll see a hazy, gauzy area, which is a point where formation is occurring, though the bone hasn't yet hardened. At still another place, you'll see a much more dense and solid substance—where the matrix has hardened or calcified.

What regulates the bone-construction process? Bone formation doesn't just happen all by itself. In other words, those "construction crews" consisting of demolition-osteoclasts and builder-osteoblasts don't run around on their own, without any direction from what you might call the "higher corporate executives" in your body.

Specifically, a number of these "executives," in the form of hormones, play important roles in causing the demolition and builder cells to do their tasks. For example, when the osteoclasts come in to create those cavities in the bone, their activity is triggered by hormones from the parathyroid glands and the thyroid gland, which are located near one another in your neck. Besides hormones produced by glands outside bone, bone itself may produce "executives" to direct demolition of bone. One of these is a substance called "prostaglandin."

When these glands or the bone itself become overactive, the osteoclasts will start working too hard to excavate and destroy old bone tissue. As a result, excessive amounts of bone will be resorbed into the body, not enough new bone tissue will be available to fill the empty spaces, and the density of the bone will decrease. But when your parathyroid and thyroid glands are operating properly, the demolition-cells (osteoclasts) get the appropriate messages. Then, they dig out just the right cavities required to achieve a balanced bone-building cycle.

Also, there are "executive ombudsmen" that check the "executives" from demolishing the bone too much. These agents, which block the activity of the osteoclasts, include estrogen and calcitonin, another hormone produced by the thyroid gland.

In the other part of the construction process—bone formation—fluoride is one substance that will stimulate the builder-cells, the osteoblasts, to work overtime. But this substance is generally available only through special experimental programs for osteoporosis patients. One of these is a research project being conducted by Dr. Charles Pak.

As for substances produced by your body, there is evidence that the male hormone testosterone and another female hormone, progesterone, may enhance bone building. Also, bone produces certain agents that stimulate the bone-building osteoblasts, and at that same time there are substances such as the steroid hormone that may control or limit bone building.

As you can see, the metabolism of bone—or the process of "remodeling"—is a process that is carefully controlled from several sources in the body. The result is a series of checks and balances designed to ensure that bone won't be lost too rapidly.

Also, vitamin D may lend a hand by serving as a kind of overseeing "construction boss" for bone formation. But this is a subject that requires a little more explanation.

Vitamin D as a major "construction boss." Vitamin D, in its various forms, plays a major role in calcium absorption and bone formation and destruction. In the first place, vitamin D comes into the body through the ultraviolet radiation absorbed by the skin and also through our diets. Although the vitamin in this form is relatively

.nactive, it becomes much more active—and usable in the bone-building process—as its chemical composition is changed in the liver and kidneys.

Without vitamin D, the calcium you take in through your diet wouldn't get absorbed into your body for use in bone building. Also, there is evidence that various types of vitamin D may:

- Stimulate the demolition capacity of osteoclasts

- Stimulate the bone-building work of osteoblasts

- Stimulate the absorption of calcium and phosphate from the food that's in the intestines so that these minerals can help to harden the skeleton through calcification

Clearly, vitamin D appears to have a big role in orchestrating important aspects of the bone "construction crews." You might say that this vitamin is not only a construction boss but a hirer and trainer of the crews as well.

These different "workers" are constantly on the job in your body as they tear down and build up bone and in various ways regulate the entire process. The first major job that you, as your body's chief executive officer, should assign your Bone Construction Company is to work hard early in your life to build the skeletal structure according to what I've called the Principle of Peak Bone Mass.

The Principle of Peak Bone Mass

Generally speaking, there are two types of bone made by those construction crews in your body.

1. The first is *trabecular* bone, which is softer, loosely packed tissue found in the inner part of most bones. In fact, this type of bone comprises a large part of the vertebrae. I refer to this as "sponge" bone because it's more or less porous. *But note:* trabecular bone is *not* the same thing as bone marrow, which is the soft organic tissue inside the bone that manufactures blood cells.

2. The second type of bone in your body is *cortical* or "long" bone, which can be found on the hard outer surface of many bones, such as the femur, in the thigh. A good way to describe this tissue is to call it "pipe" bone because it often resembles the curved outer shell of metal pipes used in construction.

In the long bones such as the femur or the radius, the outer portion of cortical "pipe" tissue may comprise 80 percent of the entire bony tissue. On the other hand, in bones such as the vertebrae, the ribs, or the breastbone (sternum), most of the tissue may be trabecular "sponge," with only a thin outer coating of hard, cortical bone. Bones of the skull are probably about half "sponge" and half "pipe." In any event, every bone will contain some percentage of both cortical and trabecular tissue.

As the construction crews work in your body in the first three to four decades of life, they concentrate on making as much of these sponge (trabecular) and pipe (cortical) tissues as possible. But the crews build up the two different types of bone at different rates.

The hard, cortical bones usually reach their peak mass or density around ages 35 to 40. Those construction crews, consisting of demolition-osteoclasts and builder-osteoblasts, have packed as much bone tissue as possible into those hard pipes by then. This density typically stays fairly constant until about age 45, when the cortical tissue begins to decline in mass.

In contrast, the spongy trabecular bones reach their peak density at about ages 25 to 30—or approximately ten years earlier than the cortical pipe tissue. From this point in time, the trabecular bones in the lower back (lumbar spine), the ribs, and elsewhere begin a gradual decline in density, which continues throughout life.

What are the practical implications of this growth of your bones toward a peak mass? Here is where the Principle of Peak Bone Mass becomes most relevant. Remember: according to this principle, up to about age 40, you must do everything in your power to help those crews working for the Bone Construction Company in your body. Through adequate calcium intake in your diet, sufficient weight-bearing exercise, and other measures we'll discuss later, you should do the best job possible to shore up your skeletal structure.

As I've already indicated, a corollary to this principle is that you must recognize that your peak bone mass is *really* a peak—and you should do everything you can to stay as close to that peak as possible as you get older.

But after age 40, bone loss is inevitable, and planning and discipline are required to prevent it. Soon after reaching maximum bone density at age 40, everyone, male and female, will begin to lose bone mass. First, the spongy trabecular bone in the spine, sternum, ribs, and other such areas begins to go. Then, by about age 45, the harder cortical pipe starts to decline in density. As people get older, the bone loss may increase to such a level that it's regarded as a disease.

At about age 40, bone loss for both men and women proceeds at an annual rate of 0.3 to 0.5 percent of a person's total bone mass. Then, for women who have just gone through menopause, bone loss may accelerate at a rate of 2 to 3 percent of the entire bone mass each year. This rate will normally decline after about eight to ten years, but by then, significant damage may have been done.

As reported in *New England Journal of Medicine*, 1986, during their entire life spans, women lose about 35 percent of their cortical or pipe bone, and about 50 percent of their trabecular or sponge bone. Men lose nearly one-fourth of their cortical bone mass and about one-third of their trabecular bone.

But even though it's possible to make certain generalizations about bone loss, an understanding of what's likely to happen to you personally requires a closer look at problems with specific sex and age groups. For example, typically a small percentage of men in their forties—say about 5 percent of the population—may be struck by bone-loss disease of unknown origin. This is an example of the so-called idiopathic osteoporosis. But what *is* known is that this type of bone loss whittles away mainly at trabecular bone and can put the victim at serious risk of fractures of the vertebrae, the wrist, and other spongy bone areas.

Another group seriously at risk is postmenopausal women, or those roughly 50 to 70 years old. With these people, the most serious bone loss also occurs in the spongy trabecular bone in the spine and similar spots elsewhere in the skeletal structure. Probably, a woman's loss of estrogen at this time of life is a key factor in causing this type of osteoporosis. The result may be serious back problems including crushed vertebrae, loss of teeth due to a more porous lower jawbone (mandible), broken ribs, and fractures of the wrist.

Still another older group that may run into serious problems with bone loss includes men and women over age 70. Here, though, the problem arises not so much from hormonal changes as from ongoing, gradual bone loss due to aging. The main target of this type of bone deterioration is the cortical pipe bones, though spongy trabecular bones also remain at risk.

As a result of this decrease in bone mass, both men and women older than 70 may experience an increasing number of hip fractures—and especially fractures of the upper femur, which fits into the hip socket. The femur, you'll recall, consists primarily of the hard, cortical bone, though there is plenty of trabecular tissue near the end of it. Also, among older people the spine remains at risk because of the long-term bone loss occurring after the achievement of peak bone mass. It's at this stage of life, for instance, that the so-called dowager's hump becomes a problem with certain women, as the weakened, porous vertebrae in their spines begin to become "wedged" through a crushing process.

If any bones get to a point of a "fracture threshold" or "critical mass," where any part of the skeleton is too weak to support the normal functions of the body, cracks and breaks may occur. At this point, the odious work of osteoporosis will become a major health hazard.

What can you do to prevent the onset of excessive bone loss and osteoporosis? There is a two-pronged strategy that everyone, male and female, should keep in mind.

First: Do everything you can to achieve the greatest possible bone mass by the peak years of 25 to 40. The stronger a substructure your "construction crews" have built in the early years, the less likelihood there is that later bone loss will reduce your density to dangerously weak levels.

Second: Continue to take steps to hold off bone loss after you've reached your peak.

There are several tactics in the following pages to help you succeed with these two strategies, including calcium-rich diets, weight-bearing exercise, estrogen and other drug treatments, and various preventive programs to retard bone loss. But before we delve into the specifics of prevention, it's important to go into a little more detail on the exact causes of bone loss and the way various diseases of the bone may put you at risk.

The Robber Baron of Bone Loss

Like the robber barons who preyed on business interests and on the public in a bygone era of American capitalism, osteoporosis will do everything in its power to steal your bone deposits, undercut "corporate communications" in your body, and ultimately destroy the entire bone-building process.

People have been examining bone growth and bone-related problems for hundreds of years. Galileo, for example, reported in 1683 a direct relationship between a person's bone size and body weight: the bigger the person, the bigger his bones. In succeeding years, a variety of scientists recognized that there's a bone-demolishing and bone-building process going on in our bodies. Then, in *The Law of Bone Transformation*, published in 1892, Julius Wolff, a German anatomist, concluded that human beings can actually change their bone structure, for better or worse, by the amount of weight-bearing exercise they do.

The stage was thus set for someone to identify a lack of sufficient bone density—whether from too little exercise or some other cause—as a disease state. That someone was Dr. Fuller Albright, who in 1940 first used the term *osteoporosis* and described it as a pathologic or disease-related process of bone loss.

But before you can begin to discuss this greatest "bone robber baron," osteoporosis, it's necessary first to mention a preliminary condition called "osteopenia." Osteopenia refers to reduced bone mass that hasn't yet resulted in any fractures. Osteopenia can be a problem with very young people or at any time during a person's life. Most important, osteopenia marks the first stages of bone deterioration that may eventually lead to osteoporosis.

But generally speaking, osteopenia may be difficult to identify, and most doctors don't even try to treat it because, by definition, there are no clear-cut symptoms. In fact, the only way you *can* treat it is to employ preventive medicine techniques like a good, high-calcium diet and a regular, weight-bearing-exercise program.

When a symptom such as a broken bone occurs, however, the situation abruptly changes, at least from the prevailing medical point of view. With the onset of symptoms, bone loss enters what many doctors regard as a disease state—the condition they call "osteoporosis."

What exactly happens in your bones with osteoporosis? And how does this condition "rob" your skeletal structure of its much-needed mass?

The main idea in osteoporosis is that over a period of years, there is more destruction or resorption of the bone than formation. In other words, the demolition crews, the osteoclasts, do more work than the builders, the osteoblasts. As a result, bone density decreases, and the bone gets more porous and brittle—until fractures and breaks may occur.

To put this another way, the ratio of mineralized bone to collagen (or nonmineralized bone) stays the same over the years in a given segment of bone—such as the outer bone of the forearm (the radius). In other words, bone that is left is adequately hardened or mineralized. But as the years pass, there is less total bone tissue present in that forearm. The amount of bone mass lost each year may be relatively small, perhaps less than half of 1 percent. But over a period of decades, enough of the bone mineral may disappear to put you at serious risk and even cause the symptoms that signal the onset of osteoporosis.

What causes osteoporosis? In chapter 2, we discussed a number of factors that may put you at high risk for osteoporosis. In many scholarly articles and summaries, these factors are also typically listed as *causes* of bone-loss disease. Often, the risks for a disease and the causes of that disease are just two sides of the same coin—and that's certainly the case with osteoporosis.

To summarize, then, the possible causes of osteoporosis—as well as the factors that put you at risk—include:

- Cigarette smoking

- Alcohol abuse

- Failure to follow sound, calcium-rich nutritional guidelines

- Failure to engage regularly in weight-bearing exercise

- Too much exercise by women who then fail to menstruate

- Eating disorders

- Diets high in animal protein

- Consuming too much salt

- Eating a vegetarian diet

- Consuming high amounts of fiber

- Drinking excessive amounts of caffeine

- Having a family with a history of osteoporosis

- Being of white, northern European, or Asian ethnic background

- Having a fair complexion

- Having a small-boned frame

- Having a very low percentage of body fat

- Being over 40 years of age

- Being a woman who has gone through menopause

- Being over 70 years of age

- Having had your ovaries removed

- Having breast-fed one child

- Being allergic to milk or other dairy products

- Having had no children

- Having undergone an early menopause

- Using steroid drugs

- Having an overactive thyroid gland

- Having excessive secretions of the parathyroid glands

- Having biliary cirrhosis, or an inflammatory disease of the bile system

- Having chronic kidney disease

- Using anticonvulsants

- Having a history of stomach or small-bowel disease

As I said, you've encountered most of these problems as risk factors in the Bone-Loss Risk Factors Evaluation in chapter 2. Also, it's very important to recognize that alone or in combination, they can be direct causes of bone loss—which may result in osteoporosis. Furthermore, these problems may involve a wide array of attacks through the body's hormones, blood composition, and other channels.

Clearly, the assaults that result in osteoporosis threaten us on a broad front and may undercut the entire metabolism or remodeling of bone. When one or more of these causes have done their work, the demolisher-osteoclasts and builder-osteoblasts typically don't work together as well as they should. The former may work too well, the latter too poorly. Consequently, the bone loses more density than it gains, and it becomes more brittle and subject to breaks.

In addition to osteoporosis, some other important enemies of your bones—though less widespread than osteoporosis—can be just as devastating in their impact. It's important for you to understand something about two of the most significant of these diseases—*osteomalacia* and *osteitis fibrosa*—so that you can get a better idea of how osteoporosis fits into the entire panoply of bone-loss diseases.

Two Other Enemies

Osteomalacia—which in children is called "rickets"—is a bone disease involving a different physiologic process from osteoporosis. There is still a loss of bone, but it occurs differently from osteoporosis. While the ratio of collagen (or matrix) to mineralized bone remains the same with osteoporosis, the ratio changes with osteomalacia. Specifically, in osteomalacia, or rickets, there's proportionately more collagen or matrix than mineralized bone. In other words, osteomalacia involves a defect in the process of hardening or calcification of bone.

The practical consequences of osteomalacia are that the person's bones become softer or spongier. As a result, the person suffering from this disease may experience bone tenderness or muscle weakness. The bone tenderness may be especially pronounced in the rib cage and along the flank of the hip bone. In children, rickets may produce deformities of the legs and joints; the child may develop bow legs, among other things.

Also, you find what are called "pseudofractures" in osteomalacia. These are softenings and indentations in the bones, especially the long bones like the thighbone and forearm bones. But with pseudofractures, there are typically no breaks—not even stress fractures. Still, these "fake fractures" can signal a serious underlying problem with your bones.

The causes of osteomalacia, or rickets, include vitamin D deficiency, severe calcium deficiency, aluminum poisoning, the side effects of certain drugs that impair bone mineralization, and low phosphorus levels in the blood.

Still another form of "stealing" from our bone tissues may occur through the action of an enemy called *osteitis fibrosa*. The problem with osteitis fibrosa begins with the all-important parathyroid glands. An excessive production of hormone by the parathyroids, as we've already seen, can promote osteoporosis, and the same sort of problem can lead to osteitis fibrosa.

Two Possible Problems with the Parathyroid Glands

There are four parathyroid glands, two on each side of the thyroid gland, which is located in the neck. Each of the parathyroid glands is about the size of a pea. These glands are extremely important because they secrete the parathyroid hormone (PTH), which regulates the metabolism of calcium and phosphorus in your body.

But sometimes these PTH glands become enlarged; or perhaps they develop a benign tumor. When this happens, they may begin to produce excessive amounts of PTH—and that's where the trouble starts. These turncoat "corporate executives" in your internal Bone Construction Company in effect begin to sabotage the bone metabolism or "remodeling" process.

Specifically, the extra PTH hormone stimulates the osteoclasts, the bone-demolisher teams on the construction crews. The osteoclasts then work harder than normal digging out cavities in the bone. Before long, they create so many cavities that the other members of the crew, the builder-osteoblasts, are unable to fill them in with their collagen. As a result, more bone is resorbed into the system than is replaced. One of the reasons for the devastating work of osteoporosis, the premier Bone Robber Baron, is the existence of such problems with the parathyroid glands.

But your body and bones may head in a somewhat different direction in response to a parathyroid malfunction. Rather than an over-all bone loss as is the case with osteoporosis, the cavities created by overactive osteoclasts may be filled in with fibrous tissue. This is a signal of the onset of osteitis fibrosa. Such an invasion of fibrous matter, which resembles scar tissue, produces weaker bone because it contains less mineral than regular hardened bone.

There are many other types of related bone problems, with such exotic names as osteogenesis imperfecta, Paget's disease of bone, homocystinuria, juvenile osteoporosis, and Sudeck's atrophy. The latter problem, by the way, is a form of local osteoporosis often limited to the hands and feet. But most of these maladies are rather rare. Most people should focus primarily on the main Bone Robber Baron, osteoporosis.

As we proceed, I'll next provide you with some exercise strategies to help you build strong bones. Then we'll explore the pros and cons of using drugs to fight bone loss. There is also a section on dietary guidelines and menus, which have been designed to enhance your skeletal structure. You'll also find a variety of additional preventive information on such subjects as smoking, alcohol abuse, bone-loss problems in children, and some basics of body mechanics.

Finally, remember this: Underlying all this advice and information—as a kind of thread that ties together this entire topic of osteoporosis—I always make one main set of assumptions: to achieve and maintain healthy, tough bones, you must do all you can to achieve your peak bone density when you're young, and also take every possible step to maintain and conserve your skeletal structure as you grow older. That, after all, is what the Principle of Peak Bone Mass is all about.

FOUR

Exercise:
The First Answer
to Osteoporosis

Why do I regard exercise as the first answer to osteoporosis?

Most bone specialists agree that the two essential ingredients in reaching your peak bone mass in the first 25 to 40 years of life are weight-bearing exercise and calcium intake. Furthermore, after age 40, these same two factors—exercise and calcium—continue to be essential in preventing bone loss and maintaining the highest possible density in your skeletal structure.

For centuries, scientific observers have been aware of how weight-bearing exercise can increase the size of our bones. As I mentioned in chapter 3, the great seventeenth-century Italian physicist and astronomer Galileo observed this connection. So did Julius Wolff, the anatomist from Berlin, who wrote in 1892:

"Every change in the function of a bone is followed by certain definite changes in internal architecture and external conformation in accordance with mathematical laws." (See Frederick S. Kaplan, M.D., "Osteoporosis: Pathophysiology and Prevention," Clinical Symposia, CIBA-GEIGY Corporation, vol. 39, no. 1, 1987, p. 13.)

Put in simpler language, this means that the size and shape of your bones will change as you use them in different ways. Anthropologists have also long been aware of this link between the use of bones and the way they develop and change. For example, Dr. Kenneth A. R. Kennedy of Cornell University has compiled a list of more than 140 "markers" on skeletons that indicate what he calls signs of "occupational stress." (The New York Times, Oct. 27, 1987.)

Among other things, Dr. Kennedy has noted the increased size of the upper part of the forearm among people who constantly throw things. The body of one unidentified modern man, who had apparently frozen to death, was brought to him, and he deduced that the man could have been a left-handed baseball pitcher. In fact, later identification confirmed that the person had been an amateur softball pitcher for twenty years!

Also, Dr. Kennedy has found that skeletons of Ice Age men have the same enlargement on the forearm—where muscles used in throwing are attached to the bone. As a result, he has concluded that these men were hunters who threw spears, bolas, slings, or boomerangs.

The important practical implications of this research for the development and health of our bones have become quite clear: If you put weight on your bones or use your muscles in such a way that the bones are put under stress, the density and size of those bones will increase. Conversely, if you don't exercise so as to put weight or pressure on your bones, they will fail to develop to their maximum mass. As a consequence, later in life your bone loss may reach a critical level much sooner, and fractures may start occurring.

Although researchers such as Dr. Kennedy have contributed a great deal to our understanding of this subject, the support for a link between exercise and bone density is by no means limited to anthropological data. In fact, the great weight of modern medical research shows that exercise is an essential element in building and maintaining maximum bone mass—*and* preventing osteoporosis.

The Evidence for Exercise

What is the evidence that exercise, and especially weight-bearing exercise, can increase the density of your bones and help prevent bone loss? Following are some of the most important recent findings.

Support for the spine. A Danish study, conducted by Dr. Bjorn Krolner and several of his colleagues, evaluated the effect of exercise on bone mineral content in 31 healthy women, ages 50 to 73 years. Specifically, the researchers measured the bone mineral content of the lumbar spine (lower back) and also the forearm near the wrist. All of the women, by the way, had suffered a Colles's fracture of the forearm, near the wrist. (*Clinical Science*, 1983.)

After taking the bone measurements, Dr. Krolner and his team divided the women into two sections. The first section, a physical-exercise group, followed an exercise program that required them to work out for one hour twice a week for eight months. The program included (1) walking, (2) running, (3) exercises while standing, sitting, lying down, and kneeling, and (4) ball games. The second section of participants, a "control" group with whom the exercisers were compared, continued their generally sedentary way of life.

The results? Bone mineral content in the lower spine—an indication of bone mass or density—increased by 3.5 percent in the exercise group, while it decreased by 2.7 percent in the control group. The bone mineral forearm measurements didn't change in response to exercise.

These researchers concluded: "The data suggest that physical exercise can inhibit or reverse the . . . bone loss from the lumbar vertebrae in normal women. Physical exercise may prevent spinal osteoporosis."

Exercise was the key factor in this study because none of the participants was given calcium supplements, and they continued with their normal medications. The only unusual change that took place in the lives of the exercise group was the increase in weight-bearing activity. And obviously, their spines were major beneficiaries.

Long-distance running: an aerobic answer to osteoporosis—without arthritis! Opponents of long-distance running have sometimes raised the specter that such athletes run a serious risk of developing osteoarthritis—the wear-and-tear degeneration of the joints. But a recent study reported in the *Journal of the American Medical Association* (March 7, 1986) indicates the opposite.

In that study, conducted by Dr. Nancy E. Lane and several colleagues from Stanford, 41 male and female long-distance runners, ages 50 to 72 years, were compared with 41 "controls" who didn't run. The runners averaged 286 minutes per week in exercise, as compared with 81 minutes a week for the nonrunners.

The researchers, who had no knowledge of the individual participants' running status, then evaluated both the runners and the controls and found that both the male and female runners had about 40 percent more bone mineral content than the controls. Also, in checking for arthritis, they found no difference in the spaces between the joints, in noises in the bones, in joint stability, or other symptoms. In other words, there was no evidence of arthritis among the runners.

In summing up their findings, Dr. Lane and her colleagues said, "Running is associated with increased bone mineral but not, in this cross-sectional study, with clinical osteoarthritis."

So the evidence continues to pile up: In the first place, a long-term physical impact activity such as long-distance running clearly helps stave off bone loss among older people. At the same time, however, it carries no added risk of osteoarthritis.

Exercise: an antidote for bone loss in postmenopausal women.

When doctors and other researchers use the term *postmenopausal,* they usually mean "women who have just gone through menopause"— and that's the way I'm using the word here. For women in this age group, exercise can be a major antidote to the problem of bone loss.

Dr. John F. Aloia—of the Department of Medicine, Nassau County Medical Center, East Meadow, New York—and some colleagues studied 18 women whose ages averaged 52 to 53 years. These women had gone through menopause about five and a half years earlier. Aloia's purpose was to see whether exercise could prevent bone loss due to aging. (*Annals of Internal Medicine,* 1978.)

To check this question, he put 9 of the women on an exercise regimen, which required them to engage in athletic activity for one hour three times a week over a one-year period. The exercises, which were done under medical supervision in a gymnasium, were those recommended by the President's Council on Physical Fitness and included warm-ups, muscle-conditioning work, and aerobic activities. The other 9 women continued with their usual, sedentary lifestyle. All the participants stayed on their regular diets, with no increase in their calcium intake.

At the end of the one-year test period, the researchers found that total body calcium—an indicator of bone mass—increased from 781 grams to 801 grams in the exercise group. In contrast, the total body calcium decreased in those who weren't exercising.

What do these findings mean? Dr. Aloia and his colleagues wrote, "Our study supports the hypothesis that . . . bone loss [through aging] may be modified in postmenopausal women by increased physical activity."

As you already know, bone loss often accelerates in women who have just gone through menopause, apparently due to the decline in the levels of estrogen in their bodies. This encouraging study suggests that even without therapy designed to replace the lost estrogen, exercise may prevent bone loss in women.

Exercise can also toughen older bones. Younger postmenopausal women are not the only ones whose bones can benefit from exercise. In a three-year study of 80 women, ages 69 to 95, Everett L. Smith, Jr., and two other researchers from the Department of Preventive Medicine at the University of Wisconsin, Madison, discovered that exercise could increase the density of older females' bones. (*Medicine and Science in Sports and Exercise,* 1981.)

Smith and his colleagues divided the women into four groups—a control group; a group that participated in a specially designed physical exercise program; a group that received calcium and vitamin D supplements; and a group that both exercised and received the supplements.

The exercise group, who regularly exercised thirty minutes a day, three days a week, did light to moderate exercises around a chair. These included sideward leg spreads, leg "walks" around the chair, running in place while holding on to the chair, and side bends.

Interestingly, in this study bone density declined slightly in the participants who both exercised and took the supplements. Those who only took the supplemental calcium and vitamin D experienced an average 1.58 percent increase in bone density in the radius bones of their forearms. But the major "winners" in the project were those who participated only in the exercise: their bone density increased by 2.29 percent!

What this seems to say is that exercise is no respecter of persons or ages when it comes to preventing the onset of osteoporosis. Or, as those who conducted the research put it:

"The present study clearly indicates that bone loss in the aged female may be reversed and maintained at a higher level of BMC [bone mineral content] through physical activity or calcium and vitamin D supplementation. Through these inverventions, the bone mineral content increased in this elderly female population."

There's a wide selection of sports to combat bone loss. As long as the physical activity you choose involves pitting your bones against pressure, gravity, or weight, you'll most likely experience some benefits in preventing bone loss.

For example, people used to think that swimming—which involves floating in water, rather than causing the impact of the body against the ground or gravity—would not be too helpful in fighting osteoporosis. But recent research by Dr. Eric S. Orwoll, a Portland endocrinologist, indicates that swimming may in fact help a great deal.

Dr. Orwoll evaluated the bone mineral content of 58 men over 40 years old who had been swimming at least three years for a minimum of three hours a week. When he compared these swimmers' results with those of 78 men the same age who didn't exercise, he discovered that the swimmers' bone mineral content was considerably higher. (*American Health,* June 1987.)

But of course, swimming is only one possibility. As we've already seen, long-distance running, walking, and even rather limited conditioning exercises—if done regularly over a year or more—can have a beneficial effect on many people's bones. And I'm talking about benefits *regardless of your age!*

Some other studies indicate similar results in a variety of exercise activities:

• When 84 active professional tennis players were studied, researchers found a pronounced increase in the size of the humerus (the bone extending from the shoulder to the elbow) in the playing arms of nearly 35 percent of the men and more than 28 percent of the women. (*Journal of Bone Joint Surgery*, vol. 59A, 1977, pp. 204–08.)

• A study of 203 baseball players, ages 8 through 19, revealed a significant increase in the bone mineral content of the throwing arm as compared with the nonthrowing arm. (R.C. Watson, "Bone Growth and Physical Activity," International Conference on Bone Mineral Measurements, 1973, pp. 380–85.)

• Other researchers have evaluated the bone density in the thighbone in 64 male athletes and 39 male nonathletes. They found that the legs used most by the athletes had higher bone density, and also they reported greater bone mass in the nonathletes who exercised, as compared with those who didn't exercise at all. (*Clinical Orthopedics*, vol. 77, 1971, p. 179.)

• Marathon runners have been found to have both a higher total bone mass and also a higher "regional" bone mass in the bones in their legs. Furthermore, the marathoners typically don't experience the decrease in total body calcium or potassium that characterizes normal sedentary men. (*Metabolism*, 1978, vol. 27, p. 1973.)

Clearly, then, there are many ways to reach peak bone mass and maintain that mass—and perhaps even reverse the process of bone loss after you've reached your peak. If you're 50 years old or older and you've never exercised regularly, you'll want to start off slowly, probably with walking. Also, be sure to have a thorough medical exam and get the approval of your physician before embarking on an exercise program.

As you gain endurance and your strength increases, you'll probably be able to increase the time and distance of your exercise sessions. But take it easy! Usually I recommend that older people stick to walking or some other activity that will give them plenty of bone-enhancing exercise—but in a way that will be completely safe. There's no reason to try to break world records as you get older unless you're a serious competitive senior athlete! The exercises in the next two chapters have been designed with a variety of these safety considerations in mind.

Before we get into these practical exercise programs, however, a little more needs to be said about the present direction of research into the relationship between exercise and bone loss.

Where Is Exercise Research Going?

In a recent "Commentary" article entitled "Does Exercise Prevent Osteoporosis?" in the *Journal of the American Medical Association,* June 12, 1987, Dr. Jon Block and several colleagues offer a few words of caution. They note that there have been some conflicting findings: Studies show that bone mass sometimes increases with exercise and physical fitness, but sometimes it doesn't. Also, in some cases one part of the skeleton may increase in density with exercise and another part may not—though no one can explain why.

Among other things, these researchers note that "uncovering such information is complicated by the enormous variation in the type, duration, and intensity of exercise programs."

The writers do acknowledge the validity of some of the studies I've mentioned above. But to ascertain the precise benefits of exercise on bone density, they call for more well-designed longitudinal studies, conducted with large numbers of people over long periods of time.

Although we lack definitive longitudinal studies, we are beginning to see some informative preliminary reports from the space program. Usually, prolonged periods of weightlessness produce physiological changes in the body comparable to complete inactivity or bedrest. To counteract this, a variety of exercise programs using different types of equipment have been used over the years. But they have met with minimal success. For example, two Russian cosmonauts who spent 211 days in space had a major loss of bone mass and couldn't walk normally for a week.

Yet, recent advances in the Russian program have improved this situation. Cosmonaut Yuri Romanenko returned from 326 days in space on December 29, 1987, and had only minimal signs of bone loss or deconditioning. He lost only 5 percent of his bone calcium—much less than what was lost by cosmonauts on other missions. Also, he could run a hundred meters the day following his return to earth.

His secret? To prevent deconditioning and bone loss, Romanenko's waking hours were spent in a "penguin suit," which resembles a sweatsuit laced with elastic cords. This contraption provides extra resistance and requires additional exertion anytime a movement is made. In addition, the cosmonaut ran two miles daily while strapped to a treadmill.

What lesson can we learn from this illustration? This Russian's experience clearly illustrates the value of resistance-type exercise coupled with an aerobic component in maintaining both bone mass and cardiovascular fitness.

There are implications from this study that need further research and documentation, and I certainly support the need for such studies, particularly large, well-controlled, longitudinal efforts. In fact, we're moving in this direction at the Aerobics Center in Dallas, though the final results on our research are still months and in some cases years away. In the meantime, however, I believe that the evidence is overwhelming that weight-bearing exercise is a key factor in developing and maintaining healthy bones. So I heartily recommend exercise as an important response to the threat of osteoporosis. But still, I want to share with you now a few cautionary words about athletic activity.

Some Words of Caution

Regular exercise, which puts pressure on your bones, is certainly one of the key solutions to osteoporosis. But like all good things, it's possible to go too far. In particular, problems have developed in two areas: (1) female athletes who exercise so much that they stop menstruating, and (2) male athletes who exercise too much and eat too little.

The woman who goes too far. In general, there's nothing wrong with a woman's exercising vigorously—as long as she doesn't become amenorrheic, or stop menstruating. But women who exercise to the point where they stop menstruating may begin to suffer bone loss similar to that which afflicts older women after menopause.

In a 1984 study, researchers at the University of California Medical School in San Francisco reported on the bone mass in the spines of 38 women under age 50 who had stopped menstruating for a variety of reasons. Ten of the women had become amenorrheic because of their participation in strenuous exercise.

The researchers found that the density of the nonmenstruating women's spines was 22 to 29 percent lower than normal. Also, these women had very little body fat and relatively low levels of estrogen—factors that can contribute to bone loss. (*The Wall Street Journal,* February 3, 1984.)

"Any factor that irreversibly decreases bone mass in women

before the normal menopausal age of 50 years will predispose these women to osteoporosis," the researchers said. Also, the combination of bone loss and strenuous exercise "may increase the risk of stress fractures in these women during exercise or osteoporotic fractures later in life."

In another study of 28 women runners in the Boston area, researchers at the Tufts University Human Nutrition Research Center on Aging found a link tying together distance running, diet, amenorrhea, and bone loss. (*American Journal of Clinical Nutrition*, June 1986.)

Specifically, they discovered that the 11 women runners in the group who were not menstruating had a significantly lower mineral density in the lumbar spine—which is located along the lower back. Also, these amenorrheic women reported a significantly lower daily energy intake than the menstruating runners, though there was no difference in their calcium consumption.

These researchers concluded that when weight-bearing exercise and a low energy intake are associated with amenorrhea, younger women may face the prospect of lower bone density. And of course, lower bone density puts you at greater risk of developing osteoporosis. As you already know, if your bone mass is relatively low when you're young, you're much more likely to run into serious bone-loss problems when you get older. Remember: The lower your bone density in youth, the more quickly you'll tend to reach that "fracture threshold" later in life—or the time when bones become so brittle and porous that they begin to break under relatively mild stress.

"The results of this study suggest that amenorrhea in athletes may have deleterious long-term health consequences by reducing the mineral content of trabecular [spongy] bone many years before menopause and old age," these Tufts researchers concluded.

Some of the best advice I've encountered in this area comes from Dr. Jill S. Lindberg and her colleagues at the Letterman Army Medical Center in San Francisco. Reporting in the *Western Journal of Medicine* (January 1987), Dr. Lindberg said, "We found that early osteopenia associated with exercise-induced menstrual dysfunction improved when runners reduced their running distance, gained weight and became eumenorrheic [began menstruating]."

She noted that the 7 female runners participating in the study had exercise-induced amenorrhea and also showed a relatively low bone mineral content. But then, over a fifteen-month period, 4 of the women reduced their running distance by 43 percent and took supplemental calcium. The result was that they increased their body weight by an average of 5 percent, experienced an increase in estrogen levels—and began to menstruate. Perhaps most significant of all, their bone mineral content also increased.

So if you're a woman who hasn't yet reached menopause, by all means, exercise! But pursue your exercise program with some restraint and good sense—and pull back if you become amenorrheic.

The man who goes too far. It's quite unusual for a male athlete to develop bone-loss problems to the point that he begins to suffer skeletal fractures. But it can happen—as was the case with one 22-year-old man examined by Dr. Nancy A. Rigotti and other doctors at Massachusetts General Hospital and Harvard Medical School. (*Journal of the American Medical Association*, July 18, 1986.)

In this case, as with many women involved in strenuous exercise, the man was not only a marathon runner but had very poor nutritional habits. In fact, he was diagnosed as suffering from anorexia nervosa.

Because of his poor nutrition combined with his rigorous running regimen, he developed a prolonged deficiency of the male hormone testosterone—a condition that's associated with reduced bone mass. The researchers surmised that his extensive exercise probably also contributed to his weight loss.

As a result of this combination of factors, this young man suffered significant losses in bone density in both his cortical (pipe) and trabecular (spongy) bone. His problems became evident when he developed both a fracture of his pelvis and multiple compression fractures of his vertebrae.

As I said, this sort of problem is unusual for men. But a case like this should serve to remind us that we need to design and follow *sensible* exercise and nutrition programs. If we go too far in any direction and lose the over-all balance that is so important to our health, a stealthy destroyer like osteoporosis could easily enter the picture.

What Exercise Program Is Best for You?

The time has come to move on to the exercise programs described in chapters 5 and 6. They have been set up so that men and women of different ages and athletic interests can select the individual approach that is most interesting and appropriate for them.

Before you do any exercise, however, it's essential that you have a medical exam by a qualified physician. Increasing your physical activity while you have an untreated health problem is not only unwise but dangerous! After you receive the go-ahead from your doctor, you'll be ready to embark on your own tough bones exercise program.

Specifically, I've divided the exercise plan into two parts: (1) the Weight-Bearing Aerobics Program; and (2) the High-Rapidity Weight-Training and Calisthenics Program.

The first emphasizes endurance exercises such as walking, jogging, swimming, and cycling. Where possible, I've included recommendations about using small handweights—weighing no more than three pounds—during the workout routines.

In the second part of the program, I've included calisthenics and exercises that can be used with weights to ensure that you'll put as much healthy stress as possible on your bones. Obviously, you don't want to push too far or too fast in this area because if you're at risk for osteoporosis, a broken bone could result. That's why it's important to take it easy and proceed with this program step by step, in consultation with your physician.

Now, let's get started on building up those bones!

FIVE

The Weight-Bearing and Non-Weight-Bearing Aerobics Programs

The first part of your bone-building exercise program involves "aerobics"—endurance exercises done at a level where the amount of oxygen you expend is balanced by the amount you take in through breathing.

Most aerobic exercises are "weight-bearing" in the sense that they involve putting pressure on your bones either through the force of gravity or by the exertion of your muscles. But some activities put more pressure on your bones than others—and it's those exercises that are emphasized in this chapter. Typical weight-bearing aerobic exercises include walking, jogging, bicycling, or dancing over an extended period of time.

If you try to exercise too intensely and feel yourself getting out of breath, then you're no longer involved in aerobic activity. You're doing "anaerobic" exercise, which will quickly expend your reserves of oxygen and put you in a state of oxygen debt. Anaerobic exercises involve activities such as sprinting or otherwise pushing your body beyond its capacity to process oxygen in a balanced way.

For our purposes, there are two main advantages to weight-bearing aerobic exercise: First, the more weight or resistance you apply to your skeletal structure, the more likely you are to build up your bone mass, or at least maintain the mass you already have. Second, endurance exercises improve your cardiovascular fitness and can help protect you against heart disease and other health problems.

In this chapter, you can choose your preferred form of aerobic exercise from a number of progressive programs, all of which have been adjusted according to age. These include:

• Walking (with or without handweights)

- Running or jogging

- Aerobic dancing (both regular and low-impact)

- Stair climbing

- Stationary running

- Rope skipping

- Stationary cycling

- Cycling

- Swimming

The main idea with any program you choose is to take it easy and move gradually from one level of difficulty to the next. That way, you'll minimize the possibility of injury and maximize the benefits to your bones and your cardiovascular system.

As you do these exercises, you should perform them in three stages:

1. First, warm up your body by doing light calisthenics or walking for about 3 to 5 minutes.

2. Second, do your chosen exercise at the lowest level first. Then, as prescribed, move up to the next week's level. If you find it to be too difficult to move up to the next week, repeat the exercise schedule you've just performed for an additional week.

3. Finally, cool down for about 5 minutes by walking about slowly and swinging your arms back and forth.

The Weight-Bearing Aerobics Programs

Walking Exercise Program
(Under 35 years of age)

Week	Distance (miles)	Time Goal (minutes)	Frequency/Week
1	2.0	35:00	3–5 sessions
2	2.0	32:30	3–5
3	2.0	30:00	3–5
4	2.5	38:30	3–5
5	2.5	38:00	3–5
6	2.5	37:30	3–5
7	3.0	46:00	3–5

Week	Distance (miles)	Time Goal (minutes)	Frequency/Week
8	3.0	45:00	3–5
9	3.0	44:00	3–5
10	3.0	43:00	3–5

Handweight Option for Last 4 Weeks
(With 3-pound weight in each hand, actively swinging the arms)

7	2.0	30:00	4 sessions
8	2.0	29:00	4
9	2.5	37:00	4
10	2.5	36:00	4

By the tenth week, an adequate level of aerobic conditioning will be reached. This level can be maintained on a schedule that involves four sessions per week. Adding the handweights will decrease both the required duration of the activity and the number of times per week it's necessary to work out to achieve an adequate training effect.

Walking Exercise Program
(35–50 years of age)

Week	Distance (miles)	Time Goal (minutes)	Frequency/Week
1	2.0	36:00	3–5 sessions
2	2.0	35:00	3–5
3	2.0	34:00	3–5
4	2.0	33:00	3–5
5	2.5	40:00	3–5
6	2.5	39:00	3–5
7	2.5	38:00	3–5
8	3.0	46:00	3–5
9	3.0	45:00	3–5
10	3.0	44:30	3–5

Handweight Option for Last 4 Weeks
(With 3-pound weight in each hand, actively swinging the arms)

7	2.0	32:00	4 sessions
8	2.0	30:00	4

Week	Distance (miles)	Time Goal (minutes)	Frequency/Week
9	2.5	38:00	4
10	2.5	37:00	4

By the tenth week, an adequate level of aerobic conditioning will be reached. This level can be maintained on a schedule that involves four sessions per week. Adding the handweights will decrease both the required duration of the activity and the number of times per week that it's necessary to work out to achieve an adequate training effect.

Walking Exercise Program
(51–65 years of age)

Week	Distance (miles)	Time Goal (minutes)	Frequency/Week
1	1.5	30:00	3–5 sessions
2	1.5	28:00	3–5
3	2.0	38:00	3–5
4	2.0	36:00	3–5
5	2.0	34:00	3–5
6	2.5	42:00	3–5
7	2.5	40:00	3–5
8	2.5	38:00	3–5
9	3.0	47:00	3–5
10	3.0	46:30	3–5
11	3.0	45:00	4
12	3.0	45:00	4

Handweight Option for Last 4 Weeks
(With 3-pound weight in each hand, actively swinging the arms)

Week	Distance (miles)	Time Goal (minutes)	Frequency/Week
9	2.0	32:00	4 sessions
10	2.0	30:00	4
11	2.5	39:00	4
12	2.5	38:00	4

By the twelfth week, an adequate level of aerobic conditioning will be reached. This level can be maintained on a schedule that involves four sessions per week. Adding the handweights will decrease both the required duration of the activity and the number of times per week it's necessary to work out to achieve an adequate training effect.

Walking Exercise Program
(Over 65 years of age)

Week	Distance (miles)	Time Goal (minutes)	Frequency/Week
1	1.0	24:00	3–5 sessions
2	1.0	22:00	3–5
3	1.0	20:00	3–5
4	1.5	32:00	3–5
5	1.5	31:00	3–5
6	1.5	30:00	3–5
7	2.0	40:00	3–5
8	2.0	39:00	3–5
9	2.0	38:00	3–5
10	2.5	47:00	3–5
11	2.5	45:00	4
12	2.5	43:00	4

Handweight Option for Last 4 Weeks
(With 3-pound weight in each hand, actively swinging the arms)

Week	Distance (miles)	Time Goal (minutes)	Frequency/Week
9	1.5	32:00	4 sessions
10	1.5	30:00	4
11	2.0	40:00	4
12	2.0	39:00	4

By the twelfth week, an adequate level of aerobic conditioning will be reached. This level can be maintained on a schedule that involves four sessions per week. Adding the handweights will decrease both the required duration of the activity and the number of times per week it's necessary to work out to achieve an adequate training effect.

Running/Jogging Exercise Program
(Under 35 years of age)

Week	Distance (miles)	Time Goal (minutes)	Frequency/Week
1	2.0 (walk)	30:00	3–4 sessions
2	3.0 (walk)	45:00	3–4
3	2.0 (walk/jog)	26:00	3–4
4	2.0 (walk/jog)	24:00	3–4
5	2.0 (jog)	22:00	3–4
6	2.0	20:00	4
7	2.5	25:00	4
8	2.5	23:00	4
9	3.0	29:00	4
10	3.0	27:00	4
11	3.0	25:00	4
12	3.0	24:00	4

By the sixth week, a satisfactory level of aerobic conditioning will be reached. But it's advisable for you to go on to achieve a higher level of fitness. Time goals are projected to be reached by the end of each week. If you haven't achieved the goal, repeat the week's program.

Running/Jogging Exercise Program
(35–50 years of age)

Week	Distance (miles)	Time Goal (minutes)	Frequency/Week
1	2.0 (walk)	32:00	3–4 sessions
2	2.5 (walk)	40:00	3–4
3	3.0 (walk)	48:00	3–4
4	2.0 (walk/jog)	27:00	3–4
5	2.0 (walk/jog)	25:00	3–4
6	2.0 (jog)	24:00	3–4
7	2.5	22:00	4
8	2.5	20:00	4
9	3.0	26:00	4
10	3.0	25:00	4
11	3.0	30:00	4

Week	Distance (miles)	Time Goal (minutes)	Frequency/Week
12	3.0	28:00	4
13	3.0	26:00	4
14	3.0	24:00	4

By the eighth week, a satisfactory level of aerobic conditioning will be reached. But it's advisable for you to go on to achieve a higher level of fitness. Time goals are projected to be reached by the end of each week. If you haven't achieved the goal, repeat the week's program.

Running/Jogging Exercise Program
(51–59 years of age)

Week	Distance (miles)	Time Goal (minutes)	Frequency/Week
1	1.0 (walk)	18:00	5 sessions
2	1.5 (walk)	27:00	4
3	2.0 (walk)	36:00	4
4	2.5 (walk)	45:00	3
5	3.0 (walk)	54:00	3
6	2.0 (walk/jog)	28:00	4
7	2.0 (walk/jog)	26:00	4
8	2.0 (jog)	24:00	4
9	2.5	30:00	4
10	2.5	28:00	4
11	2.5	27:00	4
12	3.0	33:00	4
13	3.0	31:30	4
14	3.0	30:00	4

By the ninth week, a satisfactory level of aerobic conditioning will be reached. But it's advisable for you to go on to achieve a higher level of fitness. Time goals are projected to be reached by the end of each week. If you haven't achieved the goal, repeat the week's program.

Running/Jogging Exercise Program
(Age 60 and older)

This type of physical activity is not recommended for the totally inactive individual. But jogging is acceptable for the individual who has been jogging or running prior to age 60 and who wishes to continue. Even progressive jogging programs are permitted for those past 60 years of age, provided the exercise is conducted in a medically supervised environment and preceded by an adequate medical examination.

Aerobic Dancing and Other Exercise Programs Conducted to Music
(Under 35 years of age)

Week	Time (minutes)	Maximum Heart Rate* (Beats/Minute)	Frequency/Week
1	15:00	120–130	3 sessions
2	20:00	120–130	3
3	20:00	130–140	3
4	25:00	130–140	3
5	30:00	140–150	3
6	35:00	140–150	3
7	40:00	150–160	3
8	45:00	150–160	3

By the eighth week, an adequate level of aerobic fitness will be reached, consistent with a good level of over-all fitness for women.

Aerobic Dancing and Other Exercise Programs Conducted to Music
(35–50 years of age)

Week	Time (minutes)	Maximum Heart Rate* (Beats/Minute)	Frequency/Week
1	15:00	110–120	3 sessions
2	20:00	110–120	3
3	20:00	120–130	3
4	25:00	120–130	3
5	25:00	130–140	3

*Heart rates should be determined by taking your pulse at three or more equal intervals during exercise. To get the rate, count your pulse for 10 seconds, then multiply by 6.

Week	Time (minutes)	Maximum Heart Rate* (Beats/Minute)	Frequency/Week
6	30:00	130–140	3
7	30:00	140–150	3
8	35:00	140–150	3
9	40:00	140–150	3
10	45:00	140–150	3

By the tenth week, an adequate level of aerobic fitness will be reached, consistent with a good level of over-all fitness for women.

Aerobic Dancing and Other Exercise Programs Conducted to Music
(51–59 years of age)

Week	Time (minutes)	Maximum Heart Rate* (Beats/Minute)	Frequency/Week
1	12:00	100–110	3 sessions
2	15:00	100–110	3
3	18:00	110–120	3
4	20:00	110–120	3
5	20:00	120–130	3
6	25:00	120–130	3
7	25:00	130–140	3
8	30:00	130–140	3
9	35:00	130–140	3
10	35:00	140–145	3
11	40:00	140–145	3
12	45:00	140–145	3

By the twelfth week, an adequate level of aerobic fitness will be reached, consistent with a good level of over-all fitness for women.

*Heart rates should be determined by taking your pulse at three or more equal intervals during exercise. To get the rate, count your pulse for 10 seconds, then multiply by 6.

Aerobic Dancing and Other Exercise
Programs Conducted to Music
(Age 60 and older)

This type of physical activity is not recommended for the totally inactive individual. But the individual who has been involved in aerobic dancing prior to age 60 and who wishes to continue with it can do so. Even progressive programs are permitted past 60 years of age, provided the exercise is conducted in a medically supervised environment and preceded by an adequate medical examination.

Stair-Climbing Exercise Program
(Under 35 years of age)

Week	Round Trips (Average no. per week)	Time Goal (minutes)	Frequency/Week
1	5	10:00	3–5 sessions
2	5	11:00	3–5
3	5	12:00	3–5
4	6	12:00	3–5
5	6	14:00	3–5
6	7	14:00	3–5
7	7	16:00	3–5
8	7	18:00	3–5
9	8	18:00	3–5
10	8	20:00	3–5

During the first six weeks, you should exercise the required number of minutes, but not continuously. Rest frequently and as long as necessary, but walk slowly while resting. The time goal is the combined time for both stair climbing and resting. Beginning with the seventh week, the time goals refer to continuous exercise. Warm up for 3 to 5 minutes by walking briskly. Cool down for 5 minutes after exercise by walking slowly.

This program assumes that the exercise will be done on 10 steps, 6 to 7 inches in height, at a 25-to-30-degree incline. Use of a banister is acceptable and encouraged. If a stair-climbing machine is used, exercise the required time, adjusting the speed in such a way that your time goal can be reached.

Stair-Climbing Exercise Program
(35–50 years of age)

Week	Round Trips (Average no. per week)	Time Goal (minutes)	Frequency/Week
1	5	7:30	3–5 sessions
2	5	7:30	3–5
3	5	10:00	3–5
4	5	12:00	3–5
5	5	14:00	3–5
6	6	14:00	3–5
7	6	16:00	3–5
8	7	16:00	3–5
9	7	17:00	3–5
10	7	18:00	3–5
11	8	18:00	3–5
12	8	20:00	3–5

During the first six weeks, you should exercise the required number of minutes, but not continuously. Rest frequently and as long as necessary, but walk slowly while resting. The time goal is the combined time for both stair climbing and resting. Beginning with the seventh week, the time goals refer to continuous exercise. Warm up for 3 to 5 minutes by walking briskly. Cool down for 5 minutes after exercise by walking slowly.

This program assumes that the exercise will be done on 10 steps, 6 to 7 inches in height, at a 25-to-30-degree incline. Use of a banister is acceptable and encouraged. If a stair-climbing machine is used, exercise the required time, adjusting the speed in such a way that your time goal can be reached.

Stair-Climbing Exercise Program
(51–59 years of age)

Week	Round Trips (Average no. per week)	Time Goal (minutes)	Frequency/Week
1	4	5:00	3–5 sessions
2	4	6:00	3–5
3	4	7:00	3–5

Week	Round Trips (Average no. per week)	Time Goal (minutes)	Frequency/Week
4	4	8:00	3–5
5	4	10:00	3–5
6	5	10:00	3–5
7	5	11:00	3–5
8	5	12:00	3–5
9	6	12:00	3–5
10	6	14:00	3–5
11	7	14:00	3–5
12	7	16:00	3–5
13	8	16:00	3–5
14	8	18:00	3–5

During the first six weeks, you should exercise the required number of minutes, but not continuously. Rest frequently and as long as necessary, but walk slowly while resting. The time goal is the combined time for both stair climbing and resting. Beginning with the seventh week, the time goals refer to continuous exercise. Warm up for 3 to 5 minutes by walking briskly. Cool down for 5 minutes after exercise by walking slowly.

This program assumes that the exercise will be done on 10 steps, 6 to 7 inches in height, at a 25-to-30-degree incline. Use of a banister is acceptable and encouraged. If a stair-climbing machine is used, exercise the required time, adjusting the speed in such a way that your time goal can be reached.

Stair-Climbing Exercise Program
(Age 60 and older)

Not recommended, unless a stair-climbing exercise machine is used. If one is available, use the program for the 51-to-59-year age group.

Stationary Running Exercise Program
(Under 35 years of age)

Week	Time Goal (minutes)	Steps/Minute*	Frequency/Week
1	7:30	70–80	4–5 sessions

Week	Time Goal (minutes)	Steps/Minute*	Frequency/Week
2	7:30	70–80	4–5
3	10:00	70–80	4–5
4	12:30	70–80	4–5
5	15:00	70–80	4–5
6	10:00	80–90	4–5
7	12:30	80–90	4–5
8	15:00	80–90	4–5
9	15:00	80–90	4–5
10	15:00	90–100	4–5

During the first six weeks, you should exercise the required number of minutes, but not continuously. Rest frequently and as long as necessary, but continue to walk slowly while resting. The time goals represent the combined stationary running and rest periods. Beginning with the seventh week, the time goals represent continuous exercise. Warm up for 3 to 5 minutes by walking briskly. Cool down for at least 5 minutes after exercise by walking slowly. Exercise on a cushioned surface (e.g., a thick carpet) in athletic shoes that have either rippled or deep-cushioned soles.

Stationary Running Exercise Program
(35–50 years of age)

Week	Time Goal (minutes)	Steps/Minute*	Frequency/Week
1	6:00	70–80	4–5 sessions
2	7:30	70–80	4–5
3	7:30	80–90	4–5
4	10:00	70–80	4–5
5	12:30	70–80	4–5
6	15:00	70–80	4–5
7	10:00	80–90	4–5
8	12:30	80–90	4–5
9	12:30	80–90	4–5
10	15:00	90–100	4–5

*Count only when your left foot hits the floor. You must lift your feet at least 8 inches off the floor.

Week	Time Goal (minutes)	Steps/Minute*	Frequency/Week
11	15:00	80–90	4–5
12	15:00	90–100	4–5

During the first six weeks, you should exercise the required number of minutes, but not continuously. Rest frequently and as long as necessary, but continue to walk slowly while resting. The time goals represent the combined stationary running and rest periods. Beginning with the seventh week, the time goals represent continuous exercise. Warm up for 3 to 5 minutes by walking briskly. Cool down for at least 5 minutes after exercise by walking slowly. Exercise on a cushioned surface (e.g., a thick carpet) in athletic shoes that have either rippled or deep-cushioned soles.

Stationary Running Exercise Program
(51–59 years of age)

Week	Time Goal (minutes)	Steps/Minute*	Frequency/Week
1	5:00	70–80	4–5 sessions
2	7:30	70–80	4–5
3	10:00	70–80	4–5
4	10:00	70–80	4–5
5	12:30	70–80	4–5
6	12:30	70–80	4–5
7	10:00	80–90	4–5
8	10:00	80–90	4–5
9	10:00	80–90	4–5
10	12:30	80–90	4–5
11	12:30	80–90	4–5
12	12:30	80–90	4–5
13	15:00	80–90	4–5
14	15:00	90–100	4–5

During the first six weeks, you should exercise the required number of minutes, but not continuously. Rest frequently and as long as necessary, but continue to walk slowly while resting. The time goals

*Count only when your left foot hits the floor. You must lift your feet at least 8 inches off the floor.

represent the combined stationary running and rest periods. Beginning with the seventh week, the time goals represent continuous exercise. Warm up for 3 to 5 minutes by walking briskly. Cool down for at least 5 minutes after exercise by walking slowly. Exercise on a cushioned surface (e.g., a thick carpet) in athletic shoes that have either rippled or deep-cushioned soles.

Stationary Running Exercise Program
(Age 60 and older)

Not recommended.

Rope-Skipping Exercise Program
(Under 35 years of age)

Week	Time Goal (minutes)	Steps/Minute	Frequency/Week
1	10:00	70–90	4–5 sessions
2	10:00	70–90	4–5
3	10:00	70–90	4–5
4	12:30	70–90	4–5
5	12:30	90–110	4–5
6	15:00	70–90	4–5
7	15:00	90–110	4–5
8	12:30	70–90	4–5
9	12:30	90–110	4–5
10	15:00	90–110	4–5

During the first six weeks, you should exercise the required number of minutes, but not continuously. Rest frequently and as long as necessary, but continue to skip very slowly or to walk while resting. The time goals represent the combined time for rope skipping and resting. Beginning with the seventh week, the time goals represent continuous exercise. Warm up for 3 to 5 minutes by walking briskly. Cool down for at least 5 minutes after exercise by walking slowly.

Exercise on a cushioned surface (e.g., a thick carpet) in athletic shoes. Skip with both feet together, or step over the rope, alternating feet.

Rope-Skipping Exercise Program
(35–50 years of age)

Week	Time Goal (minutes)	Steps/Minute	Frequency/Week
1	8:00	70–90	4–5 sessions
2	8:00	70–90	4–5
3	9:00	70–90	4–5
4	10:00	70–90	4–5
5	12:30	70–90	4–5
6	12:30	70–90	4–5
7	10:00	90–110	4–5
8	10:00	90–110	4–5
9	12:30	90–110	4–5
10	12:30	90–110	4–5
11	15:00	90–110	4–5
12	15:00	90–110	4–5

During the first six weeks, you should exercise the required number of minutes, but not continuously. Rest frequently and as long as necessary, but continue to skip very slowly or to walk while resting. The time goals represent the combined time for rope skipping and resting. Beginning with the seventh week, the time goals represent continuous exercise. Warm up for 3 to 5 minutes by walking briskly. Cool down for at least 5 minutes after exercise by walking slowly.

Exercise on a cushioned surface (e.g., a thick carpet) in athletic shoes. Skip with both feet together, or step over the rope, alternating feet.

Rope-Skipping Exercise Program
(51–59 years of age)

Week	Time Goal (minutes)	Steps/Minute	Frequency/Week
1	6:00	70–90	4–5 sessions
2	8:00	70–90	4–5
3	10:00	70–90	4–5
4	10:00	70–90	4–5
5	12:30	70–90	4–5
6	12:30	70–90	4–5
7	10:00	90–110	4–5

Week	Time Goal (minutes)	Steps/Minute	Frequency/Week
8	10:00	90–110	4–5
9	11:00	90–110	4–5
10	11:00	90–110	4–5
11	12:00	90–110	4–5
12	13:00	90–110	4–5
13	14:00	90–110	4–5
14	15:00	90–110	4–5

During the first six weeks, you should exercise the required number of minutes, but not continuously. Rest frequently and as long as necessary, but continue to skip very slowly or to walk while resting. The time goals represent the combined time for rope skipping and resting. Beginning with the seventh week, the time goals represent continuous exercise. Warm up for 3 to 5 minutes by walking briskly. Cool down for at least 5 minutes after exercise by walking slowly.

Exercise on a cushioned surface (e.g., a thick carpet) in athletic shoes. Skip with both feet together, or step over the rope, alternating feet.

Rope-Skipping Exercise Program
(Age 60 and older)

Not recommended.

The Non-Weight-Bearing Aerobics Programs

The following programs typically involve progressive non-weight-bearing activities. But they still have aerobic benefit and are somewhat beneficial in counteracting or slowing the development of osteoporosis.

The exercises in this section include stationary cycling, cycling, and swimming. If you choose one of these activities, follow the same basic guidelines that have been recommended for the other programs—including adequate warm-up and cool-down periods.

Stationary Cycling Exercise Program
(Under 35 years of age)

Week	Speed (mph/rpm)	Time Goal (minutes)	Pulse Rate* (after exercise)	Frequency/Week
1	15/55	8:00	<140	4–5 sessions
2	15/55	10:00	<140	4–5
3	15/55	12:00	<140	4–5
4	17.5/65	12:00	<150	4–5
5	17.5/65	14:00	<150	4–5
6	17.5/65	16:00	<150	4–5
7	17.5/65	18:00	>150	4–5
8	17.5/65	20:00	>150	4–5
9	20/75	20:00	>160	4–5
10	20/75	22:30	>160	4–5
11	25/90	25:00	>160	4–5
12	25/90	30:00	>160	4–5

During the first six weeks, warm up before beginning the actual workout by cycling for 3 minutes at 17 to 20 mph, without resistance on the bike. At the conclusion of the exercise, cool down by cycling for 5 minutes with no resistance.

Stationary Cycling Exercise Program
(35–50 years of age)

Week	Speed (mph/rpm)	Time Goal (minutes)	Pulse Rate* (after exercise)	Frequency/Week
1	15/55	6:00	<140	4–5 sessions
2	15/55	8:00	<140	4–5
3	15/55	10:00	<140	4–5
4	15/55	12:00	<150	4–5
5	15/55	14:00	<150	4–5
6	15/55	16:00	<150	4–5
7	15/55	18:00	<150	4–5
8	15/55	20:00	<150	4–5

*Add enough resistance to the bike so that your pulse rate (PR), counted for 10 seconds immediately after exercise and multipled by 6, equals the specified rate. If your pulse is higher than the specified rate, lower the resistance before cycling again. If your pulse rate is lower, add resistance to the bike.

Week	Speed (mph/rpm)	Time Goal (minutes)	Pulse Rate* (after exercise)	Frequency/Week
9	17.5/65	20:00	<150	4–5
10	17.5/65	22:00	>150	4–5
11	20/75	22:00	>150	4–5
12	20/75	25:00	>150	4–5
13	20/75	27:30	>150	4–5
14	25/90	30:00	>150	4–5

During the first six weeks, warm up before beginning the actual workout by cycling for 3 minutes at 17 to 20 mph, without resistance on the bike. At the conclusion of the exercise, cool down by cycling for 5 minutes with no resistance.

Stationary Cycling Exercise Program
(51–59 years of age)

Week	Speed (mph/rpm)	Time Goal (minutes)	Pulse Rate* (after exercise)	Frequency/Week
1	15/55	6:00	<135	4–5 sessions
2	15/55	8:00	<135	4–5
3	15/55	10:00	<135	4–5
4	15/55	12:00	<140	4–5
5	15/55	14:00	<140	4–5
6	17.5/65	16:00	<140	4–5
7	17.5/65	18:00	<140	4–5
8	17.5/65	20:00	<140	4–5
9	20/75	20:00	<150	4–5
10	20/75	20:00	<150	4–5
11	20/75	22:00	<150	4–5
12	25/90	22:00	<150	4–5
13	25/90	25:00	>150	4–5
14	25/90	30:00	>150	4–5

*Add enough resistance to the bike so that the pulse rate (PR), counted for 10 seconds immediately after exercise and multipled by 6, equals the specified rate. If your pulse is higher than the specified rate, lower the resistance before cycling again. If your pulse rate is lower, add resistance to the bike.

During the first six weeks, warm up before beginning the actual workout by cycling for 3 minutes at 17 to 20 mph, without resistance on the bike. At the conclusion of the exercise, cool down by cycling for 5 minutes with no resistance.

From the tenth week on, the exercise periods can be divided into two equal periods, performed twice daily.

Stationary Cycling Exercise Program
(Age 60 and older)

Week	Speed (mph/rpm)	Time Goal (minutes)	Pulse Rate* (after exercise)	Frequency/Week
1	15/55	4:00	<100	4–5 sessions
2	15/55	6:00	<100	4–5
3	15/55	8:00	<100	4–5
4	15/55	10:00	<110	4–5
5	15/55	12:00	<110	4–5
6	15/55	14:00	<110	4–5
7	15/55	16:00	<120	4–5
8	15/55	16:00	<120	4–5
9	17.5/65	18:00	<120	4–5
10	17.5/65	20:00	<120	4–5
11	17.5/65	22:30	<120	4–5
12	20/75	22:30	<120	4–5
13	20/75	25:00	<130	4–5
14	20/75	26:00	<130	4–5
15	20/75	28:00	<130	4–5
16	20/75	30:00	<130	4–5

During the first six weeks, warm up before beginning the actual workout by cycling for 3 minutes at 17 to 20 mph, without resistance on the bike. At the conclusion of the exercise, cool down by cycling for 5 minutes with no resistance.

From the tenth week on, the exercise periods can be divided into two equal periods, performed twice daily.

*Add enough resistance to the bike so that the pulse rate (PR), counted for 10 seconds immediately after exercise and multipled by 6, equals the specified rate. If your pulse is higher than the specified rate, lower the resistance before cycling again. If your pulse rate is lower, add resistance to the bike.

Cycling Exercise Program
(Under 35 years of age)

Week	Distance (miles)	Time Goal (minutes)	Frequency/Week
1	5.0	30:00	4–5 sessions
2	5.0	25:00	4–5
3	5.0	20:00	4–5
4	6.0	26:00	4–5
5	6.0	24:00	4–5
6	7.0	30:00	4–5
7	7.0	28:00	4–5
8	8.0	35:00	4–5
9	8.0	32:00	4–5
10	8.0	30:00	4–5

By the seventh week, an adequate level of aerobic fitness has been reached by exercising four days a week. Higher levels of fitness can be achieved by exercising over longer distances, at faster speeds, or for more days per week.

Cycling Exercise Program
(35–50 years of age)

Week	Distance (miles)	Time Goal (minutes)	Frequency/Week
1	4.0	20:00	4–5 sessions
2	4.0	18:00	4–5
3	5.0	24:00	4–5
4	5.0	22:00	4–5
5	5.0	20:00	4–5
6	6.0	26:00	4–5
7	6.0	24:00	4–5
8	7.0	30:00	4–5
9	7.0	28:00	4–5
10	8.0	33:00	4–5
11	8.0	32:00	4–5
12	8.0	30:00	4–5

By the eighth week, an adequate level of aerobic fitness has been reached by exercising four days a week. Higher levels of fitness can be achieved by exercising over longer distances, at faster speeds, or for more days per week.

Cycling Exercise Program
(51–59 years of age)

Week	Distance (miles)	Time Goal (minutes)	Frequency/Week
1	3.0	20:00	4–5 sessions
2	3.0	18:00	4–5
3	4.0	25:00	4–5
4	4.0	24:00	4–5
5	5.0	32:00	4–5
6	5.0	28:00	4–5
7	5.0	24:00	4–5
8	6.0	30:00	4–5
9	6.0	26:00	4–5
10	7.0	32:00	4–5
11	7.0	30:00	4–5
12	7.0	28:00	4–5
13	8.0	33:00	4–5
14	8.0	32:00	4–5

By the tenth week, an adequate level of aerobic fitness has been reached by exercising four days a week. Higher levels of fitness can be achieved by exercising over longer distances, at faster speeds, or for more days per week.

Cycling Exercise Program
(Age 60 and older)

It's not recommended that a progressive cycling program, such as those for younger age groups, be used by people over 60 years of age. But when a regular cyclist reaches 60, the cycling may be continued without restrictions. To avoid problems, including falls and fractures, 3-wheeled cycling or cycling on a stationary cycle are good alternatives.

Swimming Exercise Program
(Under 35 years of age)

Week	Distance (yards)	Time Goal (minutes)	Frequency/Week
1	400	10:30	4 sessions
2	600	15:00	4
3	800	20:00	4
4	1000	25:00	4
5	1200	30:00	4
6	1400	35:00	4
7	1500	37:30	4
8	1600	40:00	4
9	1700	42:30	4
10	1800	45:00	4

Use any stroke that enables you to swim the required distance in the allotted time. Resting is permissible during the initial weeks. The objective is to reach the distance–time goals at the end of a week. This program ultimately meets the requirements of Dr. Eric Orwoll for maintaining necessary bone mineral content—i.e., a minimum of 3 hours of swimming per week.

Swimming Exercise Program
(35–50 years of age)

Week	Distance (yards)	Time Goal (minutes)	Frequency/Week
1	300	8:15	4 sessions
2	400	11:30	4
3	600	16:30	4
4	800	22:00	4
5	900	25:00	4
6	1000	27:30	4
7	1100	30:30	4
8	1200	33:15	4
9	1300	36:00	4
10	1400	38:00	4
11	1500	41:30	4
12	1600	45:00	4

Use any stroke that enables you to swim the required distance in the allotted time. Resting is permissible during the initial weeks. The objective is to reach the distance–time goals at the end of a week. This program ultimately meets the requirements of Dr. Eric Orwoll for maintaining necessary bone mineral content—i.e., a minimum of 3 hours of swimming per week.

Swimming Exercise Program
(51–65 years of age)

Week	Distance (yards)	Time Goal (minutes)	Frequency/Week
1	200	6:00	4 sessions
2	300	9:00	4
3	400	12:30	4
4	500	15:00	4
5	600	18:00	4
6	700	21:00	4
7	800	24:30	4
8	900	27:30	4
9	1000	30:00	4
10	1100	33:30	4
11	1200	36:30	4
12	1300	39:30	4
13	1400	42:00	4
14	1500	46:00	4

Use any stroke that enables you to swim the required distance in the allotted time. Resting is permissible during the initial weeks. The objective is to reach the distance–time goals at the end of a week. This program ultimately meets the requirements of Dr. Eric Orwoll for maintaining necessary bone mineral content—i.e., a minimum of 3 hours of swimming per week.

Swimming Exercise Program
(Over 65 years of age)

Week	Distance (yards)	Time Goal (minutes)	Frequency/Week
1	200	7:30	4 sessions
2	200	6:30	4
3	300	11:00	4
4	300	10:00	4
5	400	13:20	4
6	500	16:30	4
7	600	20:00	4
8	700	23:00	4
9	800	26:30	4
10	900	30:00	4
11	1000	33:30	4
12	1100	36:30	4
13	1200	40:00	4
14	1300	43:00	4
15	1400	46:30	4

Use any stroke that enables you to swim the required distance in the allotted time. Resting is permissible during the initial weeks. The objective is to reach the distance–time goals at the end of a week. This program ultimately meets the requirements of Dr. Eric Orwoll for maintaining necessary bone mineral content—i.e., a minimum of 3 hours of swimming per week.

SIX

The High-Rapidity Weight-Training and Calisthenics Program

As we've just seen, any sound strategy to combat osteoporosis should begin with a solid aerobics program. In addition, you should engage in a separate muscle- and bone-building program that focuses on specific areas of the body.

To this end, I've designed two types of programs, one involving the use of light dumbbells and the other based on calisthenics and some simple surgical tubing. Feel free to choose either of these approaches as a backup to your aerobics routine.

General Guidelines

What equipment is required? The Weight-Training Program involves the use of two dumbbells, which you can purchase in most sporting-goods stores. The recommended starting weight for women is 1.5 to 3 pounds, and progresses to a 5-pound dumbbell. Men should begin with 3-to-5-pound dumbbells and progress to 10-to-15-pound weights.

It's important not to become "weight conscious"! Put the emphasis not on the amount of weight you use, but rather on performing the exercises correctly. It doesn't take much weight to do your bones and muscles plenty of good.

The second group of exercises—the Calisthenics Program—involves the use of a springy, rubbery surgical tubing that can be bought at a medical-supply store. The exercises designed to be used with this material involve using the resistance provided by the tubing, much as you might stretch a rubber band by holding one end of it in each hand and then pulling it in opposing directions. As with a rubber band, the resistance provided by the tubing can be increased by stretching a relatively short portion of the tube, or decreased by stretching a relatively long portion.

Exercise experts in our Aerobics Center have found that this surgical tubing will retain its strength and elasticity for a long time, even when it's used over and over again. Also, the material costs much less than the exercise springs and chest expanders that are typically advertised on television or radio or in the print media. Dealers who sell surgical tubing for rehabilitation and exercise may suggest the purchase of a 50-foot box at a price of $20 to $40. If you choose not to buy an entire box, you can buy this material by the foot. Usually, a six-to-seven-foot piece of tubing is quite adequate for exercise purposes. The usual thickness for this tubing is 3/16th of an inch for the inside diameter, and 3/8th of an inch for the outside diameter.

Finally, both the weight-training and the calisthenics programs require a low, sturdy bench.

Don't forget the warm-up! Before you begin any of these exercises, spend a few minutes warming up. One purpose of the warm-up is to reduce the likelihood that you'll pull a muscle or otherwise injure yourself during the exercise program. Another purpose is to get your body "revved up" to enhance your performance.

Any combination of *slow* stretching exercises, such as toe touching or side bends, for five minutes or so just before the workout should be adequate for these programs.

Sets and repetitions. Throughout these two programs you'll find references to "repetitions" and "sets." A repetition is simply a repeating of an exercise a designated number of times in a row, without any rest. A set refers to a group of repetitions. If more than one set of an exercise is supposed to be performed, then you should take a short rest of one to two minutes between each set.

For example, if an exercise calls for 2 sets of 8 to 12 repetitions, that means that you repeat the exercise 8 to 12 times in a row. Then you rest for a minute or two. Finally, you do the exercises again (the second set) for another 8 to 12 repetitions.

Stick to the program! Each of these programs has been designed so that all of the large and small groups of muscles in the body get a workout. Also, it's best to exercise a large muscle group first and then to finish with a small muscle group. In any event, you shouldn't concentrate on just one group of exercises and neglect the rest of the body.

The exercise programs in this book have been designed with all these considerations in mind. So be sure to do all the exercises in the order suggested to get the maximum benefits.

The benefits of good breathing. Good breathing is important for two reasons:

• You need an adequate supply of oxygen for your muscles to work efficiently.

• Holding your breath will stabilize the muscles of your chest and allow a greater force to be generated—but this may also cause heart irregularities to occur. So it's important to inhale as you perform an exercise, and then to exhale immediately after a movement has been completed.

The range-of-motion rule. It's important for each of these exercises to be performed completely, with the targeted muscle groups getting a full workout. There may be a temptation to swing your body to make the completion of a repetition easier—but avoid this temptation! To give each muscle an adequate workout and to put maximum pressure on your bones, it's important to use a full extension and contraction of each muscle group, with as little extra body motion as possible.

How long should you work out? Start with a 5-to-10-minute workout three times a week, and then slowly work up to a minimum of 20 minutes three times a week. The six-week conditioning programs in this chapter have been designed with these time considerations in mind.

As you progress, this schedule can be extended, depending on your ultimate goals of fitness and strength. For example, individuals who like to focus on weight training usually exercise for 20 to 45 minutes per session, three times a week.

Both the Calisthenics and the Weight-Training Programs should be done *in addition to* the aerobics workout programs described in chapter 5. Typically, these muscle- and bone-building activities will be performed on the days when you're not doing your aerobics. If you want to do these weight-training or calisthenics exercises on the same day as your aerobic workout, it's best to do them *after* the aerobics. That way, you're less likely to tire out your muscles or lower your endurance before you go out for your walk, run, swim, or other endurance activity.

The Weight-Training Program

To make it easier to use this program, I've first included descriptions of each exercise, with stick-figure drawings to illustrate the various positions and movements. After these descriptions, you'll find charts of the set and repetition requirements for each exercise for four separate age groups.

When you reach the maximum number of sets and repetitions in the sixth week, you can continue with that level indefinitely, three days a week. If you become particularly interested in this type of exercise, you can increase your time and weight levels under the supervision of a qualified physician or exercise physiologist. But remember: Keep doing your aerobics program on alternate days.

Exercise 1: Lying Bench Press

Lie flat on a bench, with your knees bent and feet flat on the bench. Hold the dumbbells against your upper chest in each hand. Your hands should be held shoulder-width apart, with the palms facing toward your feet, and your back should be flat on the bench. Remember: The recommended starting weights are 1.5 to 3 pounds for women and 3 to 5 pounds for men.

Push the dumbbells straight up until your arms are fully extended. Then return slowly to the starting position, with the dumbbells against your upper chest.

This exercise will build up the muscles of your chest and arms.

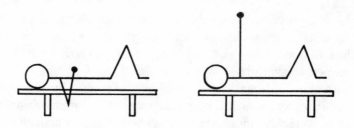

Exercise 2: Bent-over Rowing

Stand bent over at the waist, with one hand on the bench for balance. Hold one dumbbell in your free hand, with the arm fully extended.

Pull the dumbbell up to your shoulder, then lower it to the starting position. When you've done the required number of repetitions and sets with one arm, repeat the exercises with the other arm.

These movements will strengthen your arm and back muscles.

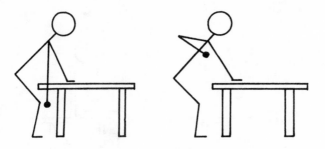

Exercise 3: Shoulder Shrugs

Stand upright with your knees slightly bent for support. Hold one dumbbell in each hand, with your arms fully extended.

Lift your shoulders as high as possible in a "shrug," at the same time keeping your arms and elbows straight. Then, lower your shoulders to the starting position and repeat the exercise.

These movements will tone up the trapezius muscles of your upper shoulders.

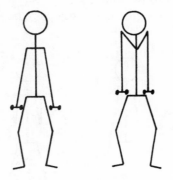

Exercise 4: Seated Overhead Press

Sit on a bench with your back supported, if possible. Hold a dumbbell in each hand, with your arms bent, palms facing forward close to the sides of your upper chest.

Push the dumbbells straight up over your head until your arms are fully extended. Then slowly lower the dumbbells to the starting position. If you prefer, you can alternate the raising of your arms. But in that case, be sure you exercise both arms before you count 1 repetition.

Your upper back, arm, and shoulder muscles will benefit from this exercise.

Exercise 5: Standing Dumbbell Curls

Stand upright with your knees slightly bent to give you support. Hold a dumbbell in each hand with an underhand grip and your forearms turned toward the front.

Raise both dumbbells to the tops of your shoulders, always holding your body steady through the movement. Your elbows should remain stationary, as a kind of pivot point just above your hips. Then, slowly lower the dumbbells to the starting position.

This exercise strengthens the biceps muscles on the fronts of the upper arms.

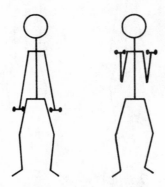

Exercise 6: Bent-over Triceps Kickback

Stand bent over at the waist, with one hand on the bench for balance. Hold a dumbbell in your free hand, with your arm bent at the elbow against your side. The hand holding the dumbbell should face toward the back.

Move the dumbbell in a backward and upward motion by straightening your elbow. Only your forearm should move; the upper arm should remain stationary. Then slowly return the dumbbell to the starting position.

The word triceps is used to describe this exercise because the movement builds up the triceps muscles on the backs of the upper arms, as well as the shoulder muscles.

Exercise 7: Abdominal Crunch

Lie flat on a mat or a carpet-covered floor, with your knees bent up toward your chest and your arms flat against the floor at your sides. You don't need any weights for this exercise.

Lift your head and shoulders up to a 45-degree angle, until your shoulder blades rise from the floor. Then slowly lower your head and shoulders back to the starting position on the floor.

This exercise is excellent for strengthening your stomach muscles.

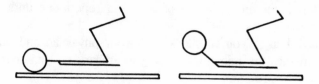

Exercise 8: The Lunge

Stand with your feet together and a dumbbell in each hand at your sides. Your arms should be fully extended downward, with your palms pointing toward your body, as if you were holding the handle of a briefcase in each hand.

Step forward, bending your stepping leg in a "lunge" movement, with the knee bent as though you were lowering yourself to the floor. The back leg should be kept straight at the knee. Then, push your body back up to the starting position by using only the muscles of the bent leg. Keep your back straight throughout the exercise. Then repeat the movement using the opposite leg. When you've done a lunge with each leg, count that as 1 repetition.

This exercise, which will strengthen the muscles in your legs and lower torso, is an excellent conditioning exercise for skiing.

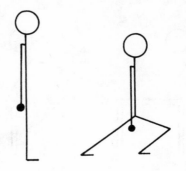

Following are the set-and-repetition schedules for my six-week Weight-Training Program for four different age groups. Throughout, the letter *s* refers to "set" or "sets," and the letter *r* refers to "repetitions."

As you'll see, the number of sets and repetitions increases gradually through the six-week program. As you get stronger from week to week, you should find it relatively easy to move from one exercise level to the next. But if you should discover at any point that you're not quite ready to graduate to the next level of difficulty, feel free to continue your current schedule of sets and repetitions until you feel ready to move on.

Finally, I urge you to check with your physician and undergo a thorough medical examination before you embark on this or any other physical fitness program.

Weight-Training Exercises
(Under 35 years of age)

s = sets
r = repetitions

Exercises	Week 1	2	3	4	5	6
Lying Bench Press	1s/8–12r	2s/8–12r	2s/15r	2s/18r	3s/20r	3s/25r
Bent-over Rowing	1s/8–12r	2s/8–12r	2s/15r	2s/18r	3s/20r	3s/25r
Shoulder Shrugs	1s/8–12r	2s/8–12r	2s/15r	2s/18r	3s/20r	3s/25r
Seated Overhead Press	1s/8–12r	2s/8–12r	2s/12r	2s/12–15r	3s/15r	3s/15r
Standing Dumbbell Curls	1s/8–12r	2s/8–12r	2s/15r	2s/18r	3s/20r	3s/25r

Exercises	Week 1	2	3	4	5	6
Bent-over Triceps Kickback	1s/8–12r	2s/8–12r	2s/15r	2s/18r	3s/20r	3s/25r
Abdominal Crunch	10–15r	15–18r	18–20r	20–25r	25–30r	30r
Lunge	1s/12–15r	2s/12–15r	2s/15r	2s/15–20r	3s/25r	3s/30r

Weight-Training Exercises
(35–50 years of age)

s = sets
r = repetitions

Exercises	Week 1	2	3	4	5	6
Lying Bench Press	1s/8–12r	1s/12–15r	2s/10–12r	2s/12–15r	3s/12r	3s/15r
Bent-over Rowing	1s/8–12r	1s/12–15r	2s/10–12r	2s/12–15r	3s/12r	3s/15r
Shoulder Shrugs	1s/8–12r	1s/12–15r	2s/10–12r	2s/12–15r	3s/12r	3s/15r
Seated Overhead Press	1s/8–10r	1s/8–10r	2s/8–10r	2s/8–10r	3s/10r	3s/12r
Standing Dumbbell Curls	1s/8–12r	1s/12–15r	2s/10–12r	2s/12–15r	3s/12r	3s/15r
Bent-over Triceps Kickback	1s/8–12r	1s/12–15r	2s/10–12r	2s/12–15r	3s/12r	3s/15r
Abdominal Crunch	10–15r	15–18r	18–20r	20–25r	25–30r	30r
Lunge	1s/8–12r	1s/12–15r	2s/10–12r	2s/12–15r	3s/12r	3s/15r

Weight-Training Exercises
(51–65 years of age)

s = sets
r = repetitions

Exercises	Week 1	2	3	4	5	6
Lying Bench Press	1s/6–8r	1s/8–12r	2s/8–12r	2s/12–15r	3s/10r	3s/12r
Bent-over Rowing	1s/6–8r	1s/8–12r	2s/8–12r	2s/12–15r	3s/10r	3s/12r
Shoulder Shrugs	1s/6–8r	1s/8–12r	2s/8–12r	2s/12–15r	3s/10r	3s/12r
Seated Overhead Press	1s/6–8r	1s/8–10r	2s/8–10r	2s/8–10r	3s/8r	3s/10r
Standing Dumbbell Curls	1s/6–8r	1s/8–12r	2s/8–12r	2s/12–15r	3s/10r	3s/12r
Bent-over Triceps Kickback	1s/6–8r	1s/8–12r	2s/8–12r	2s/12–15r	3s/10r	3s/12r
Abdominal Crunch	10–15r	15–18r	18–20r	20–25r	25–30r	30r
Lunge	1s/6–8r	1s/8–12r	2s/8–12r	2s/12–15r	3s/10r	3s/12r

Weight-Training Exercises
(Over 65 years of age)

s = sets
r = repetitions

Exercises	Week 1	2	3	4	5	6
Lying Bench Press	1s/6–8r	1s/8–10r	1s/10–12r	2s/8–10r	2s/10r	2s/12r
Bent-over Rowing	1s/6–8r	1s/8–10r	1s/10–12r	2s/8–10r	2s/10r	2s/12r
Shoulder Shrugs	1s/6–8r	1s/8–10r	1s/10–12r	2s/8–10r	2s/10r	2s/12r
Seated Overhead Press	1s/6–8r	1s/8–10r	1s/10–12r	2s/6–8r	2s/8r	2s/10r
Standing Dumbbell Curls	1s/6–8r	1s/8–10r	1s/10–12r	2s/8–10r	2s/10r	2s/12r
Bent-over Triceps Kickback	1s/6–8r	1s/8–10r	1s/10–12r	2s/8–10r	2s/10r	2s/12r
Abdominal Crunch	8–10r	10–12r	12–15r	15–18r	18–20r	25r
Lunge	1s/6–8r	1s/8–10r	1s/10–12r	2s/8–10r	2s/10r	2s/12r

The Calisthenics Program

As with the Weight-Training Program, I've first included descriptions of each calisthenic exercise, followed by stick-figure drawings to show you the various positions and movements. After this section, you'll once again find charts of set and repetition requirements for each calisthenic exercise, to be used with the four separate age groups.

When you reach the maximum number of sets and repetitions in the sixth week, you can continue with that level indefinitely, three days a week.

As you'll recall from the General Guidelines section (p. 75), you'll need some surgical tubing to perform a number of these exercises. Finally, remember that you must continue doing your aerobics program on alternate days.

Exercise 1: Push-ups

Get down on the floor in a "baby crawl" position, with your arms and upper legs perpendicular to the floor, and your body supported on your hands, knees, and feet. Your hands should be about shoulder-width apart and should be placed just below your head, with the fingers pointed forward. Tuck your buttocks in and straighten your spine so that your back is parallel to the floor.

Now, keeping your back straight, lower your body toward the

floor until your chin touches the floor. Then push your body up again to the starting position.

If your strength increases sufficiently over the six-week program—or if you're strong enough at the outset of this calisthenics program—you can modify this exercise by doing regular push-ups. These involve pushing up while you keep the entire body straight. Also, with a regular push-up, you support the body only by the hands and toes (not the knees).

This exercise is excellent for strengthening the chest, arms, back, and stomach.

Exercise 2: Reverse Fly

Sit on a bench with your back straight and grip the ends of your surgical tube with each of your hands. Your hands should be turned palms down, and your elbows should be bent at a 90-degree angle, with your forearms parallel to the floor.

Now, keeping your elbows bent, stretch out the surgical tubing, away from the sides of your body. At the same time, press your elbows toward the middle of your back as you squeeze your shoulder blades together.

This exercise will strengthen your wrists, arms, and back.

Exercise 3: Bent-over Rowing

Kneel on a bench with your back parallel to the floor. Support your body with your right arm and knee on the bench, and place your left foot on the floor, with the surgical tubing securely under that foot.

Grasp the other end of the surgical tubing with your left hand. Your left arm should be fully extended, perpendicular to the floor.

Pull the surgical tubing up with your left hand until the left hand touches the side of your body. Then return your left hand and arm slowly to the starting position.

After you've completed the required number of sets and repetitions with your left arm, switch positions so that the right foot is on the floor and the right hand is holding the surgical tube. Then do the same number of sets and repetitions with the right arm.

This exercise will strengthen your arms, wrists, hands, back, legs, and hips.

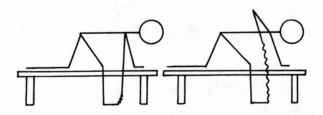

Exercise 4: Front Lateral Raise

Stand with your knees slightly bent and one end of the surgical tubing placed firmly under your right foot. Grasp the other end of the surgical tubing in your right hand.

With a slight bend in your right elbow, raise your right arm until it is even with your shoulder and parallel to the floor. Then slowly return your arm to the starting position. Do the required number of repetitions and sets, then repeat the exercise with the left arm.

This exercise will strengthen your wrists, arms, and shoulders.

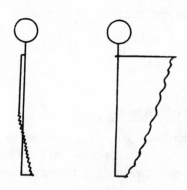

Exercise 5: Triceps Extension

Kneel on the bench, with your body supported by your knees and by your left arm, which should be extended perpendicular to the floor. Your back should be parallel to the floor. Grip one end of the surgical tube with the left hand, which is supporting you on the bench, and the other end of the tube with your free right hand, which should be resting on the bench.

Holding one end of the surgical tube, raise your right arm backward, with the elbow bent at about a 90-degree angle, until your right hand touches the side of your body. Then return your right hand and arm to the starting position.

Repeat this exercise the required number of sets and repetitions, then follow the same procedure with the left hand and arm.

This exercise will strengthen your hands, arms, and shoulders.

Exercise 6: Biceps Curl

Stand with your knees slightly bent and your feet about 1 foot apart. Place the center of a piece of surgical tubing, which should be approximately 6 feet long, under both feet. Grip one end of the tube with each of your hands, and hold your elbows at the sides of your body.

Curl your hands upward to your shoulder, always keeping your

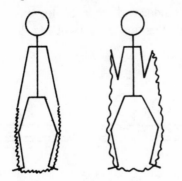

elbows at the sides of your body. Then slowly return your hands to the starting position.

This exercise will provide a good workout for your arms—and especially your biceps muscles on the fronts of your upper arms. Also, you'll strengthen your wrists and your forearm muscles.

Exercise 7: Shoulder Shrugs

Stand with your knees slightly bent and your feet about 1 foot apart. As with the previous exercise, place both feet on top of the center of the surgical tubing. Grip the other ends of the tubing with each of your hands, and allow your arms to hang straight down at your sides.

Keeping your arms straight, raise your shoulders toward your ears, as in a shrug. Then slowly lower your shoulders to the starting position. Repeat for the required number of sets and repetitions.

This exercise will build up your upper shoulder muscles and will also increase the power of your grip.

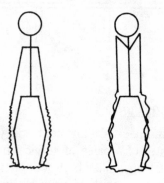

Exercise 8: Leg Lift

Lie on your left side, with your left leg extended straight down in line with your body. Position your right leg directly out in front at a

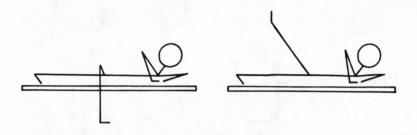

90-degree angle to your body. Support your body by placing your hands and left elbow firmly on the floor in front of your chest and head.

Raise your right leg toward the ceiling without bending your knee. Keep your right foot flexed toward the ceiling during the movement. When you've completed the required number of sets and repetitions with the right leg, turn over onto your right side and repeat the procedure with the left leg.

Exercise 9: Scissor Leg Lift

Lie on your left side, with your left leg straight down in line with your body. Bend your right knee and place your right foot behind the knee of your left leg.

Supporting yourself with your hands and elbows, raise your right leg straight upward, and then return your right leg to the starting position. Repeat this movement for the required number of sets and repetitions. Then shift to the right side and repeat.

This exercise will build up the muscles in your legs, hips, abdomen, and lower back.

Exercise 10: Rear Leg Lift

Kneel with your elbows and knees on the floor in a "baby crawl" position.

Keeping the left leg bent, extend your right leg straight back and raise it toward the ceiling as far as you can. Then return your right leg to the starting position. When you've finished the required number of sets and repetitions for the right leg, go through these same movements with the left leg.

This exercise will strengthen the muscles of the back of the leg and the lower back.

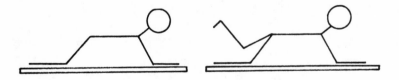

Following are the set-and-repetition schedules for my six-week Calisthenics Program for four different age groups. Throughout, the letter *s* refers to "set" or "sets," the letter *r* refers to "repetitions," and the letters *s.t.* refer to "surgical tubing."

The number of sets and repetitions increases gradually through the six-week program. As you get stronger from week to week, you should find it relatively easy to move from one exercise level to the next. But if you discover at any point that you're not quite ready to begin the next level of difficulty, just continue the schedule of sets and repetitions that you've been working on for a longer period of time.

Finally, as always, I urge you to check with your physician and undergo a thorough medical examination before you embark on this or any other physical fitness program.

Calisthenics Exercise Routine
(Under 35 years of age)

s = sets
r = repetitions
s.t. = surgical tubing

Exercises	Week 1	2	3	4	5	6
Push-ups	1s/8–12r	2s/8–10r	2s/10–12r	2s/12–15r	3s/10r	3s/12r
Reverse Fly (s.t.)	1s/8–12r	2s/8–10r	2s/10–12r	2s/12–15r	3s/10r	3s/12r
Bent-over Rowing (s.t.)	1s/8–12r	2s/8–10r	2s/10–12r	2s/12–15r	3s/10r	3s/12r
Front Lateral Raise (s.t.)	1s/8–12r	2s/8–10r	2s/10–12r	2s/12–15r	3s/10r	3s/12r
Triceps Extension (s.t.)	1s/8–12r	2s/8–10r	2s/10–12r	2s/12–15r	3s/10r	3s/12r
Biceps Curl (s.t.)	1s/8–12r	2s/8–10r	2s/10–12r	2s/12–15r	3s/10r	3s/12r
Shoulder Shrugs (s.t.)	1s/8–12r	2s/8–10r	2s/10–12r	2s/12–15r	3s/10r	3s/12r
Leg Lift	2s/10–15r	2s/20r	2s/25r	3s/20r	3s/25r	3s/30r
Scissor Leg Lift	2s/10–15r	2s/20r	2s/25r	3s/20r	3s/25r	3s/30r
Rear Leg Lift	2s/10–15r	2s/20r	2s/25r	3s/20r	3s/25r	3s/30r

Calisthenics Exercise Routine
(35–50 years of age)

s = sets
r = repetitions
s.t. = surgical tubing

Exercises	Week 1	2	3	4	5	6
Push-ups	1s/8–10r	1s/10–15r	2s/8–10r	2s/10–12r	2s/12r	3s/10r
Reverse Fly (s.t.)	1s/8–10r	1s/10–15r	2s/8–10r	2s/10–12r	2s/12r	3s/10r
Bent-over Rowing (s.t.)	1s/8–10r	1s/10–15r	2s/8–10r	2s/10–12r	2s/12r	3s/10r
Front Lateral Raise (s.t.)	1s/8–10r	1s/10–15r	2s/8–10r	2s/10–12r	2s/12r	3s/10r
Biceps Curl (s.t.)	1s/8–10r	1s/10–15r	2s/8–10r	2s/10–12r	2s/12r	3s/10r
Triceps Extension (s.t.)	1s/8–10r	1s/10–15r	2s/8–10r	2s/10–12r	2s/12r	3s/10r
Shoulder Shrugs (s.t.)	1s/8–10r	1s/10–15r	2s/8–10r	2s/10–12r	2s/12r	3s/10r
Leg Lift	2s/8–12r	2s/15r	2s/20r	2s/25r	3s/20r	3s/25r
Scissor Leg Lift	2s/8–12r	2s/15r	2s/20r	2s/25r	3s/20r	3s/25r
Rear Leg Lift	2s/8–12r	2s/15r	2s/20r	2s/25r	3s/20r	3s/25r

Calisthenics Exercise Routine
(51–65 years of age)

s = sets
r = repetitions
s.t. = surgical tubing

Exercises	Week 1	2	3	4	5	6
Push-ups	1s/6–10r	1s/8–12r	1s/15r	2s/6–10r	2s/12r	2s/15r
Reverse Fly (s.t.)	1s/6–10r	1s/8–12r	1s/15r	2s/6–10r	2s/12r	2s/15r
Bent-over Rowing (s.t.)	1s/6–10r	1s/8–12r	1s/15r	2s/6–10r	2s/12r	2s/15r
Front Lateral Raise (s.t.)	1s/6–10r	1s/8–12r	1s/15r	2s/6–10r	2s/12r	2s/15r
Triceps Extension (s.t.)	1s/6–10r	1s/8–12r	1s/15r	2s/6–10r	2s/12r	2s/15r
Shoulder Shrugs (s.t.)	1s/6–10r	1s/8–12r	1s/15r	2s/6–10r	2s/12r	2s/15r
Biceps Curl (s.t.)	1s/6–10r	1s/8–12r	1s/15r	2s/6–10r	2s/12r	2s/15r
Leg Lift	1s/8–10r	1s/15r	2s/10r	2s/12r	2s/15r	2s/20r
Scissor Leg Lift	1s/8–10r	1s/15r	2s/10r	2s/12r	2s/15r	2s/20r
Rear Leg Lift	1s/8–10r	1s/15r	2s/10r	2s/12r	2s/15r	2s/20r

Calisthenics Exercise Routine
(Over 65 years of age)

s = sets
r = repetitions
s.t. = surgical tubing

Exercises	Week 1	2	3	4	5	6
Push-ups	1s/6–8r	1s/8–10r	1s/12r	2s/6–8r	2s/10r	2s/12r
Reverse Fly (s.t.)	1s/6–8r	1s/8–10r	1s/12r	2s/6–8r	2s/10r	2s/12r
Bent-over Rowing (s.t.)	1s/6–8r	1s/8–10r	1s/12r	2s/6–8r	2s/10r	2s/12r
Front Lateral Raise (s.t.)	1s/6–8r	1s/8–10r	1s/12r	2s/6–8r	2s/10r	2s/12r
Triceps Extension (s.t.)	1s/6–8r	1s/8–10r	1s/12r	2s/6–8r	2s/10r	2s/12r
Biceps Curl (s.t.)	1s/6–8r	1s/8–10r	1s/12r	2s/6–8r	2s/10r	2s/12r
Shoulder Shrugs (s.t.)	1s/6–8r	1s/8–10r	1s/12r	2s/6–8r	2s/10r	2s/12r
Leg Lift	1s/8–10r	1s/15r	1s/18r	2s/10r	2s/12r	2s/15r
Scissor Leg Lift	1s/8–10r	1s/15r	1s/18r	2s/10r	2s/12r	2s/15r
Rear Leg Lift	1s/8-10r	1s/15r	1s/18r	2s/10r	2s/12r	2s/15r

By combining either the Weight-Training Program or the Calisthenics Program with an aerobic activity described in chapter 5, you'll find that your endurance will increase *and* the tone and strength of your muscles will improve. These changes in your body are a good sign that your bones are also benefiting from the weight-bearing exercises that have now become an important part of your life.

But as important as exercise is, it's only the first step in building tough bones. Let's move on to some of the other important strategies that can help you maintain a healthy level of bone mass.

SEVEN

The Promise of Estrogen Replacement

Whenever possible, I recommend natural, nonprescriptive preventive strategies for people facing any health challenge—including the challenge of osteoporosis. Consequently, as far as I'm concerned, the first answer to bone loss should be exercise, and the second should be calcium taken into your body through a well-balanced diet.

But sometimes nature needs a little help. Fortunately, modern medicine has developed a number of weapons that are demonstrating a powerful potential to combat osteoporosis. Some of the treatments designed to stop bone loss include:

- The female hormone estrogen

- Thiazide diuretics

- Calcitonin, a hormone produced in the thyroid gland, which helps maintain calcium in our bones

Other treatments, which may actually increase bone mass after it has been lost, include:

- Sodium fluoride, an experimental drug that has been used with considerable success by my consultant, Dr. Charles Pak

- Parathyroid hormones

- "Coherence therapy," which combines the timed administration of various medications

Of course, some of these new treatments are more promising than others, and a number have yet to reach their full potential. The most promising, which are still relatively unknown or are currently being developed in experimental programs, have been highlighted in chapter 8 as "secret weapons" against osteoporosis.

One of the most successful treatments, however, is in many ways an "open secret." I'm referring, of course, to estrogen replacement therapy, which has received a considerable amount of publicity in recent years.

Estrogen: The Open Secret

There is now unequivocal evidence that taking the female hormone estrogen can prevent bone loss both in long, cortical bones and in "spongy" trabecular skeletal tissue, such as the vertebrae. Estrogens, by the way, are hormones produced principally by the ovaries and to some extent in fat tissue. So women whose ovaries aren't functioning— because of recent menopause, surgery, or some other cause—are especially at risk for osteoporosis.

Why is estrogen so important?

At this stage of research, the answer to this question isn't entirely clear. But specialists in the area have suggested a number of ideas about how estrogen works to prevent bone loss.

One possibility is that estrogen may modify or reduce bone resorption or loss that occurs in response to the activity of the parathyroid hormones (PTH). As you'll recall, the hormones from the parathyroid glands stimulate the osteoclasts, or bone-demolishing cells on your "bone-construction crews." Estrogen helps to control this PTH activity. But when the ovaries have been removed or are no longer functioning, there's much less estrogen in a woman's body. So the parathyroid hormones begin to "run wild" and break down too much bone—and osteoporosis may be the end result.

In any event—whatever the precise mechanism—the loss of estrogen that occurs with menopause or with ovary removal puts women at greater risk for osteoporosis. In particular, estrogen loss just after menopause can increase the risks associated with a loss of spongy trabecular bone, which is found in the spine, ribs, and other such areas. Consequently, some sort of estrogen replacement therapy is often advisable for women who have recently gone through menopause or who have had their ovaries removed.

But now, how about you? How can you tell whether you should receive estrogen replacement therapy? And if you are a candidate, what sort and amount of medication or hormone supplementation should you receive?

To answer these questions, it's helpful to divide women who may be eligible for estrogen replacement into a number of categories. Specifically, I think in terms of four types of women:

• 1. Women who may face special dangers if they receive extra estrogen.

• 2. Healthy postmenopausal women, who have no special estrogen-related problems. These women have recently gone through menopause and usually will be in their early fifties.

• 3. Women who are "perimenopausal." These individuals are on the verge of going through menopause or are in the process of going through it. In general, this category includes women who are approximately three years away from the full onset of menopause.

• 4. Women who have reached the ages of 65 to 70.

Now, let's take a closer look at the advisability of estrogen replacement therapy for women in each of these categories. Again, however, I must remind you that it's essential to check with your physician both to ascertain exactly what your status is and to receive guidance in your treatment.

Women who face special dangers from estrogen. For some women, estrogen can cause a rise in blood pressure. The reason for this is that the estrogen tends to increase the amount of "renin substrate," an enzyme produced in the liver. The increase in this substance may contribute to hypertension.

Women who are prone to this problem, or who have a history of hypertension, should usually avoid estrogen therapy. If estrogen is used in this situation, it's important for the physician to follow the patient closely, to be sure the high blood pressure doesn't get out of control. Even with those patients who don't have a history of high blood pressure, the physician should monitor the blood pressure to make sure it doesn't rise during the estrogen therapy.

Other women may experience increased blood-clotting activity in the liver with estrogen therapy. The result may be an increased danger of clotting in the blood veins (called "venous thrombosis,") or a blockage in the pulmonary artery leading from the heart to the lungs (a "pulmonary thrombosis" or "embolism"). These dangers may be life-threatening, so if you have a history of blood clotting, it's usually best to avoid estrogen.

Estrogen preparations may also increase the incidence of gallstones in certain patients because estrogen increases the amounts of saturated cholesterol in the bile produced by the liver. Unfortunately, there's no way to predict the onset of gallstones unless you've already suffered from this problem.

Finally, the administration of estrogen may cause "withdrawal bleeding," or unnatural bleeding in a woman whose uterus is still intact. Because this factor should be of concern to most healthy women, it deserves further, special discussion under our next topic.

Healthy postmenopausal women, who have no special estrogen-related problems. Estrogen replacement treatment can be a tremendous boon to many postmenopausal women—and especially to those who are at high or very high risk for osteoporosis. But still, *every* woman, no matter what her medical history or risk status, should be careful about estrogen replacement therapy.

The biggest concern for most healthy women who take estrogen preparations is the problem of endometrial cancer, or cancer of the uterus. In fact, the only women who don't need to be worried are those who have had their uteri removed through surgery (i.e., who have undergone a hysterectomy).

But the concerns are different for those whose uteri are still intact. If some women take estrogen continuously, without any other hormone or medication, abnormal bleeding called "withdrawal bleeding" may occur. Unlike premenstrual bleeding, which occurs predictably once a month, withdrawal bleeding may happen constantly or irregularly. This type of bleeding may signal the presence of cancer or precancerous lesions in the uterus.

To prevent this type of bleeding and minimize the risk of endometrial cancer, most physicians these days prescribe estrogen *plus* the hormone progesterone. Progesterone in effect intervenes in the woman's body to produce predictable bleeding, as in a regular menstrual cycle.

How are these hormones administered and in what doses?

In general, estrogen treatments should be started as soon as possible after menopause, or after the ovaries have stopped functioning as a result of surgery or some other cause. The longer a postmenopausal woman waits to begin this therapy, the less effect the estrogen will have in preventing bone loss. In fact, women who wait until they have reached their sixties may find that the estrogen provides no help at all in the fight against osteoporosis.

A woman who has just passed through menopause will usually receive estrogen for 25 days, beginning on the first day of the month, in the form of 0.625 mg. a day of equine estrogen or 0.05 mg. a day of ethinyl estradiol. During the last 10 days of the estrogen, the woman will *also* typically receive progesterone. For example, the progesterone may be administered in the form of 10 mg. a day of Provera.

Then, after the 25 days are finished, she will go off all hormones until the first of the following month, when the cycle should begin again. During that 5 to 6 days of "rest" without any treatment, most women experience bleeding that mimics a normal menstrual period.

After starting estrogen therapy, all women should continue with it for at least 7 to 10 years. Furthermore, if you are at high or very high risk for osteoporosis—according to the Bone-Loss Risk Factors Evaluation in chapter 2—you should plan on staying with the estrogen treatment indefinitely. Many doctors recommend that regardless of your risk level, once you start estrogen, you should stay on it for life. The reason for this is that stopping the estrogen after you've started it may cause you to suffer increased bone loss.

In addition to receiving the estrogen and progesterone, the average woman should also consume 1,000 to 1,500 mg. of calcium a day. By following the suggestions in the nutrition section of this book, you should easily be able to achieve this amount in your daily diet.

Women on estrogen therapy should also take in at least 400 international units of vitamin D each day, either through supplements or regular exposure to sunlight. A lack of estrogen in your body will decrease your ability to make a highly active form of vitamin D, which is essential to helping you absorb and use calcium in bone mineralization. Any vitamin D supplements should be taken regularly throughout the year, without regard to the cyclical administration of estrogen and progesterone.

There are some other factors that must be considered with this estrogen replacement therapy. In the first place, estrogen tends to have a beneficial effect on a person's cholesterol balance. Specifically, it raises the levels of "good" cholesterol—the high-density lipoproteins (HDLs)—which are associated with a lower incidence of clogging of the arteries and coronary heart disease. Also, estrogen lowers the levels of "bad" cholesterol, or low-density lipoproteins (LDLs), which have been linked to a higher risk of coronary artery problems.

But there's also another edge to the sword of this therapy: Progesterone has been found to have the opposite effect from estrogen on blood cholesterol! That is, progesterone lowers the "good" HDLs and raises the "bad" LDLs.

What are the implications of these findings for your use of estrogen and progesterone? It's difficult to generalize because so many of the facts now available have individual applications to specific people in specific circumstances. But we do know this:

Each woman who undergoes estrogen-progesterone replacement therapy should have her cholesterol balances checked regularly, to be sure that she is not exposing herself to undue risks of atherosclerosis, or hardening of the arteries. After you've had a complete cholesterol and blood lipid test, you may find it helpful to consult my previous book in this Preventive Medicine Program series, *Controlling Cholesterol,* to see whether you are undergoing any unhealthy changes in your cholesterol levels.

For many women, the results of estrogen replacement therapy in reducing bone loss have been rather dramatic. In one group, which included both healthy postmenopausal women and women who had had their ovaries removed (by the operation known as "oophorectomy"), estrogen treatments were given for two to six years after the ovaries ceased to function. As a result, the women experienced an average 1 to 3 percent rise *per year* in bone density in their arms and legs— though this increase in density occurred only during the first three years of therapy.

Also, other studies have shown that estrogen can prevent fractures of the hips and spine. In fact, one study has shown a 78 percent reduction in the fracture rate of the vertebrae for those who were treated with calcium plus estrogen.

To understand how estrogen treatment can help an individual, consider the situation faced by Lois, a 52-year-old woman who went through menopause at age 49. Lois seemed to be in rather good health until she leaned over to pick up a piece of paper on the floor one day and felt a sharp pain shoot through her back.

She tried to "shake off" the pain for several days, but it got worse. Finally, she went to see her doctor, and he sent her to the local hospital—where she got the bad news: X rays showed that she had compression fractures of two thoracic vertebrae in her mid-to-upper back.

Further tests, including bone-densitometry studies, showed that her bone mass was lower than it should have been for her age. Specifically, her spine was only about 72 percent of normal density. Also, the density of bones in her hips ranged from about 46 percent to 60 percent of what would have been expected. As is characteristic of a woman of her age, most of the bone loss in both the spine and hips was spongy trabecular bone, rather than the harder cortical type. Clearly, Lois was suffering from a severe but classic form of postmenopausal osteoporosis.

As it happened, Lois had no family history of bone disease, and she had a dark complexion and a normal, medium-size frame. But further investigation revealed that she had typically avoided dairy products in an attempt to control her weight. A nutritional evaluation of her eating habits showed that she consumed an average of only about 400 mg. of calcium each day—well below the 1,000 to 1,500 mg. recommended by many bone experts.

As for estrogen, Lois had been on very small doses of the hormone since she had passed through menopause. But they were well below the 0.625 mg. per day of equine estrogen recommended by many experts in the field.

To deal with her bone problems, Lois was placed on a full dose of estrogen with progesterone. She was also given 800 mg. of calcium citrate daily, a readily absorbable form of calcium. This supplement, when combined with an increased intake of calcium through her meals, brought her up well within the recommended daily range of 1,000 to 1,500 mg.

In addition to these medical treatments, Lois was placed in a class for patients with osteoporosis. There, she learned how to walk, sit, sleep, and move about by putting as little pressure and stress as possible on vulnerable bones and joints.

Within a year, the physical and emotional changes in this woman were startling. Bone studies taken one year after she had embarked on the estrogen and calcium therapy showed that the density of the trabecular tissue in her hips and spine had increased by nearly 4 percent. Also, as a result of these treatments and what she had been learning about decreasing the pressure on her bones, she reported a significant decrease in pain in her back.

If she continues to progress as expected, her bone density will most likely increase for another two years. Also, I expect she'll become even more knowledgeable about how to live a full life without putting undue stress on her bones. That way, she may escape much of the additional suffering usually associated with osteoporosis.

The perimenopausal woman. The prefix *peri* means "around" or "near," so perimenopausal means that time of life when a woman is approaching or just going through menopause. For most women, this means the 45-to-50-year age range—a time when you can expect significant additional bone loss due to a lack of estrogen.

In general, women of this age who undergo estrogen replacement therapy will be in the high risk or very high risk categories for osteoporosis. The idea is for those in the greatest danger to use estrogen as a preventive tool against bone loss as early as possible. As with postmenopausal women, those in the perimenopausal category will be more likely to hold off further bone loss, and perhaps even experience some increase in bone density, if they begin early with estrogen treatment than if they wait.

Estrogen treatment should begin at the first signal of approaching menopause—or as soon as a woman begins to experience irregular menstrual periods. The perimenopausal woman should take the same hormonal doses of estrogen and progesterone—and also the same amounts of calcium and vitamin D—as the woman who has already gone through menopause.

In effect, these treatments will normalize the perimenopausal woman's erratic menstrual cycle, as the progesterone causes her to have regular bleeding at the end of each month. The result will be healthy estrogen levels in the body—and less bone loss.

Women who have reached the ages of 65 to 70. Unfortunately, the benefits that estrogen replacement therapy affords to younger women seem not to apply to those who are older. As we've seen, the main impact of estrogen occurs in the first few years after menopause. When a woman grows older, the turnover rate of her bone decreases, and the benefits of estrogen wane.

The main advantage of estrogen is that it prevents further bone loss. But this advantage becomes less and less important as a woman grows older.

So, as you can see, it's important to determine which of the foregoing four categories you fall into before you consider embarking on estrogen replacement therapy. With two of these categories—the postmenopausal and the perimenopausal—estrogen may be highly beneficial. With one category, those in the 65-plus age bracket, estrogen probably won't be much help. And for those who are at high risk from estrogen, the hormone may be downright dangerous.

Of course, there may be other types of women whose bones may benefit from estrogen treatments. For example, estrogen may help the amenorrheic younger woman, whose menstrual cycle has stopped as a result of excessive exercise. On the other hand, as we've already seen in an earlier chapter, when such women simply reduce the amount of their exercise and put on extra weight, they often succeed in bringing back regular menstruation and increasing their estrogen levels and bone density. In such cases, determining whether to go on estrogen therapy—and what doses to use—is a highly individual decision that must be left up to you and your physician.

Estrogen, however, is not the only answer for those with bone-loss problems. Modern science has been quietly assembling an array of treatments that, though still experimental in some cases, have demonstrated considerable success. So now let's consider some of these "secret weapons" in the war against osteoporosis.

EIGHT

The New Secret Weapons of Drug and Hormone Therapy

In recent years, a great deal of research has been done into the use of drug and hormone treatments to combat the ravages of osteoporosis. Some of these techniques are still in the experimental stage, while others have been approved for general use by the Federal Drug Administration.

Over all, the success of many of these new approaches, or "secret weapons" as I sometimes call them, has been encouraging in two areas: (1) preventing bone loss before it occurs, and (2) increasing bone mass after it's been lost. The first of these, the prevention of bone loss, has been especially promising.

The Weapons to Prevent Bone Loss

As you know, bone loss may be reduced or prevented by the use of estrogen or by various applications of calcium. (We'll go into considerably more detail about calcium when we discuss the Tough Bone Diet Program and the use of calcium supplements.) But there are also a number of other ways that physicians may try to combat osteoporosis in people who already have the disease, or prevent it in those who are at high risk of getting it. Two of the most commonly used of these preventive techniques involve calcitonin and thiazide diuretics.

Calcitonin—a possible alternative to estrogen. In some cases, a physician may decide to treat postmenopausal women with the hormone calcitonin. Calcitonin may be especially useful for those who, for one reason or another, have some resistance to taking estrogen. Also, unlike some of the other experimental treatments, calcitonin is generally available to the public because it's been approved by the Federal Drug Administration.

The purpose of this hormone, which is produced in the thyroid gland, is to maintain proper calcium levels in our bones. To achieve this goal, one of the main activities of calcitonin is to *oppose* the activity of the parathyroid hormone, which promotes the bone-demolition work of the osteoclasts. So, if calcitonin can be applied effectively in the body, less bone should be broken down, and bone mass should stay the same or increase.

I emphasize the word *should* here because the benefits of calcitonin haven't been proved as solidly as have the benefits of estrogen. In fact, there are many indications that the effects of calcitonin in warding off bone loss may be only temporary in many patients. One study, for example, showed that there may be an increase in the body's calcium for up to two years from the time calcitonin is administered. But then the amount of calcium in the body may decrease again.

Another possible problem with calcitonin may be the development of what's called "secondary hyperparathyroidism." This condition, which involves overactive parathyroid glands, can occur through a four-step process:

1. The additional calcitonin in the system from hormone injections causes reduced breakdown of bone.

2. Less bone resorption into the blood means a decrease in calcium concentrations in the blood.

3. Then, the opposite of what you want to happen begins to occur: the lower calcium levels in the blood stimulate the parathyroid glands to increase their secretions.

4. Finally, you find yourself losing everything you may have gained: the extra parathyroid hormone in the blood overwhelms the calcitonin; the osteoclasts are freed to proceed with their bone demolition; and bone loss marches ahead, hardly missing a beat.

Also, the tendency of calcitonin to encourage less activity by the bone-destroying osteoclasts probably simultaneously reduces the bone-building action of the osteoblasts. So, even though calcitonin may cause less bone to be broken down for a time, your "bone-construction crews" may also be forming less bone!

Even with these limitations, however, some osteoporosis patients may find calcitonin therapy helpful. In certain cases, calcitonin may successfully limit bone loss, though the treatment probably won't increase your bone mass. If you're a candidate for this approach, your physician will probably give it to you by injection—approximately 100 units per dose, given every other day.

Another short-term solution—the thiazide diuretic. The thiazide diuretic is a so-called water pill that has been used to treat high blood pressure and other circulatory and heart problems. But thiazide also has the unusual quality of being able to prevent the loss of calcium through the urine. Specifically, thiazide decreases calcium in the urine by acting directly on the kidneys. This action causes the calcium to back up into the person's bloodstream, and possibly to be deposited in the bones.

For a short period—say, up to six months—this impact of thiazide can actually increase bone density, though in the long run the effects of thiazide tend to recede. Some experts, including Dr. Charles Pak, recommend thiazide in some cases with women who have kidneys that "leak" too much calcium from their system. In technical terms, such women may have what's called "renal hypercalciuria." Such persons generally have excessive parathyroid hormone secretions, which may cause too much demolition of bone. Thiazide could correct this condition.

Here's a summary of how thiazide works:

1. First, thiazide lowers the calcium levels in the urine.

2. This action tends to raise calcium levels in the blood.

3. When calcium goes up in the blood, hormone secretions of the parathyroid glands decrease.

4. At the same time, the levels of the most active form of vitamin D in the blood go down.

5. Finally, calcium absorption will also begin to decrease—and it's at this point that the benefits of thiazide begin to disappear.

To sum up, then, you can expect thiazide to help for a while, but then the good effects trail off. For example, in one study of postmenopausal women, thiazide prevented a decline in the bone density of the women's forearm bones during the first six months of treatment. But after six months, the bone density declined at the same rate as a "control" group of women who were not being treated with thiazide.

A typical medication schedule for a woman with a kidney "leak" might be 25 mg. doses, twice daily, of hydrochlorothiazide, *or* 2 to 4 mg. per day of trichlormethiazide. Such thiazide treatments might be appropriate for a woman with actual symptoms of osteoporosis. Or they might be taken by a perimenopausal woman (one who is approaching or going through menopause) or a postmenopausal woman who seems to be particularly at risk.

Of course, I'm just mentioning these doses as general guidelines. You should take these medications or any others mentioned in this book only under the supervision and direction of your physician.

Weapons to Increase
Your Bone Mass

In most cases, if you are at risk for osteoporosis, you should adopt a gradual, step-by-step approach to the problem. First, you should use the most conservative preventive techniques, and only when all else has failed should you move on to the more experimental treatments.

Generally speaking, it's best to keep this sequence in mind:

1. First, concentrate on exercise and calcium consumption.

2. Second, try established drug or hormone treatments, such as estrogen therapy, which are designed to prevent further bone loss.

3. Finally, as a last resort, check the more experimental techniques to increase bone mass, such as fluoride treatments.

Take this typical case, for example:

One woman in her late thirties—because of her slight stature, fair complexion, family history of bone loss, and other such factors—knew she was at relatively high risk for osteoporosis. So she began to do regular, weight-bearing exercises and increased the intake of calcium in her diet. Because she had no symptoms of bone-loss disease, such as fractures, this approach made a lot of sense.

But then a few years later, when she was perimenopausal (i.e., in the midst of menopause), she began to complain of a consistent pain in her back. X rays showed a possible compression fracture of one of her vertebrae. Also, a bone-density evaluation through dual-photon absorptiometry showed that the bone density in her spine was 0.8 grams per square centimeter—a relatively low reading for someone her age. So her physician placed her on estrogen replacement therapy, along with additional supplements of calcium and vitamin D.

With some women, this estrogen approach could succeed in increasing bone density in the first two years, perhaps by as much as 15 percent. With most, estrogen should at least prevent further loss of bone mass. But when this woman was measured again at the end of a year, her bone density had actually *decreased* even further. She also broke her wrist during a fall on some icy steps. Clearly, she was in the throes of a serious case of osteoporosis, and none of the more conservative treatments were working.

What was the next logical step? She was a prime candidate for one of the more experimental treatments, such as sodium fluoride. This therapy hasn't yet been approved by the FDA, but it is available in certain research facilities.

The sodium fluoride solution. The woman in our illustration was placed on an experimental sodium fluoride program that required her to take 25 mg. of sodium fluoride twice a day. She also continued with her estrogen, calcium, and vitamin D. As a result, her bone loss was stopped, and she actually began to put on additional bone mass. During a lifestyle therapy program—in which she was taught how to move, sleep, and exercise with maximum safety and benefit to her bones— she reported that her back pains had subsided.

What exactly happens during sodium fluoride therapy?

Fluoride treatments tend to stimulate the work of the bone-building cells, the osteoblasts, as they get involved in the making of matrix or collagen. If fluoride is given alone or in excessive amounts, the result may be the development of a kind of "false bone," which has hardened or calcified poorly and may be relatively weak. In other words, this type of bone may be too weak to sustain normal skeletal stresses. But when the right amount of fluoride is combined with adequate amounts of calcium, estrogen, and sometimes vitamin D, the result may be much stronger, mineralized bone that serves as a good counter to osteoporosis.

In one study by B. Lawrence Riggs, of the Mayo Clinic in Rochester, Minnesota, and a number of his colleagues, postmenopausal women with osteoporosis were divided into three groups: (1) one that received no special treatment; (2) one that was treated with calcium alone or with estrogen; and (3) one that received sodium fluoride combined with other treatments such as calcium and estrogen. Riggs found that the combination of sodium fluoride, calcium, and estrogen was the most effective of the three treatments.

"These results provide grounds for optimism about the efficacy of combinations of available agents with sodium fluoride for fracture in postmenopausal osteoporosis," Riggs concluded.

The benefits of sodium fluoride have also become apparent in men who have been treated with this therapy. One 50-year-old businessman had been suffering from "idiopathic osteoporosis," or bone loss that was occurring without any identifiable cause. As a result, two of his vertebrae had cracked and a bone in one of his legs had been fractured.

He was placed in a sodium fluoride therapy program, with supplements of calcium and a small amount of vitamin D. Within ten years, the density of his bones had increased by 60 percent! The rise in bone mass was so dramatic that the physician treating the man said, "His bones are now better than mine are!"

In fact, the treatment was so successful that the physician stopped the sodium fluoride therapy. Now, two years later, the patient's bone mass is still well within the normal, healthy range, with only minimal bone loss recorded each time the man goes in for a density test.

If sodium fluoride is so helpful, why is it still considered to be in an experimental stage? Why hasn't the FDA moved to approve it?

One of the problems with sodium fluoride is that a number of patients, estimated at 5 to 30 percent, are resistant to the treatment. Furthermore, the resistant patients often can't be identified before the treatments begin.

Second, there is still some controversy about how the treatments should be given to minimize the side effects. For example, with some recommended dosages, as many as 40 to 50 percent of the patients involved have reported indigestion and joint problems, such as arthritis. Others may experience diarrhea, bleeding in the stomach or intestines, muscle tenderness, and swelling of the feet.

On the other hand, Dr. Charles Pak has reported that the use of slow-release preparations of sodium fluoride can reduce or eliminate many side effects. In 101 patients with postmenopausal osteoporosis, he found that a slow-release approach resulted in only "minor" side effects in a small number of patients. These included diarrhea in 2 patients; nausea in 2; abdominal pain and cramping in 2; foot pain in 2; and joint pain in 6—or only 14 patients with side effects out of the total 101.

A final question that has been raised about the ultimate benefits of sodium fluoride has been whether the type of bone produced by this treatment is really strong enough to ward off osteoporosis. There are strong indications in some studies that sodium fluoride therapy does inhibit skeletal fractures after one year of treatment. Also, in a related development, one Finnish study has reported that fluoridated drinking water can result in stronger bones.

That investigation, which was reported by Olli Simonen in 1985 in *The Lancet*, evaluated the incidence of fragile bones, as measured by fractures of the neck and of the femur (the thighbone), in two towns, one with and one without fluoridated water. The results? Bone fragility was significantly less in Kuopio, a town that had fluoridated its drinking water since 1959, than in Jyväskylä, a town with only traces of fluoride in its water.

Clearly, sodium fluoride holds great promise, for both the present and the future. If you have a serious problem with osteoporosis that could benefit from this type of treatment—and the side effects can be minimized or eliminated—then the sodium fluoride approach may be just right for you. On the other hand, you and your physician may want to consider a couple of other new treatments—parathyroid hormone therapy and "coherence" therapy—which also have the potential to increase bone mass.

The parathyroid hormone approach. It may seem strange to suggest that parathyroid hormones (PTH) may be able to increase bone mass when we've already discussed in some detail how they help trigger the breaking down of bone through the activity of the bone-demolishing cells, the osteoclasts. But in fact, as the PTH activates the osteoclasts, this process also helps stimulate the osteoblasts, which are the bone-building cells. Because the active life of osteoblasts is about twice as long as the life of osteoclasts, any means of stimulating both should help to increase over-all bone mass. This is because the bone-building osteoblasts will continue to operate after their osteoclast counterparts have expired.

Some studies of postmenopausal women with osteoporosis have already shown that PTH can result in a net increase in new bone— especially the "soft" trabecular bone found in places such as the spine and ribs. Also, in a 1986 study reported in the *Journal of Bone and Mineral Research,* Dr. David Slovik and some of his colleagues from the Massachusetts General Hospital in Boston saw a similar effect in men.

These researchers treated their eight male participants with parathyroid hormone and also with an active form of vitamin D. The eight men, who ranged in age from 37 to 62, had osteoporosis of the spine. As a consequence of the treatments, the density of the trabecular bone in the men's spines increased significantly. Also, the therapy improved the men's ability to absorb calcium and phosphorus in their intestines. In addition, their ability to retain dietary calcium and phosphorus increased.

These researchers found that the "increases in spinal bone mineral were marked and progressive during a year of treatment." Furthermore, they concluded that their findings "indicate that increasing intestinal absorption of dietary calcium while simultaneously stimulating new bone formation with small doses of parathyroid hormone can restore spinal bone in osteoporotic men."

In short, we have here one more potentially powerful tool to increase bone density in both sexes. But considerably more research will have to be done before we can evaluate the full impact of this parathyroid hormone therapy.

"Coherence" therapy. Another very promising treatment designed to increase bone mass involves a *sequential* application of drugs, hormones, and vitamins to enhance the rhythm of bone formation. The coherence approach is often summed up by the acronym ADFR, which stands for *a*ctivation, *d*epression, *f*ormation, and *r*est.

Specifically, therapists stimulate the bone-remodeling process for about three to five days with an *activating* agent, such as parathyroid hormone, which triggers the action of the bone-demolishing osteoclasts. Then, a drug such as oral calcium or diphosphonate is given for up to one month to *depress* the action of the osteoclasts—and stop the bone-destruction process. Next, no drug is given for about two to three months, a kind of *rest* period, so that the osteoblasts can go about their work of *forming* new bone. The idea here is to encourage more bone formation than destruction—and to produce an overall increase in bone mass.

Does it work? Tests are still being conducted, but so far the results are encouraging. In one ongoing project conducted at the University of Colorado Health Sciences Center in Denver, seventeen women, ages 52 to 77, have increased their bone mass by as much as 36 percent.

In this study, which was reported in 1987, the women first took oral phosphate for three days to activate the demolition action of the osteoclasts. Then they took the drug Didronel for fourteen days to depress the action of the osteoclasts. Finally, for the next seventy-two days, the women went off the drugs, but took vitamin D and calcium supplements and exercised daily. Although the preliminary reports on this study are quite encouraging, experts in the field are eagerly awaiting the final results and also the results of similar coherence-type studies currently scheduled in six other research centers around the country.

Clearly, there are some exciting developments taking place in the drug and hormone therapy arena, and medical researchers continue to report new breakthroughs.

Some interesting work has been done with a kind of "combined" therapy involving calcitonin and phosphates at the Yale University

School of Medicine. There, Dr. H. Rasmussen and some colleagues conducted a study with twenty-six patients who were divided into three groups. The first received only a placebo; the second got an oral placebo and a calcitonin injection; and the third group was given an oral phosphate and a calcitonin injection.

The first two groups showed no significant increase in their bone mass. But the third group, who had taken the phosphate and calcitonin, showed a 36 percent increase in their trabecular bone mass. They also experienced an 85 percent increase in their bone-formation surfaces, without any significant increase in their bone-demolishing osteoclasts or bone resorption.

Although much more study needs to be done in these and other areas, the outlook for the future seems quite bright for drug and hormone therapy. But still, we don't want to lose perspective. After all, many of these treatments are still experimental and haven't received FDA approval. Even more important, whenever possible, it's always best first to try a more conservative, preventive approach before you resort to any drugs. And with osteoporosis, the most fundamental preventive measures involve good nutrition, and especially adequate calcium in the diet—topics that we'll now consider in some detail.

NINE

The Tough Bone Diet Program

There's no question that calcium is absolutely necessary in building and maintaining a good, solid bone mass—or what I call "tough bones." Unfortunately, however, the average person consumes far less calcium than needed in his or her daily diet.

How much calcium do you need each day? The Recommended Daily Allowance (RDA) suggested by the U.S. government is 800 mg. of calcium. In fact, for full bone development and protection against bone loss at all stages of life, you really need more—preferably 1,000 to 1,500 mg. daily. That's the range that has been identified by a National Institutes of Health Consensus Conference on Osteoporosis as the necessary amount required to prevent bone-loss disease.

But how much calcium do people really get? Various dietary surveys show that the typical person gets 450 to 550 mg. per day. Our studies at the Aerobics Center, where we have done nutritional analyses on the diets of thousands of men and women of all ages, support these findings.

The consequences of inadequate calcium consumption are clear and disturbing. In what has been called a "classic study" done in Yugoslavia a number of years ago, Dr. V. Matkovic and a number of colleagues have given a typical picture of the potential power of calcium in the diet. In that investigation, the researchers focused on two parts of the country: one where milk and dairy products were consumed in relatively large quantities, and another where less of these foods were eaten.

In the nondairy region, the average daily calcium intake was 445 mg. for women between 40 and 42 years old, and 343 mg. for women 70 to 72 years old. In the area where more dairy products were consumed, the younger women took in 940 mg. of calcium, and the older women 812 mg.

The final results of this study were decidedly "pro-calcium": The Yugoslavian scientists found that the women who had the most calcium in their diets had significantly greater bone mass and fewer fractures after age 65 than did the women whose diets contained less calcium.

As we'll see, calcium by itself—especially in the form of certain supplements—won't necessarily help you develop the tough bones you need to fight osteoporosis. But in general, if you consume your calcium wisely, in line with the principles and guidelines outlined in this chapter and the following ones, you'll most likely strengthen your defenses against bone loss.

Now, let's move on to the practical question of the best way for you to incorporate an adequate amount of calcium in your diet. As you'll see later in this section, I've included two sets of diets—a regular diet with normal amounts of dairy foods, and a lactose-restricted diet. One of the first decisions you'll have to make is which diet is best for you.

Why Two Types
of Tough Bone Diets?

The main sources of calcium in most people's diets are dairy foods, and especially milk. Skim milk in particular is a great source of calcium, with about 300 mg. in an 8-ounce glass. Whole milk has about 10 mg. less. Yogurt is also a good source of calcium.

So why not just load up on three glasses of milk and maybe some yogurt each day to meet your minimum quota of 1,000 mg. of calcium? For some people, this solution may work quite well. But other people just don't like dairy products. Still others—an estimated 60 percent or more of the population—*can't* consume many dairy products in their diets because of gastrointestinal discomforts such as gas and cramps, which arise from what's known as a "lactose intolerance." This problem involves an inability to digest the sugar lactose in milk products because of a deficiency in the enzyme lactase.

Because of many people's aversion to dairy products, I've included some lactose-restricted diets in addition to a set of regular dairy-oriented diets. Each diet includes a set of two-week menus at a 1,500-calorie level and a set of two-week menus at 2,200 calories. The lower calorie levels are appropriate for most reasonably active women, and the higher levels should be used by reasonably active men.

Of course, if you're very active or athletic, you may find you can maintain your present weight while consuming more calories. However, if you need to lose weight, you may decide—under the supervision of your physician—to cut down on your total number of calories, though you should be careful *not* to reduce your calcium intake.

As you'll see, the lactose-intolerant diets include much of their calcium in the form of various supplements, as well as calcium-carrying nondairy foods such as broccoli and collards. But still, these diets do include some dairy products. The reason for this—as we'll discuss in more detail a little later—is that almost all lactose-intolerant people, even those with significant deficiencies in the enzyme lactase, can still handle a certain amount of dairy foods.

In general, the older you are, the more likely you are to turn to the lactose-restricted diets. But it's important to examine yourself as an *individual* to see which diet best suits you. For example, an estimated 25 percent of people up to about age 40 have some degree of lactose intolerance. By their fifties, about 50 percent begin to experience some gastrointestinal problems from dairy products, such as gas or cramping. Then, by age 65 or 70, the lactose intolerance may increase to 65 or 70 percent of the elderly population.

On the other hand, even if a younger person is able to tolerate dairy products, he or she may not like them or want to eat them for a variety of reasons. Such behavioral considerations may keep consumption of dairy products almost as low among young people as among the elderly. So, in picking the type of calcium diet program that's best for you, you'll have to be honest in evaluating your needs and preferences.

One way to make this choice is to focus on a number of factors, both behavioral and physical, that affect calcium intake and needs in a variety of different age groups. Here are some of the most important factors, and how younger people and older people often respond to them:

Factor 1: The ability of the body to absorb calcium. In most younger people, calcium absorption is adequate, so if they consume a reasonable amount of calcium in their diets, they can be fairly sure that their bones will benefit.

Older people, in contrast, tend to have less ability to absorb calcium. For example, postmenopausal women may not have the estrogen necessary to encourage the production of active vitamin D in the body—and thus to facilitate calcium absorption.

Factor 2: Lactose intolerance. Typically, older people have more problems ingesting milk sugars than do younger people. Later in this chapter we'll examine this problem in more detail. In any case, you'll have to be sure you make an honest evaluation of your needs in this regard.

Factor 3: The need for calcium to promote bone growth. Since children and teenagers are still growing, their bones have a special need for adequate calcium. Also, as you already know from our discussion of the Principle of Peak Bone Mass, young adults up to about 40 years of age are still increasing the density of their skeletal structure. So they, too, need plenty of calcium, preferably in the range of 1,000 to 1,500 mg. daily.

After about age 40, bone growth stops. Therefore, while calcium is still necessary for older people to maintain their bone mass, they don't need it for bone growth.

Factor 4: The need for extra calcium to meet bodily deficiencies. Most young people's bodies absorb calcium efficiently, so they don't need to take in extra calcium to balance out any problems their bodies have processing it. But as you get older, your body tends to have more problems with calcium absorption. For this reason, it's important for older people to be sure their calcium intake stays sufficiently high, to compensate for their decreasing ability to process this nutrient.

Factor 5: Weight consciousness and diet practices. Young and middle-aged people are often quite conscious about the way they look. So, to enhance their appearance, they often turn to various diets. Unfortunately, they may cut calories at the expense of their calcium intake—and dairy products are often among the first foods to go. If you fall into this weight-conscious category, be especially careful *not* to cut down your calcium to dangerous levels that may result in bone loss.

Another related problem here is the tendency for many young people—and some older ones as well—to go on faddish "health" diets. These may include radical vegetarian regimens containing a great deal of fiber, which can "bind" calcium, thus making it inaccessible for use in bone building.

Also, studies have shown that vegetarian diets may cause an increased fecal output, including increased excretion of estrogen. Remember: The less estrogen a woman has, the less capable her body is of absorbing and using calcium for bone building.

These and other factors should be taken into consideration as you choose which of the two diets—the regular dairy or the lactose-restricted—is best for you.

Now, to give you a better idea of some of the thinking that has gone into the preparation of these diets, I'll summarize some of the principles that underlie the Tough Bone Diet Program. A number of these principles, such as the amount of calcium in the daily menus, have been mentioned—but they are important enough to deserve further emphasis.

Some Key Principles of the Program

Principle 1. Each day's menus contain 1,000 to 1,500 mg. of calcium.

As I've already said, the U.S. RDA for calcium is 800 mg. But I prefer to go with the higher 1,000-to-1,500 range, which has been endorsed by the National Institutes of Health, as well as by Dr. Charles Pak and other osteoporosis experts.

The reason for choosing the higher amount is that it's important to be certain that you reach at least a "zero calcium balance" in your body. That is, you should be retaining at least as much calcium as you're losing. If you're consuming only the average amounts of 450 to 550 mg. a day that many Americans take in, you're in danger of losing bone mass. Furthermore, you are putting yourself at greater risk for osteoporosis.

In addition, recent studies have shown that under some circumstances, increasing your calcium consumption may lower your risk of hypertension. For example, one study of pregnant women suggested that high blood pressure was associated with low calcium intake. Also, nationwide surveys and clinical studies have indicated that as a group, those who have high blood pressure take in less calcium than do those who have normal blood pressure. Specifically, one study revealed that people who consume fewer than 300 mg. of calcium daily have a two to three times greater risk of developing hypertension than do those consuming 1,500 mg. a day.

Of course, hypertension is a complex disease, and there's no one solution to it for everybody. But the general trend of scientific investigation points toward a definite link between low calcium intake and the risk of high blood pressure.

To help you monitor the exact amounts of calcium you're consuming, the daily menus in this book show how much calcium is contained in various foods.

Principle 2. It's best to take your calcium on an empty stomach.

Admittedly, there is some disagreement on this point. One group of researchers feels that calcium supplements—and, by implication, calcium contained in foods—should be taken with meals because they're absorbed better that way. This contention is based on the fact that certain foods, such as meats, will stimulate secretions such as hydrochloric acid, and thereby enhance the solubility of calcium salts. In this way, more calcium supposedly is absorbed into the system and becomes available for use in bone formation.

A second group, which includes my consultant, Dr. Charles Pak, takes the opposite position. They feel that calcium is best consumed on an empty stomach because some other foods may interfere with its absorption. For example, the oxalates or organic salts in foods such as spinach may tie up the calcium so that it never gets into the bloodstream. A similar process may occur with certain types of fiber, which "bind" the calcium and cause it to be excreted from the body before it can get to the bones. Also, these scientists fear that taking calcium with other foods may interfere with the body's absorption of certain minerals such as phosphate and iron. Remember: Phosphate, as well as calcium, is needed for hardening!

On balance, I believe that the arguments of this second group are the strongest. As a result, we've designed the diet menus so that as often as possible, high-calcium snacks and supplements can be taken on an empty stomach. Obviously, however, for you to get the necessary amounts of calcium, often you must consume your calcium at mealtimes as well.

Principle 3. Divide your calcium consumption into at least two separate "doses" each day.

It's a well-established fact that the more you can spread out your calcium intake over the day, the more likely it is that you'll absorb maximum amounts. Most people who take supplements find that it's most convenient to take a tablet or other form of calcium before breakfast and a second one at bedtime.

On the other hand, if you're including your calcium as snacks in the middle of the day or as part of your regular meals, you can spread it out into even more "doses." That approach will promote absorption by your body even better.

Principle 4. Limit the sodium in your diet—especially if you're a postmenopausal woman.

In general, it's best to limit your salt intake for your overall good health. But there's a particular reason for you to pay attention to this principle if you're a woman who has gone through menopause: You'll put yourself at greater risk for lower calcium absorption and the development of osteoporosis if you consume too much sodium.

To understand how this can happen, let's first look at the way the typical *pre*menopausal woman reacts to salt. Then we'll contrast that with the reaction of the *post*menopausal woman.

• *Salt and the premenopausal woman.* When the typical, estrogen-producing woman who hasn't yet gone through menopause consumes salt in her diet, here's a summary of what happens inside her body:

1. First, the salt goes into her stomach, intestinal tract, and bloodstream.

2. The excess salt causes more calcium than normal to be lost from her body through her urine.

3. Next, the calcium levels in the blood fall a bit as a consequence of this process.

4. This reduction of calcium in the blood triggers a response by the parathyroid glands, which secrete more parathyroid hormone (PTH).

5. As a result of the increase in PTH, the body produces more of an active form of vitamin D if there is an adequate amount of estrogen present.

6. Finally, with adequate amounts of vitamin D in their systems, these premenopausal women can absorb additional amounts of calcium for use in bone formation—even though some calcium was initially lost through their increased salt intake.

But the situation is far different with the postmenopausal woman.

• *Salt and the postmenopausal woman.* In the following sequence, you can see the special problems that salt poses for women who have gone through menopause:

1. As with premenopausal women, postmenopausal women take in excessive amounts of salt through their diets.

2. As a result, they also lose extra calcium through their urine.

3. Again, the loss of calcium in the urine leads to a lowering of calcium in their blood.

4. Next, the lower blood calcium levels trigger an increase in the parathyroid hormone (PTH).

5. At this point, the experiences of the pre- and postmenopausal women diverge. First of all, the postmenopausal woman, lacking estrogen, can't produce the active vitamin D that's necessary for calcium absorption.

6. Consequently, her calcium absorption doesn't increase to compensate for the calcium that was originally lost in the urine.

7. The end result is that the postmenopausal woman will go into a negative calcium balance—and will be at risk of accelerated loss of bone mass and osteoporosis.

My conclusion: It's *very* important for postmenopausal women to restrict their salt intake. For that matter, to be on the safe side, all men and women at every stage of life should hold down their salt consumption. The diets in this book have been designed with this in mind.

Principle 5. Calcium from different sources is absorbed by the body with varying degrees of efficiency.

In other words, calcium may be more "bioavailable" from one source than from another. In general—as we'll see in chapter 10—calcium in certain supplements tends to be better absorbed or more bioavailable than in others.

The calcium contained in milk—calcium phosphate—isn't as well absorbed when it's given as a pure salt. It's much better absorbed in the form of milk. Furthermore, skim milk seems to be better than whole milk, probably because the fats in whole milk interfere with the absorption of calcium.

Spinach contains a great deal of calcium, but it has very low bioavailability—only about 3 percent of its calcium gets absorbed into the body. This is because the oxalates or organic salts in spinach operate in the intestines to prevent absorption of calcium.

Other common calcium-containing foods include yogurt, canned sardines and salmon (eaten with bones still present), canned or fresh oysters, collard greens, dandelion greens, turnips, mustard greens, broccoli, and kale. In many cases, their exact calcium bioavailability hasn't yet been ascertained through research studies. But you can assume that they compare favorably with the calcium bioavailability of milk.

Principle 6. Be *moderate* in your consumption of different types of foods.

The principle of moderation or balance, which I've advocated explicitly and vigorously in all my books beginning with *The Aerobics Program for Total Well-Being,* is especially important in any diet designed to prevent osteoporosis. Let me illustrate briefly what I mean:

Various studies have shown that a diet heavy in animal protein may encourage bone loss. The reason for this is that animal proteins are rich in sulfur-containing amino acids. These acids promote loss of calcium through the urine. Also, retention of acid in the system is thought to promote bone resorption, or destruction of bone tissue. In other words, too much animal protein may help create a negative calcium balance in the body—and a net bone loss associated with osteoporosis.

On the other hand, a vegetarian diet may bind calcium and thus prevent its absorption into the system for use in bone formation. Also, as we've seen in another context, vegetarian diets may promote the elimination of estrogens from a woman's body—a factor that may also lead to bone loss.

So, in light of these findings, what are you to do? Clearly, you can't eliminate all animal protein and all vegetables from your diet—that would create even more serious problems than osteoporosis. The answer to this nutritional dilemma, as I've said, is *moderation*. A proper balance between animal protein and vegetables will put you in the best position to prevent bone loss and osteoporosis.

To this end, the Tough Bone Diets are designed to include food in the following percentages of protein, complex carbohydrates (found mostly in vegetables and fruits), and fats:

Nutrient	% of Calories
Protein	10–20
Complex carbohydrates	50–70
Fats	20–30

Even though a major emphasis in these menus is the inclusion of adequate amounts of calcium, the diets are also low in cholesterol, fats, and sugars.

Principle 7. Lactose intolerance exists on a sliding scale of severity.

A person with lactose intolerance has trouble digesting a milk sugar called "lactose." Here's the way the problem develops: An enzyme in the body called "lactase" breaks down the lactose sugar so that it can be absorbed by the body. But some people have deficient amounts of lactase. This problem becomes especially acute for many people as they grow older and may be an inherited characteristic.

With too little lactase, the lactose sugars pass directly through the digestive tract without being broken down and absorbed. As a result, the person with this condition may begin to have problems with gas, cramps, diarrhea, or a feeling of being too "full" or bloated.

But this problem isn't an either/or kind of difficulty. In other words, there are varying degrees of lactose intolerance. So each person must monitor his or her reactions to various foods to understand the body's special responses.

In general, most lactose-intolerant people seem to be able to tolerate *some* amounts of lactose-containing foods. Specifically, the majority of those with the problem can tolerate up to a 12-gram serving of lactose at a meal, or the amount in one 8-ounce glass of milk. On the other hand, a meal that contains 50 grams or more of lactose, or the equivalent of a quart of milk, will cause problems in 80 to 100 percent of those with a degree of lactose intolerance.

In light of this "sliding scale" of lactose intolerance, you shouldn't be concerned to see that we've included a number of dairy foods as you look over the lactose-restricted menus. Even with some dairy-product dishes at a given mealtime, most lactose-intolerant people shouldn't experience any discomfort.

If you find that you do have a problem, just exchange the particular food that was giving you trouble for another with a comparable amount of calcium. For example, studies have shown that even though yogurt and milk contain similar amounts of lactose, people who are deficient in lactase can digest the lactose in yogurt more effectively than the lactose in milk.

On the other hand, if you find you can't get enough calcium through any type of dairy food, you can always use one of the supplements described in chapter 10.

What Is the Food Exchange System?

All of the following menus have been prepared in accordance with a food exchange system that I use in many of my books. The main idea is to give you an easy method for changing a day's menus without altering the calorie amounts or nutrient values. In other words, a food exchange system can give you some flexibility in preparing a meal while ensuring that you'll end up with a well-balanced diet.

In our system, the foods are divided into six exchange groups or categories: meats, breads, vegetables, milk, fats, and fruits. The foods in each exchange group contain similar amounts of proteins, fats, carbohydrates, and calories.

In the menus, the relevant exchange group is noted in parentheses after each food item. For example, (Bread) refers to breads, tortillas, cereals, crackers, or potatoes, to name just a few foods. Any differences in nutrients and/or calories are adjusted by the serving size. So, one slice of bread provides the same amount of proteins, carbohydrates, and calories as one tortilla, ½ cup of bran cereal, two graham crackers, or one small potato. Also, the foods are interchangeable on a menu or between menus—a fact that explains why the food groups are called "exchanges."

Although you can substitute one food for another in the same food exchange list, you should *not* substitute foods of one exchange list for foods of a different exchange list. In other words, you can't substitute orange juice for cottage cheese without upsetting the dietary balance or the calorie amounts.

Throughout these menus, exchange units are expressed as ounces or as standard measuring cups and spoons. It's important to keep these measures accurate if you want to keep your meals balanced. But there is some room for flexibility. At first, you may measure the servings precisely, and then as you get used to the exchange concept you may be able to estimate the amounts with a similar accuracy.

"Combination" foods, such as the recipes in the section after the menus, bring together foods from different exchange lists. But the exchanges have been carefully calculated for each recipe. So, if you want to substitute other foods for a special recipe, you'll have the information at hand to do so.

Some specifics to keep in mind about calcium when you're working with food exchanges include the following:

• Dairy foods provide the primary source of calcium in your diet. Without dairy foods, it can be difficult to obtain the recommended daily amount of 1000 to 1500 milligrams. Other nutrients commonly found in dairy products, such as lactose (milk sugar) and vitamin D (if listed on the package), will help your body use calcium more effectively.

• I encourage low-fat varieties of milk and cheese products to help you control the fat and cholesterol content of your diet.

• Nonfat powdered milk has been added to the menus and exchanges to help you boost the calcium intake of everyday foods without the liquid bulk of beverages.

• Canned salmon with the bones provides a good source of calcium. Without the bones, the calcium is limited.

• When you choose brands of tofu for recipes, check to be sure that calcium sulfate is listed on the label.

• Some leafy vegetables, such as spinach, contain moderate or even relatively large amounts of calcium. But it may not be as "bioavailable" or usable by the body as calcium from milk and other sources.

• Be alert for new products on the market which have been fortified with calcium. If you decide to include them in your diet, be certain that you exchange them in equivalent amounts suggested for similar types of foods in the following food exchange lists. These lists will provide you with a more detailed guideline for the food exchange system.

Food Exchange Lists

Milk & Milk Products
One serving contains 80–90 calories
(8 grams protein, 12 grams carbohydrate)

EAT

Milk (nonfat, skim, ½%, 1% . . . . .1 cup
    evaporated . . . . .½ cup
    powdered . . . . .¼ cup
Low-fat 2% milk . . . . .¾ cup
Buttermilk (made from nonfat milk). . . . . .1 cup
Yogurt
    from skim milk, plain, unflavored. . . . . .1 cup
    from low-fat milk, plain, unflavored .½ cup

AVOID

Whole milk products:	Flavored milk drink mixes
chocolate	Instant breakfast drinks
condensed	Flavored yogurts
dried	Eggnog
evaporated	Ice cream
Buttermilk (make from whole	Custard
milk)	Pudding

EAT

Choose 10 + meals per week:
Poultry (without skin)
    chicken, turkey, cornish hen, squab. .1 oz.

Meat/Substitutes
One serving (1 ounce) contains 60–70 calories
(8 grams protein, 3–5 grams fat)

Fish—any kind (fresh or frozen)............................1 oz.
    water-packed tuna or salmon, crab or lobster............¼ cup
    clams, oysters, scallops, shrimp....................1 oz. or 5
    sardines, drained..3
Veal—any lean cut..1 oz.
Peanut butter not hydrogenated (read labels) ....1 Tbsp.
Dried beans, peas (count as 1 meat + 1 bread) ....½ cup
Chicken or turkey cold cuts
    turkey ham, turkey bologna ....1 oz.

Limit to 4 meals per week:
Lean beef cuts
    tenderloin (sirloin, filet, T-bone, porterhouse),
    round, cube, flank ....1 oz.
    roasts, stews—sirloin tip, round, rump, chuck, arm ....1 oz.
    other—ground round or chuck (15% fat ground beef),
    chipped beef, venison ....1 oz.
Lean lamb cuts—leg, chops, loin, shoulder..................1 oz.
Lean pork & ham
    center cut steaks, loin chops, smoked ham...............1 oz.

Limit to 3–5 ounces per week:
Cholesterol-free cheese
    Cheezola, Countdown, Kraft "Golden Image", etc. ....1 oz.
Low-fat cheese
    low-fat cottage cheese, Laughing Cow, farmer's,
    skim ricotta ....1 oz. or ¼ cup
Medium-fat cheese
    Bonbel, Mozzarella, parmesan,
    Neufchâtel ....1 oz. or ¼ cup

Limit to 1–3 egg yolks per week:
Whole egg 1
Egg substitutes (cholesterol-free) ....¼ cup
Egg whites ....as desired

Limit to one 3 oz. serving per month:
Organ meats—liver, heart, brains, kidney

AVOID

Poultry—duck, goose, poultry skin

Fish—fish row (caviar); limit shrimp

Meats—fried, with gravies, sauces, breading, casseroles
   —high fat meats:
        beef—brisket, corned beef, ground hamburger, club or rib
             steaks, rib roasts, spare ribs
        pork—bacon, deviled ham, loin, spare ribs, sausage, cold cuts,
        pork—hot dogs, luncheon meats

Cheese—all except skim milk or cholesterol-free cheese

Convenience foods—canned or frozen meats, cream cheese, cheese
   spreads, dips, packaged dinners, pork and beans, pizza, fast foods,
   cold cuts

Starches
One serving contains 70 calories
(2 grams of protein, 15 grams of carbohydrate)

EAT

Bread and substitutes:

Bread, any type . . . . .1 slice
Bread, "extra thin" (30 calories/slice) . . . . .2 slices
Bread crumbs. . . . . .3 Tbsp.
Bagel, small . . . . .½
Biscuit (2″ across, made with proper fat). 1
Cornbread, 1½″ cube 1
English muffin . . . . .½
Hamburger or hot dog bun. . . . . .½
Pita or pocket bread . . . . .½
Rice Cakes 2
Roll, plain soft. 1
Tortilla (6″ diameter, made without lard) 1

Cereal and cereal products:

Bran Cereals. . . . . .½ cup
Dry cereal (flaked) . . . . .¾ cup
Dry cereal (puffed) . . . . .1 cup
Grapenuts . . . . .¼ cup
Cooked cereal (oatmeal, etc.). . . . . .½ cup
Cooked grits, noodles, rice, spaghetti .½ cup

Popcorn (popped, no fat added) . . . . .3 cups
Wheat germ or bran. . . . . .¼ cup

Starchy Vegetables:

Corn. . . . . .⅓ cup
Corn-on-the-cob (3″ long). . . . . .1 small
Mixed vegetables . . . . .½ cup
Lima Beans . . . . .½ cup
Parsnips. . . . . .½ cup
Peas, green (canned or frozen) . . . . .½ cup
Potato, white. . . . . .1 small
Potato, mashed. . . . . .½ cup
Pumpkin . . . . .¾ cup
Winter squash (acorn or butternut) . . . . .½ cup
Yam or sweet potato . . . . .¼ cup

Crackers:

Animal 10
Arrowroot 3
Bread sticks (4″ x ¼″) 2
Graham, 2½″ square 2
Hollund rusks. 1½
Matzoth, 4″ x 6″ . . . . .½
Melba Toast 4
Oyster (½ cup) 20
Pretzels, 3⅛″ x ⅛″ 25
Pretzels (unsalted small circles) 10
Rye Wafers, 2″ x 3½″ 3
Rye Krisp 3
Saltines, 2″ square 6
Soda, 2½″ square 4

Dried beans and Lentils:

Beans, Peas, Lentils
    dried and cooked . . . . .½ cup
    (½ cup = 1 meat + 1 starch)
Baked beans, no pork (if canned) . . . . .¼ cup
Chickpeas, garbanzo beans . . . . .¼ cup

Miscellaneous:

Catsup, chili sauce or BBQ sauce . . . . .¼ cup
Tomato sauce . . . . .½ cup
Cornmeal, cornstarch, flour . . . . .2 Tbsp.
Cornflake crumbs. . . . . .3 Tbsp.

Soups: . . . . .1 cup
    Broth or tomato-based (i.e. vegetable, chicken noodle)*
    Homemade, with allowed ingredients
    Canned soup—refrigerate and remove hardened fat
    Fat-free broth or consomme—eat as desired

AVOID

Butter rolls	Doughnuts
Cereals, sugar-coated	Egg & cheese bread
Coffee cake	Fried foods
Commercial baked goods	Granola cereals
Commercial popcorn	unless homemade
Cornbread, biscuit, bread,	Pancakes, waffles
cake mixes	Pastries
Crackers, flavored	Potato chips
Cream soup	Sweet rolls
Croissants	

*Note: READ FOOD LABELS CAREFULLY TO AVOID FOODS WITH UNDESIRABLE FATS.

Fruit/Juice
One serving contains 40 calories
(10 grams of carbohydrates)
Count one large fruit as 2 portions (80 calories)

EAT

Fresh, frozen, canned fruit or fruit juice without sugar or syrup; cranberries can be used as desired if no sugar is added.

Apple . . . . .½ (4″ diameter) or 1 (2″ diameter)
Applesauce . . . . .½ cup
Apricots . . . . .2 fresh
Apricots, dried . . . . .4 halves
Banana . . . . .½ (3″ long)
Berries:
    Blackberries . . . . .½ cup
    Blueberries . . . . .½ cup
    Boysenberries. . . . . .½ cup
    Raspberries. . . . . .½ cup
    Strawberries . . . . .¾ cup
Cherries . . . . .10 large

Dates 2
Figs, fresh or dried 1
Fruit cocktail. . . . . ½ cup
Grapefruit. . . . . ½
   sections . . . . ½ cup
Grapes . . . . 12 large
Kiwi . . . . ½
Mango. . . . . ½ small
Melon:
        Cantaloupe . . . . ¼ (6″ diameter)
        Casaba. . . . . ¼ (6″ diameter)
        Honeydew. . . . . ⅛ (7″ diameter)
        Watermelon . . . . .1 cup
        Melon Balls . . . . ¾ cup
Nectarine . . . . .1 small
Orange . . . . .1 small
Orange sections . . . . ½ small
Papaya . . . . ¾ cup
Peach, fresh . . . . .1 medium
Pear, fresh. . . . . .1 small
Pear, canned . . . . .2 halves
Pineapple, diced . . . . ½ cup
Pineapple, sliced . . . . 1½ slices
Plums. . . . . .2 medium
Prunes, dried . . . . .2 medium
Raisins. . . . . .2 tablespoons
Tangerine . . . . .1 medium

Juices

Apple juice . . . . ⅓ cup
Cider . . . . ⅓ cup
Cranberry juice
        low-cal . . . . ¾ cup
        regular . . . . ¼ cup
Grapefruit juice. . . . . ½ cup
Grape juice . . . . ¼ cup
Nectar . . . . ⅓ cup
Orange juice . . . . ½ cup
Pineapple juice . . . . ⅓ cup
Prune juice . . . . ¼ cup

AVOID

All sweetened frozen juice or canned fruit

Vegetables
One serving contains 25 calories
(2 grams protein, 5 grams carbohydrate)
One serving = ½ cup

EAT

Raw, baked, broiled, steamed, boiled:

Artichoke
Asparagus
Bean sprouts
Beets
Broccoli
Brussel sprouts
Cabbage
Cauliflower
Celery
Eggplant
Green pepper
Greens, all types
Kohlrabi
Mushrooms
Okra

Onions
Rhubarb
Rutabaga
Sauerkraut
String beans
  green or yellow
Summer squash
Tomatoes
Tomato juice
Turnips
Vegetable juice
  cocktail
Water chestnuts
Zucchini

Eat these raw vegetables in any quantity:

Chicory
Chinese Cabbage
Cucumbers
Endive
Escarole
Lettuce

Parsley
Pickles
  dill or sour
Radishes
Watercress
Rhubarb

AVOID

Creamed or fried vegetables; vegetables with gravies, sauces

Fats
One serving contains 45 calories
(5 grams of fat)

EAT

Margarine, soft tub or stick* ....1 tsp.
Margarine, diet* ....3 tsp.
Vegetable oils* (except coconut, palm) ....1 tsp.
Mayonnaise ....1 tsp.
Diet mayonnaise ....3 tsp.
Yogannaise..2 tsp.
Avocado ....⅛
Olives..5
Salad dressing without sour cream or cheese
   (i.e., Italian, French)* ....1 Tbsp.
Salad dressing (low-calorie)* ....2 Tbsp.
Seeds (i.e., sunflower, sesame), unsalted ....1 Tbsp.
Nuts, unsalted..6 small
Almonds, unsalted 6
Peanuts, unsalted 10
Pecans (whole), unsalted 2

AVOID

Bacon & bacon drippings
Butter
Chicken fat
Chocolate, cocoa butter
Coconut & palm oil
Commercial baked goods
Commercial popcorn
   (made w/coconut oil)
Creamy salad dressings
   (blue cheese, 1000 Island,
   sour cream, etc.)

Cream:
   Liquid, sour, whipping
   (sweet)
Desserts
Dips & chips
Gravies, sauces, meat drippings
Hydrogenated oils
   (as 1st ingredient)
Ice Cream
Lard
Margarine (regular stick)

*Made with corn, cottonseed, safflower, or sunflower oil only. Choose margarine with "liquid oil" as the first listed (predominant) ingredient on the label.

Non-dairy creamers w/coconut
    and/or palm oil
Whipped topping
Nuts: cashew, macadamia
Salt pork

Shortening
Sour cream
Food labeled with
    non-specific "vegetable oil"

The Tough Bone
Regular Diet Program

1,500-Calorie Menus

Week 1—Monday

BREAKFAST

½ grapefruit (1 Fruit)
½ cup oatmeal (1 Bread) with
2 tablespoons nonfat powdered milk (104 mg Calcium)
1 teaspoon margarine (1 Fat)
1 cup skim milk (1 Milk) (300 mg Calcium)

LUNCH

2 Veggie Burritos (3 Bread, 2 Meat, 1 Fat) (438 mg Calcium), see p. 202
1 cup fresh fruit cocktail (2 Fruit) topped with
2 tablespoons plain, nonfat yogurt (⅛ Milk) (52 mg Calcium)

SNACK

4 *tablespoons Calico Cracker Spread (½ Meat, ½ Vegetable) (132 mg Calcium), see p. 211*
4 *pieces melba toast (1 Bread)*

DINNER

1 cup Salmon Salad (1 Meat, 2 Vegetable) (140 mg Calcium), see p. 194
1 whole wheat roll (1 Bread) with
2 teaspoons margarine (2 Fat)
½ cup unsweetened peach slices (1 Fruit)

SNACK

1 *cup Strawberry Delight (1 Milk, 2 Fruit) (315 mg Calcium), see p. 209*
50 *small pretzel sticks (2 Bread)*

1,500-Calorie Menus

Week 1—Tuesday

BREAKFAST

½ cup skim milk (½ Milk) (150 mg Calcium)

½ cup bran flakes (1 Bread)

1 banana (2 Fruit)

LUNCH

Toasted Cheese Sandwich

2 slices whole wheat bread (2 Bread)

2 ounces low-fat cheese (2 Meat) (400 mg Calcium)

1 tablespoon margarine (3 Fat)

2 cups celery and carrot sticks (1 Vegetable)

1 small apple (1 Fruit)

SNACK

½ *cup skim milk (½ Milk) (150 mg Calcium)*

2 *graham crackers (1 Bread)*

DINNER

1 serving Zucchini Quiche (2 Bread, 3 Vegetable, 2 Meat, 1 Fat) (380 mg Calcium), see pp. 203–204

½ cup mandarin oranges on lettuce leaf (1 Fruit)

SNACK

1½ *cups Very Fruity Frozen Frappé (2 Fruit, 1½ Milk, 1 Fat) (288 mg Calcium), see p. 210*

1,500-Calorie Menus

Week 1—Wednesday

BREAKFAST

1   cup Fruit à la Yogurt (1 Milk, 2 Fruit) (250 mg Calcium), see p. 204

½   whole wheat English muffin (1 Bread) with

1   teaspoon margarine (1 Fat)

LUNCH

Tuna Sandwich

2   slices whole wheat bread (2 Bread)

¾   cup water-packed tuna (3 Meat)

1   teaspoon mayonnaise (1 Fat)

1   tablespoon nonfat powdered milk (52 mg Calcium)

Lettuce plus 3 tomato slices (1 Vegetable)

1   small pear (1 Fruit)

SNACK

1   *cup Pinana Frost (½ Milk, 1½ Fruit) (167 mg Calcium), see p. 209*

DINNER

1   serving Lasagna (2 Meat, 3 Bread, 1 Vegetable, 2 Fat) (306 mg Calcium), see pp. 197–198

½   cup cooked turnip greens (1 Vegetable) (126 mg Calcium) with

1   teaspoon margarine (1 Fat)

SNACK

½   *cup milk (½ Milk) (150 mg Calcium) with*

1   *tablespoon nonfat powdered milk (52 mg Calcium)*

18   *grapes (1½ Fruit)*

1,500-Calorie Menus

Week 1—Thursday

BREAKFAST

½ cup orange juice (1 Fruit)

1 scrambled egg (1 Meat) with

1 ounce low-fat cheese mixed in while cooking (1 Meat) (200 mg Calcium)

1 slice dry whole wheat toast (1 Bread)

½ cup skim milk (½ Milk) (150 mg Calcium)

LUNCH

1 cup Cream of Corn Soup (1 Bread, 1 Milk, 2 Fat) (300 mg Calcium), see p. 190

6 saltine crackers (1 Bread)

Lettuce, tomato, and cucumber salad (2 Vegetable) with

1 tablespoon French dressing (1 Fat)

SNACK

1   banana (2 Fruit)

DINNER

3 ounces baked chicken, skinless (3 Meat)

1 medium baked potato (2 Bread) with

¼ cup plain, nonfat yogurt (¼ Milk) (103 mg Calcium)

1 teaspoon margarine (1 Fat)

½ cup cooked collard greens (1 Vegetable) (180 mg Calcium) with

1 teaspoon margarine (1 Fat)

SNACK

6   cups air-popped popcorn (2 Bread) with

2   tablespoons Parmesan cheese (½ Meat) (140 mg Calcium)

¾ cup grape juice (3 Fruit)

1,500-Calorie Menus

Week 1—Friday

BREAKFAST

1   medium banana (2 Fruit)
1   whole wheat English muffin
    (2 Bread) with
2   tablespoons natural peanut
    butter (2 Meat)
½   cup skim milk (½ Milk) (150
    mg Calcium)

LUNCH

1   cup Cheese Cauliflower
    Chowder (1 Meat, 1 Vegetable,
    1 Milk) (459 mg Calcium),
    see p. 189
½   cup (20) oyster crackers
    (1 Bread)
¾   cup strawberries (1 Fruit)

SNACK

1   ounce low-fat cheese (1 Meat)
    (200 mg Calcium)
6   saltine crackers (1 Bread)

DINNER

Taco Salad
2   soft tortillas, baked and
    broken in chips (2 Bread)
2   cups shredded lettuce
½   tomato, diced (1 Vegetable)
½   cup pinto beans (1 Meat,
    1 Bread) (45 mg Calcium)
    seasoned with
1   teaspoon chili powder
1   ounce part-skim mozzarella
    cheese, shredded (1 Meat)
    (180 mg Calcium)
3   tablespoons hot sauce

SNACK

½   cup Nibbler's Surprise (½ Milk,
    ½ Meat, 2 Fat) (270
    mg Calcium), see p. 211
4   celery stalks (2 Vegetable)

1,500-Calorie Menus

Week 1—Saturday

BREAKFAST

1   cup orange juice (2 Fruit)
Cheese and Mushroom Omelet
  1 whole egg (1 Meat)
  1 ounce low-fat cheese
    (1 Meat) (200 mg Calcium)
  ¼ cup chopped fresh
    mushrooms (½ Vegetable)
  ¼ teaspoon dried oregano
  1 teaspoon margarine (1 Fat)
1   slice whole wheat toast
    (1 Bread) with
1   teaspoon margarine (1 Fat)
¾   cup low-fat buttermilk (1 Milk)
    (285 mg Calcium)

LUNCH

2   Meatless Enchiladas (2 Meat,
    3 Bread, 1 Vegetable, 2 Fat)
    (402 mg Calcium), see
    pp. 198–199
1   large kiwi, sliced (1 Fruit)

SNACK

½   *cup ice milk (1 Milk) (90 mg
    Calcium)*

DINNER

1   Cheesy Pita Pocket Sandwich
    (1 Bread, 1 Meat, 1
    Vegetable, 1 Fat) (211 mg
    Calcium), see p. 195
8   dried apricot halves (2 Fruit)

SNACK

1   *cup Hot Peppermint Patty
  ½ cup heated skim milk
    (½ Milk) (150 mg Calcium)
  ¼ cup hot water
  1 ounce sugar-free hot cocoa
    mix (1 Fruit)
  1 to 2 teaspoons peppermint
    extract*

1,500-Calorie Menus

Week 1—Sunday

BREAKFAST

1   small whole wheat bran muffin
     (1 Bread)
1   cup plain, nonfat yogurt (1
     Milk) (415 mg Calcium) with
½   cup unsweetened crushed
     pineapple (1 Fruit)

LUNCH

English Muffin Pizza
1   whole wheat English muffin,
     split (2 Bread) topped with
2   tablespoons spaghetti sauce
4   green pepper slices
     (1 Vegetable)
2   ounces part-skim mozzarella
     cheese (2 Meat) (360 mg
     Calcium)
     Broil until cheese is bubbly.
1   medium orange (2 Fruit)

SNACK

1   cup Fruity Milkshake (½ Milk,
     2 Fruit) (202 mg Calcium),
     see p. 207

DINNER

3   ounces broiled whitefish
     (3 Meat) with
1   teaspoon margarine (1 Fat)
     Lemon juice
1   cup cooked brown rice with
     parsley (2 Bread)
1   cup cooked mustard greens (2
     Vegetable) (200 mg Calcium)
1   whole wheat roll (1 Bread)
     with
1   teaspoon margarine (1 Fat)

SNACK

1   cup skim milk (1 Milk) (300 mg
     Calcium)
6   vanilla wafers (1 Bread)

1,500-Calorie Menus

Week 2—Monday

BREAKFAST

½ cup skim milk (½ Milk) (150 mg Calcium)
½ cup bran flakes (1 Bread)
1 banana (2 Fruit)

LUNCH

1 serving Pizza Olé (2 Bread, 1 Meat, 2 Vegetable, 2 Fat) (348 mg Calcium), see p. 200
Tossed greens with
1 tablespoon French dressing (1 Fat)

SNACK

1 cup Fruity Milkshake (2 Fruit, ½ Milk) (202 mg Calcium), see p. 207

DINNER

3 ounces broiled flank steak (3 Meat)
1 medium baked potato (2 Bread) with
¼ cup plain, nonfat yogurt (¼ Milk) (103 mg Calcium)
1 teaspoon margarine (1 Fat)
½ cup cooked mustard greens (1 Vegetable) (100 mg Calcium)

SNACK

¾ cup 2% low-fat milk (1 Milk) (225 mg Calcium)
4 pieces melba toast (1 Bread)
1 ounce low-fat cheese (1 Meat) (200 mg Calcium)
1 medium apple (2 Fruit)

1,500-Calorie Menus

Week 2—Tuesday

BREAKFAST

¼ cantaloupe (1 Fruit)
1   raisin English muffin (2 Bread, 1 Fruit) topped with
¼ cup part-skim ricotta cheese (1 Meat) (170 mg Calcium)
½ teaspoon cinnamon
    Heat in oven until warm.

LUNCH

1   serving Crustless Kale Pie (1 Meat, ½ Milk, 1 Vegetable, 1 Fat) (374 mg Calcium), see p. 196
    Lettuce, tomato, and green pepper salad (1 Vegetable) with
1   tablespoon Italian dressing (1 Fat)
½ cup skim milk (½ Milk) (150 mg Calcium)
1   medium pear (2 Fruit)

SNACK

8   *Skinny Nachos (1 Bread, 1 Meat) (200 mg Calcium), see pp. 212–213*

DINNER

2   ounces baked filet of sole (2 Meat) with
1   teaspoon margarine (1 Fat)
    Lemon wedge
½ cup cooked broccoli spears (1 Vegetable)
½ cup whipped potatoes (1 Bread) with
1   tablespoon nonfat powdered milk (52 mg Calcium)
1   slice whole wheat bread (1 Bread) with
1   teaspoon margarine (1 Fat)

SNACK

1   *cup Peachy Fruit Shake (1 Milk, 1 Fruit) (285 mg Calcium), see pp. 208–209*

1,500-Calorie Menus

Week 2—Wednesday

BREAKFAST

1   banana (2 Fruit)
½   cup orange juice (1 Fruit)
1   cup oat bran cereal (2 Bread)
    with
1   tablespoon nonfat powdered
    milk (52 mg Calcium)
1   cup skim milk (1 Milk) (300 mg
    Calcium)

LUNCH

Turkey Sandwich
2   slices whole wheat bread
    (2 Bread)
1   ounce low-fat cheese (1 Meat)
    (200 mg Calcium)
2   ounces sliced turkey (2 Meat)
1   teaspoon mayonnaise (1 Fat)
Lettuce and tomato slice
½   cup unsweetened peach slices
    (1 Fruit)

SNACK

½   cup Rice Pudding (½ Bread,
½ Milk, ½ Fat) (87 mg
Calcium), see p. 212

DINNER

1   serving Roni Cheese Bake (2
    Meat, 2 Bread, 2 Vegetable,
    2 Fat) (389 mg Calcium), see
    pp. 200–201
    Tossed greens with 1 cup raw
    vegetables (1 Vegetable)
    with
1   tablespoon vinaigrette dressing
    (1 Fat)

SNACK

Spicy Hot Chocolate
½ cup heated skim milk
    (½ Milk) (150 mg
    Calcium)
½ cup hot water
1 ounce sugar-free hot cocoa
    mix (1 Fruit)
⅛ teaspoon cinnamon

1,500-Calorie Menus

Week 2—Thursday

BREAKFAST

1   cup grapefruit juice (2 Fruit)
1   Cheese Toast
1   slice whole wheat toast
    (1 Bread) topped with
1   ounce low-fat cheese, melted
    (1 Meat) (200 mg Calcium)

LUNCH

1   serving Tomato Rarebit (1
    Meat, 1 Bread, 1 Vegetable)
    (277 mg Calcium),
    see pp. 201–202
2   cups celery and carrot sticks
    (1 Vegetable)

SNACK

¾   *cup low-fat buttermilk (1 Milk)*
    (285 mg Calcium)
6   *saltine crackers (1 Bread)*

DINNER

Pita Pocket Sandwich
1   whole wheat pita pocket
    (2 Bread)
¾   cup cooked, chopped chicken
    (3 Meat) with
3   teaspoons mayonnaise
    (3 Fat)
1   tablespoon nonfat powdered
    milk (52 mg Calcium)
    Lettuce, diced tomato, and
    alfalfa sprouts (1 Vegetable)
1   cup fresh fruit cup (2 Fruit)

SNACK

1   *slice angel food cake (1 Bread)*
1   *cup berries (2 Fruit)*
1   *cup skim milk (1 Milk) (300*
    mg Calcium)

1,500-Calorie Menus

Week 2—Friday

BREAKFAST

1   Open-Faced Swiss and Pear Sandwich (1 Bread, 1 Meat, 2 Fruit) (216 mg Calcium), see p. 205

½   cup skim milk (½ Milk) (150 mg Calcium) with

1   tablespoon nonfat powdered milk (52 mg Calcium)

LUNCH

1   cup Confetti Cottage Cheese Salad (1 Meat, 1 Milk) (300 mg Calcium), see p. 193 stuffed in whole tomato (2 Vegetable)

8   pieces melba toast (2 Bread)

SNACK

1   Yogurt Frozen Treat (½ Milk, ½ Fruit) (75 mg Calcium), see p. 213

DINNER

3   ounces poached salmon (3 Meat) topped with

½   cup Dilly Sauce (1 Milk, ½ Fat) (175 mg Calcium), see pp. 206–207

½   cup cooked brown rice (1 Bread)

½   cup cooked spinach (1 Vegetable) with

1   teaspoon margarine (1 Fat)

SNACK

6   ginger snap cookies (1 Bread)

1½   cups orange juice (3 Fruit) with

1   tablespoon nonfat powdered milk (52 mg Calcium)

1,500-Calorie Menus

Week 2—Saturday

BREAKFAST

1 cup orange juice (2 Fruit)
1 wedge Sunrise Pancake Stack (2 Bread, 1 Meat, ½ Fat) (216 mg Calcium), see pp. 205–206, with
1 teaspoon margarine (1 Fat)
2 tablespoons low-sugar syrup (1 Fruit)
½ cup skim milk (½ Milk) (150 mg Calcium) with
1 tablespoon nonfat powdered milk (52 mg Calcium)

LUNCH

Cheeseburger
1 bun (2 Bread)
2 ounces lean beef patty (2 Meat)
1 ounce low-fat cheese (1 Meat) (200 mg Calcium)
  Lettuce, tomato slice, and onion slice (1 Vegetable)
1 tablespoon mustard
1 medium apple (2 Fruit)

SNACK

1 cup Fruited Cocoa (1 Milk, 1 Meat) (257 mg Calcium), see p. 207

DINNER

2 ounces baked fish (2 Meat)
1 cup cooked collard greens (2 Vegetable) (360 mg Calcium)
2 whole new potatoes, boiled (1 Bread), with
2 teaspoons margarine (2 Fat)
2 teaspoons chopped chives
½ teaspoon grated lemon rind

SNACK

1 cup Pinana Frost (½ Milk, 1½ Fruit) (167 mg Calcium), see p. 209

1,500-Calorie Menus

Week 2—Sunday

BREAKFAST

1   Yogurt and Fruit Parfait
    (1 Milk, 2 Fruit) (415 mg
    Calcium), see p. 206
1   bagel (2 Bread) with
1   teaspoon margarine (1 Fat)

LUNCH

1   cup Seafood Chowder (1 Milk,
    1 Meat) (166 mg Calcium),
    see p. 192
½   cup (20) oyster crackers
    (1 Bread)

SNACK

*1   ounce low-fat cheese (1 Meat)
    (200 mg Calcium)*
1   small apple (1 Fruit)

DINNER

1   serving Chicken Broccoli
    Casserole (½ Milk, 2 Meat,
    1 Vegetable) (258 mg
    Calcium), see pp. 195–196
    Tossed greens with ½ cup raw
    carrots, green pepper, and
    tomato (1 Vegetable) with
2   tablespoons French dressing
    (2 Fat)
1   dinner roll (2 Bread) with
1   teaspoon margarine (1 Fat)

SNACK

*¾   cup orange juice (1½ Fruit)
    with*
*1   tablespoon nonfat powdered
    milk (52 mg Calcium)*
*3   cups air-popped popcorn
    (1 Bread)*

2,200-Calorie Menus

Week 1—Monday

BREAKFAST

1 cup orange juice (2 Fruit)
1 whole egg plus 1 egg white, scrambled (2 Meat), with
1 ounce low-fat cheese mixed in while cooking (1 Meat) (200 mg Calcium)
2 slices whole wheat toast (2 Bread) with
1 teaspoon margarine (1 Fat)
½ cup skim milk (½ Milk) (150 mg Calcium)

LUNCH

1 cup Cream of Corn Soup (1 Bread, 1 Milk, 2 Fat) (300 mg Calcium), see p. 190
6 saltine crackers (1 Bread)
Large lettuce, tomato, and cucumber salad (3 Vegetable) with
1 tablespoon French dressing (1 Fat)
1 medium tangerine (1 Fruit)

SNACK

1 *banana (2 Fruit)*

DINNER

4 ounces baked chicken, skinless (4 Meat)
1 large baked potato (3 Bread) with
½ cup plain, nonfat yogurt (½ Milk) (206 mg Calcium)
1 teaspoon chopped chives
1 teaspoon margarine (1 Fat)
½ cup cooked collard greens (1 Vegetable) (180 mg Calcium)
1 dinner roll (1 Bread) with
1 teaspoon margarine (1 Fat)

SNACK

9 *cups air-popped popcorn (3 Bread) with*
2 *tablespoons Parmesan cheese (½ Meat) (140 mg Calcium)*
1 *cup grape juice (4 Fruit)*

2,200-Calorie Menus

Week 1—Tuesday

BREAKFAST

1   cup skim milk (1 Milk) (300 mg Calcium)
1   cup bran flakes (2 Bread)
1   banana (2 Fruit)
1   slice whole wheat toast (1 Bread) with
1   teaspoon margarine (1 Fat)

LUNCH

Toasted Cheese Sandwich
2   slices whole wheat bread (2 Bread)
2   ounces low-fat cheese (2 Meat) (400 mg Calcium)
1   tablespoon margarine (3 Fat)
2   cups celery and carrot sticks (1 Vegetable)
1   medium apple (2 Fruit)

SNACK

1   *cup skim milk (1 Milk) (300 mg Calcium)*
4   *graham crackers (2 Bread)*

DINNER

2   servings Zucchini Quiche (4 Bread, 6 Vegetable, 4 Meat, 2 Fat) (760 mg Calcium), see pp. 203–204
½   cup mandarin oranges on lettuce leaf (1 Fruit)

SNACK

1½   *cups Very Fruity Frozen Frappé (2 Fruit, 1½ Milk, 1 Fat) (288 mg Calcium), see p. 210*

2,200-Calorie Menus

Week 1—Wednesday

BREAKFAST

1 cup Fruit à la Yogurt (1 Milk, 2 Fruit) (250 mg Calcium), see p. 204

1 whole wheat English muffin (2 Bread) with

2 teaspoons margarine (2 Fat)

LUNCH

Tuna Sandwich

2 slices whole wheat bread (2 Bread)

1 cup water-packed tuna (4 Meat)

½ cup finely chopped green onion and celery (1 Vegetable)

2 teaspoons mayonnaise (2 Fat)

1 tablespoon nonfat powdered milk (52 mg Calcium) Lettuce plus 3 tomato slices (1 Vegetable)

1 large pear (3 Fruit)

SNACK

1 *cup Pinana Frost (½ Milk, 1½ Fruit) (167 mg Calcium), see p. 209*

6 *ginger snap cookies (1 Bread)*

DINNER

1 serving Lasagna (2 Meat, 3 Bread, 1 Vegetable, 2 Fat) (306 mg Calcium), see pp. 197–198

½ cup cooked turnip greens (1 Vegetable) (126 mg Calcium)

1 large slice Italian bread (1 Bread) with

2 teaspoons margarine (2 Fat)

SNACK

½ *cup milk (½ Milk) (150 mg Calcium) with*

1 *tablespoon nonfat powdered milk (52 mg Calcium)*

18 *grapes (1½ Fruit)*

2 *rice cakes (1 Bread) with*

1 *tablespoon natural peanut butter (1 Meat)*

2,200-Calorie Menus

Week 1—Thursday

BREAKFAST

1   grapefruit (2 Fruit)
1   cup oatmeal (2 Bread) with
2   tablespoons nonfat powdered milk (104 mg Calcium)
4   tablespoons raisins (2 Fruit)
1   teaspoon margarine (1 Fat)
1   cup skim milk (1 Milk) (300 mg Calcium)

LUNCH

2   Veggie Burritos (3 Bread, 2 Meat, 1 Fat) (438 mg Calcium), see p. 202
1½ cups fresh fruit cocktail (3 Fruit) topped with
3   tablespoons plain, nonfat yogurt (¼ Milk) (78 mg Calcium)

SNACK

8   *tablespoons Calico Cracker Spread (1 Meat, 1 Vegetable) (264 mg Calcium), see p. 211*
9   *pieces Rye Krisp (3 Bread)*

DINNER

2   cups Salmon Salad (2 Meat, 4 Vegetable) (280 mg Calcium), see p. 194
1   whole wheat roll (1 Bread) with
3   teaspoons margarine (3 Fat)
½   cup unsweetened peach slices (1 Fruit)
1   cup skim milk (1 Milk) (300 mg Calcium)

SNACK

1   *cup Strawberry Delight (1 Milk, 2 Fruit) (315 mg Calcium), see p. 209*
50 *small pretzel sticks (2 Bread)*

2,200-Calorie Menus

Week 1—Friday

BREAKFAST

1 medium banana (2 Fruit)
1 whole wheat English muffin (2 Bread) with
2 tablespoons natural peanut butter (2 Meat)
¾ cup 2% low-fat milk (1 Milk) (300 mg Calcium)

LUNCH

2 cups Cheese Cauliflower Chowder (2 Meat, 2 Vegetable, 2 Milk) (918 mg Calcium), see p. 189
½ cup (20) oyster crackers (1 Bread)
¾ cup strawberries (1 Fruit)

SNACK

2 *ounces low-fat cheese (2 Meat) (400 mg Calcium)*
12 *saltine crackers (2 Bread)*
1 *medium apple (2 Fruit)*

DINNER

Taco Salad
3 soft tortillas, baked and broken in chips (3 Bread)
2 cups shredded lettuce
½ tomato, diced (1 Vegetable)
½ cup pinto beans (1 Meat, 1 Bread) (45 mg Calcium) seasoned with
1 teaspoon chili powder
2 ounces part-skim mozzarella cheese, shredded (2 Meat) (360 mg Calcium)
3 tablespoons hot sauce

SNACK

1 *cup apple juice (3 Fruit)*
½ *cup Nibbler's Surprise (½ Milk, ½ Meat, 2 Fat) (270 mg Calcium), see p. 211*
4 *celery stalks (2 Vegetable)*

2,200-Calorie Menus

Week 1—Saturday

BREAKFAST

1   cup orange juice (2 Fruit)
     Cheese and Mushroom Omelet
     1   whole egg plus 1 egg white
         (2 Meat)
     1   ounce low-fat cheese (1 Meat)
         (200 mg Calcium)
     ¼   cup fresh chopped
         mushrooms (½ Vegetable)
     ¼   teaspoon dried oregano
     1   teaspoon margarine (1 Fat)
1   slice whole wheat toast
     (1 Bread) with
1   teaspoon margarine (1 Fat)
¾   cup low-fat buttermilk (1 Milk)
     (285 mg Calcium)

LUNCH

2   Meatless Enchiladas (2 Meat,
     3 Bread, 1 Vegetable, 2
     Fat) (402 mg Calcium), see
     pp. 198–199
1   large kiwi, sliced (1 Fruit)

SNACK

½   *cup ice milk (1 Milk) (90 mg*
     Calcium) with
½   *cup blueberries (1 Fruit)*
20   *small pretzel rings (2 Bread)*

DINNER

2   Cheesy Pita Pocket Sandwiches
     (2 Bread, 2 Meat, 2
     Vegetable, 2 Fat) (422 mg
     Calcium), see p. 195
8   dried apricot halves (2 Fruit)

SNACK

1   *cup Hot Peppermint Patty*
¾   *cup heated 2% low-fat milk*
     (1 Milk) (300 mg Calcium)
1   *ounce sugar-free hot cocoa*
     mix (1 Fruit)
1 to 2 *teaspoons peppermint*
     extract
2   *graham crackers (1 Bread)*

2,200-Calorie Menus

Week 1—Sunday

BREAKFAST

2   small whole wheat bran muffins
(2 Bread) with
2   teaspoons margarine (2 Fat)
1   cup plain, nonfat yogurt (1
Milk) (415 mg Calcium) with
½   cup unsweetened crushed
pineapple (1 Fruit)

LUNCH

English Muffin Pizza
1   whole wheat English
muffin, split (2 Bread),
topped with
4   tablespoons spaghetti sauce
4   green pepper slices
(1 Vegetable)
4   ounces part-skim mozzarella
cheese (4 Meat) (720 mg
Calcium)
Broil until cheese is bubbly.
1   medium orange (2 Fruit)

SNACK

1   *cup Fruity Milkshake with
additional ½ banana (½
Milk, 3 Fruit) (202 mg
Calcium), see p. 207*

DINNER

5   ounces broiled whitefish
(5 Meat) with
2   teaspoons margarine (2 Fat)
Lemon juice
1½ cups cooked brown rice with
parsley (3 Bread)
1   cup cooked mustard greens (2
Vegetable) (200 mg Calcium)
½   cup cooked carrots
(1 Vegetable)
1   whole wheat roll (1 Bread)
with
2   teaspoons margarine (2 Fat)

SNACK

1   *cup skim milk (1 Milk) (300
mg Calcium)*
12 *vanilla wafers (2 Bread)*

2,200-Calorie Menus

Week 2—Monday

BREAKFAST

¼ cantaloupe (1 Fruit)

1 raisin English muffin (2 Bread, 1 Fruit) topped with

¼ cup part-skim ricotta cheese (1 Meat) (170 mg Calcium) and

½ teaspoon cinnamon
Heat in oven until warm.

LUNCH

2 servings Crustless Kale Pie (2 Meat, 1 Milk, 2 Vegetable, 2 Fat) (748 mg Calcium), see p. 196
Lettuce, tomato, and green pepper salad (1 Vegetable) with

1 tablespoon Italian dressing (1 Fat)

1 medium pear (2 Fruit)

SNACK

16 *Skinny Nachos (2 Bread, 2 Meat) (400 mg Calcium), see pp. 212–213*

1 *large orange (3 Fruit)*

DINNER

4 ounces baked filet of sole (4 Meat) with

2 teaspoons margarine (2 Fat)
Lemon wedge

½ cup cooked broccoli spears (1 Vegetable)

1 cup whipped potatoes (2 Bread) with

1 teaspoon margarine (1 Fat)

2 slices dry whole wheat bread (2 Bread)

½ cup skim milk (½ Milk) (150 mg Calcium)

SNACK

1 *cup Peachy Fruit Shake (1 Milk, 1 Fruit) (285 mg Calcium), see pp. 208–209*

2,200-Calorie Menus

Week 2—Tuesday

BREAKFAST

1 banana (2 Fruit)
1 cup orange juice (2 Fruit)
1 cup oat bran cereal (2 Bread)
1 cup skim milk (1 Milk) (300 mg Calcium)

LUNCH

Turkey Sandwich
  2 slices whole wheat bread (2 Bread)
  2 ounces low-fat cheese (2 Meat) (400 mg Calcium)
  2 ounces sliced turkey (2 Meat)
  1 teaspoon mayonnaise (1 Fat)
    Lettuce and tomato slice
1 cup unsweetened peach slices (2 Fruit)

SNACK

½ *cup Rice Pudding (½ Bread, ½ Milk, ½ Fat) (87 mg Calcium), see p. 212*

DINNER

2 servings Roni Cheese Bake (4 Meat, 4 Bread, 4 Vegetable, 4 Fat) (778 mg Calcium), see pp. 200–201
    Tossed greens with 1 cup raw vegetables (1 Vegetable) with
1 tablespoon vinaigrette dressing (1 Fat)
1 cup steamed zucchini (2 Vegetable) with
1 teaspoon margarine (1 Fat)

SNACK

Spicy Hot Chocolate
1 cup heated skim milk (1 Milk) (300 mg Calcium)
1 ounce sugar-free hot cocoa mix (1 Fruit)
⅛ teaspoon cinnamon

2,200-Calorie Menus

Week 2—Wednesday

BREAKFAST

1 cup grapefruit juice (2 Fruit)
2 Cheese Toasts
    2 slices whole wheat toast
       (2 Bread) topped with
    2 ounces low-fat cheese,
       melted (2 Meat) (400 mg
       Calcium)

LUNCH

2 servings Tomato Rarebit with
    extra slice of toast, cut
    diagonally (2 Meat, 3 Bread, 2
    Vegetable) (554 mg Calcium),
    see pp. 201–202
2 cups celery and carrot sticks
    (1 Vegetable)
24 grapes (2 Fruit)

SNACK

¾ *cup low-fat buttermilk (1 Milk)*
    (285 mg Calcium)
12 *saltine crackers (2 Bread)*

DINNER

Pita Pocket Sandwich
1 whole wheat pita pocket
    (2 Bread)
1 cup cooked, chopped chicken
    (4 Meat) with
3 teaspoons mayonnaise (3 Fat)
    Lettuce, diced tomato, and
    alfalfa sprouts
    (1 Vegetable)
1 cup fresh fruit cup (2 Fruit)

SNACK

2 *slices angel food cake (2 Bread)*
1 *cup blueberries (2 Fruit)*
1 *cup skim milk (1 Milk) (300*
    mg Calcium)

2,200-Calorie Menus

Week 2—Thursday

BREAKFAST

¾ cup pear nectar (3 Fruit)

1 Open-Faced Swiss and Pear Sandwich (1 Bread, 1 Meat, 2 Fruit) (216 mg Calcium), see p. 205

½ cup skim milk (½ Milk) (150 mg Calcium) with

1 tablespoon nonfat powdered milk (52 mg Calcium)

LUNCH

1 cup Confetti Cottage Cheese Salad (1 Meat, 1 Milk) (300 mg Calcium), see p. 193, stuffed in whole tomato (2 Vegetable)

8 pieces melba toast (2 Bread)

1 large apple (3 Fruit)

SNACK

½ cup skim milk (½ Milk) (150 mg Calcium)

DINNER

6 ounces poached salmon (6 Meat) topped with

½ cup Dilly Sauce (1 Milk, ½ Fat) (175 mg Calcium), see pp. 206–207

1 cup cooked brown rice (2 Bread)

1 cup cooked spinach (2 Vegetable) with

1 teaspoon margarine (1 Fat)

2 medium whole wheat dinner rolls (2 Bread) with

2 teaspoons margarine (2 Fat)

SNACK

12 ginger snap cookies (2 Bread)

1½ cups orange juice (3 Fruit) with

1 tablespoon nonfat powdered milk (52 mg Calcium)

2,200-Calorie Menus

Week 2—Friday

BREAKFAST

½   cup skim milk (½ Milk) (150 mg Calcium)
½   cup bran flakes (1 Bread)
1   banana (2 Fruit)

LUNCH

2   servings Pizza Olé (4 Bread, 2 Meat, 4 Vegetable, 4 Fat) (696 mg Calcium), see p. 200 Tossed greens with
1   tablespoon French dressing (1 Fat)
½   cup raspberries (1 Fruit)

SNACK

1   *cup Fruity Milkshake (2 Fruit, ½ Milk) (202 mg Calcium), see p. 207*

DINNER

4   ounces broiled flank steak (4 Meat)
1   large baked potato (3 Bread) with
¼   cup plain, nonfat yogurt (¼ Milk) (103 mg Calcium)
1   teaspoon margarine (1 Fat)
½   cup cooked mustard greens (1 Vegetable) (100 mg Calcium)

SNACK

¾   *cup 2% low-fat milk (1 Milk) (225 mg Calcium)*
4   *pieces melba toast (1 Bread)*
2   *ounces low-fat cheese (2 Meat) (400 mg Calcium)*
1   *medium apple (2 Fruit)*

2,200-Calorie Menus

Week 2—Saturday

BREAKFAST

1 cup orange juice (2 Fruit)
1 wedge Sunrise Pancake Stack
(2 Bread, 1 Meat, ½ Fat)
(216 mg Calcium), see
pp. 205–206, with
1 teaspoon margarine (1 Fat)
2 tablespoons low-sugar syrup
(1 Fruit)
½ cup skim milk (½ Milk) (150
mg Calcium) with
1 tablespoon nonfat powdered
milk (52 mg Calcium)

LUNCH

Cheeseburger
1 bun (2 Bread)
2 ounces lean beef patty
(2 Meat)
1 ounce low-fat cheese (1 Meat)
(200 mg Calcium)
Lettuce, tomato slice, and
onion slice (1 Vegetable)
1 tablespoon mustard
1 large apple (3 Fruit)
1 banana (2 Fruit)

SNACK

1 cup *Fruited Cocoa (1 Milk,
1 Meat) (257 mg Calcium), see
p. 207*

DINNER

4 ounces baked fish (4 Meat)
1 cup cooked collard greens (2
Vegetable) (360 mg Calcium)
4 whole new potatoes, boiled
(2 Bread), with
2 teaspoons margarine (2 Fat)
2 teaspoons chopped chives
½ teaspoon grated lemon rind
1 biscuit (1 Bread, 1 Fat) with
1 teaspoon margarine (1 Fat)

SNACK

1 cup *Pinana Frost (½ Milk,
1½ Fruit) (167 mg Calcium),
see p. 209*
50 small pretzel sticks (2 Bread)

2,200-Calorie Menus

Week 2—Sunday

BREAKFAST

1 Yogurt and Fruit Parfait (1 Milk, 2 Fruit) (415 mg Calcium), see p. 206
1 bagel (2 Bread) with
1 teaspoon margarine (1 Fat)

LUNCH

2 cups Seafood Chowder (2 Milk, 2 Meat) (332 mg Calcium), see p. 192
1 cup (40) oyster crackers (2 Bread)
   Ham Sandwich
   2 slices whole wheat bread (2 Bread)
   2 ounces lean boiled ham (2 Meat)
   2 teaspoons mayonnaise (2 Fat)

SNACK

1 *ounce low-fat cheese (1 Meat) (200 mg Calcium)*
1 *large apple (3 Fruit)*

DINNER

1 serving Chicken Broccoli Casserole (½ Milk, 2 Meat, 1 Vegetable) (258 mg Calcium), see pp. 195–196
   Tossed greens with 2 cups raw carrots, green pepper, and tomato (2 Vegetable)
2 tablespoons French dressing (2 Fat)
1 whole wheat dinner roll (2 Bread) with
1 teaspoon margarine (1 Fat)

SNACK

¾ *cup orange juice (1½ Fruit) with*
1 *tablespoon nonfat powdered milk (52 mg Calcium)*
3 *cups popcorn (1 Bread) popped with*
2 *teaspoons safflower oil (2 Fat)*

The Tough Bone Lactose-Restricted Diet Program

1,500-Calorie Menus
Lactose-Restricted

Week 1—Monday

BREAKFAST

1 cup Fruit à la Yogurt L.R. (½ Milk, 2½ Fruit) (147 mg Calcium), see p. 204

½ whole wheat English muffin (1 Bread) with

1 teaspoon margarine (1 Fat)

LUNCH

Tuna Sandwich
2 slices whole wheat bread (2 Bread)
1 cup water-packed tuna (4 Meat)
1 teaspoon mayonnaise (1 Fat)
Lettuce and 3 tomato slices (1 Vegetable)
1 small pear (1 Fruit)

SNACK

1 cup blueberries (2 Fruit)

DINNER

1 serving Lasagna (2 Meat, 3 Bread, 1 Vegetable, 2 Fat) (306 mg Calcium), see pp. 197–198

½ cup cooked turnip greens (1 Vegetable) (126 mg Calcium) with

1 teaspoon margarine (1 Fat)

SNACK

24 grapes (2 Fruit)

1,500-Calorie Menus
Lactose-Restricted

Week 1—Tuesday

BREAKFAST

½ cup oat bran cereal (1 Bread)
4 tablespoons raisins (2 Fruit)

LUNCH

Toasted Ham and Cheese
Sandwich
2 slices whole wheat bread
   (2 Bread)
1 ounce lean boiled ham
   (1 Meat)
1 ounce low-fat cheese
   (1 Meat) (200 mg Calcium)
2 teaspoons margarine (2 Fat)
2 cups celery and carrot sticks
   (1 Vegetable)
1 small apple (1 Fruit)

SNACK

¾ *cup Very Fruity Frozen Frappé*
   L.R. (¼ Milk, 2½ Fruit)
   (189 mg Calcium), see p. 210
2 *graham crackers (1 Bread)*

DINNER

1 serving Zucchini Quiche (2
   Bread, 3 Vegetable, 2 Meat,
   1 Fat) (380 mg Calcium), see
   pp. 203–204
½ cup mandarin oranges on
   lettuce leaf (1 Fruit)

SNACK

3 *cups air-popped popcorn*
   (1 Bread)

1,500-Calorie Menus
Lactose-Restricted

Week 1—Wednesday

BREAKFAST

½   cup calcium-fortified orange
     juice (1 Fruit) (133 mg
     Calcium), see p. 262
1   scrambled egg (1 Meat) with
1   ounce low-fat cheese mixed in
     while cooking (1 Meat) (200
     mg Calcium)
1   slice dry whole wheat toast
     (1 Bread)

LUNCH

1   cup Cream of Tomato Soup (1
     Meat, 3 Vegetable) (219 mg
     Calcium), see p. 190
6   saltine crackers (1 Bread)
     Lettuce, tomato, and
     cucumber salad (2 Vegetable)
     with
1   tablespoon French dressing
     (1 Fat)

SNACK

1   banana (2 Fruit)

DINNER

3   ounces baked chicken, skinless
     (3 Meat)
1   medium baked potato
     (2 Bread) with
1   teaspoon margarine (1 Fat)
1   cup cooked collard greens (2
     Vegetable) (360 mg Calcium)
     with
1   teaspoon margarine (1 Fat)

SNACK

3   cups air-popped popcorn
     (1 Bread) with
2   tablespoons Parmesan cheese
     (½ Meat) (140 mg Calcium)
¾   cup grape juice (3 Fruit)

1,500-Calorie Menus
Lactose-Restricted

Week 1—Thursday

BREAKFAST

½ grapefruit (1 Fruit)
½ cup calcium-fortified oatmeal (1 Bread) (200 mg Calcium), see p. 262, with
1 tablespoon nonfat powdered milk (52 mg Calcium)
1 teaspoon margarine (1 Fat)

LUNCH

2 Veggie Burritos (3 Bread, 2 Meat, 1 Fat) (438 mg Calcium), see p. 202
1 cup fresh fruit cocktail (2 Fruit) topped with
2 tablespoons plain, nonfat yogurt (⅛ Milk) (52 mg Calcium)

SNACK

4 pieces melba toast (1 Bread) with
2 tablespoons natural peanut butter (2 Meat)

DINNER

1 cup Salmon Salad (1 Meat, 2 Vegetable) (140 mg Calcium), see p. 194
1 whole wheat roll (1 Bread) with
2 teaspoons margarine (2 Fat)
½ cup unsweetened peach slices (1 Fruit)

SNACK

1 cup apple cider (3 Fruit)
50 small pretzel sticks (2 Bread)

1,500-Calorie Menus
Lactose-Restricted

Week 1—Friday

BREAKFAST

1   medium banana (2 Fruit)
1   whole wheat English muffin
    (2 Bread) with
2   tablespoons natural peanut
    butter (2 Meat)

LUNCH

1   cup French Onion Soup (½
    Bread, ½ Vegetable, 1 Fat)
    (99 mg Calcium), see p. 191
¾   cup strawberries (1 Fruit)

SNACK

2   *graham crackers (1 Bread)*
½   *cup grape juice (2 Fruit)*

DINNER

Taco Salad
2   soft tortillas, baked and
    broken in chips (2 Bread)
2   cups shredded lettuce
1   tomato, diced (2 Vegetable)
½   cup pinto beans (1 Meat,
    1 Bread) (45 mg Calcium)
    seasoned with
2   teaspoons chili powder
2   ounces part-skim mozzarella
    cheese, shredded (2 Meat)
    (360 mg Calcium)
3   tablespoons hot sauce

SNACK

2   *cups raw vegetables*
    (2 Vegetable)
2   *tablespoons low-calorie Ranch*
    dressing (1 Fat)

1,500-Calorie Menus
Lactose-Restricted

Week 1—Saturday

BREAKFAST

1   cup calcium-fortified orange juice (2 Fruit) (267 mg Calcium), see p. 262
Cheese and Mushroom Omelet
1   whole egg plus 2 egg whites (3 Meat)
1   ounce low-fat cheese (1 Meat) (200 mg Calcium)
½   cup fresh chopped mushrooms (1 Vegetable)
¼   teaspoon dried oregano
1   teaspoon margarine (1 Fat)
1   ounce lean grilled ham (1 Meat)
1   slice whole wheat toast (1 Bread) with
1   teaspoon margarine (1 Fat)

LUNCH

2   Meatless Enchiladas L.R. (1 Meat, 2 Bread, 1 Fat) (269 mg Calcium), see p. 199
1   large kiwi, sliced (1 Fruit)

SNACK

½   cup orange sherbet (2 Bread) (50 mg Calcium)

DINNER

1   Cheesy Pita Pocket Sandwich (1 Bread, 1 Meat, 1 Vegetable, 1 Fat) (211 mg Calcium), see p. 195
12   dried apricot halves (3 Fruit)

SNACK

1   cup Hot Peppermint Patty
¾ cup hot water
1   ounce sugar-free hot cocoa mix (1 Fruit)
1 to 2 teaspoons peppermint extract
2   sugar cookies (1 Bread)

1,500-Calorie Menus
Lactose-Restricted

Week 1—Sunday

BREAKFAST

1   small whole wheat bran muffin
    (1 Bread)
¼   cantaloupe (1 Fruit)

LUNCH

English Muffin Pizza
1   whole wheat English muffin,
    split (2 Bread), topped with
1 to 2 tablespoons spaghetti
    sauce
4   green pepper slices
    (1 Vegetable)
2   ounces part-skim
    mozzarella cheese (2 Meat)
    (360 mg Calcium)
Broil until cheese is bubbly.
1   medium orange (2 Fruit)

SNACK

1   cup Fruity Milkshake L.R.
    (½ Milk, 3 Fruit) (237 mg
    Calcium), see p. 208

DINNER

3   ounces broiled whitefish
    (3 Meat) with
2   teaspoons margarine (2 Fat)
    Lemon juice
1   cup cooked brown rice with
    parsley (2 Bread)
1   cup cooked mustard greens (2
    Vegetable) (200 mg Calcium)
1   whole wheat roll (1 Bread)
    with
1   teaspoon margarine (1 Fat)

SNACK

½   cup lime sherbet (2 Bread) (50
    mg Calcium)
6   vanilla wafers (1 Bread)

1,500-Calorie Menus
Lactose-Restricted

Week 2—Monday

BREAKFAST

⅓ cup pineapple juice (1 Fruit)
1 Open-Faced Swiss and Pear Sandwich (1 Bread, 1 Meat, 2 Fruit) (216 mg Calcium), see p. 205

LUNCH

¾ cup Chicken Salad (3 Meat, 1 Bread, 1 Fat) (64 mg Calcium), see p. 193 stuffed in whole tomato (2 Vegetable)
8 pieces melba toast (2 Bread)

SNACK

3 cups air-popped popcorn (1 Bread)
1 cup Orange Frost (1½ Fruit) (27 mg Calcium), see p. 208

DINNER

3 ounces poached salmon (3 Meat) Lemon wedge
½ cup cooked brown rice (1 Bread)
½ cup cooked spinach (1 Vegetable) with
1 teaspoon margarine (1 Fat)

SNACK

6 ginger snap cookies (1 Bread)
1 cup calcium-fortified orange juice (2 Fruit) (267 mg Calcium), see p. 262

1,500-Calorie Menus
Lactose-Restricted

Week 2—Tuesday

BREAKFAST

½ cantaloupe (2 Fruit)
1 raisin English muffin (2 Bread, 1 Fruit) with
1 teaspoon margarine (1 Fat)

LUNCH

1 serving Crustless Kale Pie (1 Meat, ½ Milk, 1 Vegetable, 1 Fat) (374 mg Calcium), see p. 196
   Lettuce, tomato, and green pepper salad (1 Vegetable) with
1 tablespoon Italian dressing (1 Fat)
1 large pear (3 Fruit)

SNACK

8 *Skinny Nachos (1 Bread, 1 Meat) (200 mg Calcium), see pp. 212–213*

DINNER

4 ounces baked filet of sole (4 Meat) with
1 teaspoon margarine (1 Fat)
   Lemon wedge
1 cup cooked broccoli spears (2 Vegetable)
1 cup whipped potatoes (2 Bread) with
1 tablespoon nonfat powdered milk (52 mg Calcium)
1 slice whole wheat bread (1 Bread) with
1 teaspoon margarine (1 Fat)

SNACK

1 *medium apple (2 Fruit)*
1 *small oatmeal cookie (1 Bread)*

1,500-Calorie Menus
Lactose-Restricted

Week 2—Wednesday

BREAKFAST

1   banana (2 Fruit)
1   cup calcium-fortified orange juice (2 Fruit) (267 mg Calcium), see p. 262
1   cup oat bran cereal (2 Bread) with
1   tablespoon nonfat powdered milk (52 mg Calcium)

LUNCH

Turkey Sandwich
2   slices whole wheat bread (2 Bread)
1   ounce low-fat cheese (1 Meat) (200 mg Calcium)
2   ounces sliced turkey (2 Meat)
1   teaspoon mayonnaise (1 Fat)
    Lettuce and tomato slice
½   cup Rice Pudding (½ Bread, ½ Milk, ½ Fat) (87 mg Calcium), see p. 212

SNACK

½   *cup unsweetened peach slices (1 Fruit)*

DINNER

Spaghetti
1   cup cooked spaghetti noodles (2 Bread)
½   cup tomato sauce (1 Bread)
2   1-ounce meatballs (2 Meat)
    Tossed greens with 2 cups raw vegetables (2 Vegetable) with
1   tablespoon vinaigrette dressing (1 Fat)
1   slice Italian bread (1 Bread) with
1   teaspoon margarine (1 Fat)

SNACK

Spicy Hot Chocolate
¾ cup hot water
1 ounce sugar-free hot cocoa mix (1 Fruit)
⅛ teaspoon cinnamon

1,500-Calorie Menus
Lactose-Restricted

Week 2—Thursday

BREAKFAST

1   cup grapefruit juice (2 Fruit)
1   Cheese Toast
   1   slice whole wheat toast
     (1 Bread) topped with
   1   ounce low-fat cheese, melted
     (1 Meat) (200 mg Calcium)

LUNCH

1   serving Tomato Rarebit (1
   Meat, 1 Bread, 1 Vegetable)
   (277 mg Calcium), see
   pp. 201–202
2   cups celery and carrot sticks
   (1 Vegetable)

SNACK

½   cup cranberry juice (2 Fruit)
16   animal crackers (2 Bread)

DINNER

Pita Pocket Sandwich
1   whole wheat pita pocket
   (2 Bread)
1   cup cooked, chopped chicken
   (4 Meat) with
3   teaspoons mayonnaise (3 Fat)
1   tablespoon nonfat powdered
   milk (52 mg Calcium)
   Lettuce, diced tomato, and
   alfalfa sprouts
   (1 Vegetable)
1   cup fresh fruit (2 Fruit)

SNACK

1   slice angel food cake (1 Bread)
1   cup blueberries (2 Fruit)

1,500-Calorie Menus
Lactose-Restricted

Week 2—Friday

BREAKFAST

1   cup calcium-fortified oatmeal (2
    Bread) (400 mg Calcium),
    see p. 262, with
1   mashed banana (2 Fruit)

LUNCH

1   serving Pizza Olé (2 Bread,
    1 Meat, 2 Vegetable, 2 Fat)
    (348 mg Calcium), see p. 200
    Tossed greens with
1   tablespoon French dressing
    (1 Fat)

SNACK

1   *cup Fruity Milkshake L.R.*
    (½ Milk, 3 Fruit) (237 mg
    Calcium), see p. 208

DINNER

3   ounces broiled flank steak
    (3 Meat)
1   medium baked potato (2
    Bread) with
2   tablespoons plain, nonfat
    yogurt (⅛ Milk) (52 mg
    Calcium)
1   teaspoon margarine (1 Fat)
1   cup cooked mustard greens (2
    Vegetable) (200 mg Calcium)

SNACK

4   *pieces melba toast (1 Bread)*
1   *medium apple (2 Fruit)*

1,500-Calorie Menus
Lactose-Restricted

Week 2—Saturday

BREAKFAST

1 cup calcium-fortified orange juice (2 Fruit) (267 mg Calcium), see p. 262
2 4-inch whole wheat pancakes (1 Bread, 1 Fat) with
1 teaspoon margarine (1 Fat)
2 tablespoons low-sugar syrup (1 Fruit)

LUNCH

Cheeseburger
1 bun (2 Bread)
3 ounces lean beef patty (3 Meat)
1 ounce low-fat cheese (1 Meat) (200 mg Calcium)
  Lettuce, tomato slice, and onion slice (1 Vegetable)
1 tablespoon mustard
1 medium apple (2 Fruit)

SNACK

1 *strawberry frozen fruit bar (1 Fruit)*

DINNER

3 ounces baked fish (3 Meat)
1 cup cooked collard greens (2 Vegetable) (360 mg Calcium)
4 whole new potatoes, boiled (2 Bread), with
2 teaspoons margarine (2 Fat)
2 teaspoons chopped chives
½ teaspoon grated lemon rind

SNACK

1 *small slice lemon sponge cake (1 Bread)*
1 *cup herbal tea*

1,500-Calorie Menus
Lactose-Restricted

Week 2—Sunday

BREAKFAST

½ cup calcium-fortified orange juice (1 Fruit) (133 mg Calcium), see p. 262
½ bagel (1 Bread) with
1 teaspoon margarine (1 Fat)

LUNCH

1 Chef's Salad (2 Meat, 3 Vegetable) (236 mg Calcium), see pp. 192–193, with
1 tablespoon Ranch dressing (1 Fat)
6 saltine crackers (1 Bread)

SNACK

1 *large apple (3 Fruit)*

DINNER

1 serving Chicken Broccoli Casserole (½ Milk, 2 Meat, 1 Vegetable) (258 mg Calcium), see pp. 195–196
   Tossed greens with 1 cup raw carrots, green pepper, and tomato (1 Vegetable), with
1 tablespoon French dressing (1 Fat)
1 whole wheat dinner roll (2 Bread)
1 teaspoon margarine (1 Fat)

SNACK

⅔ *cup pineapple juice (2 Fruit)*
6 *cups air-popped popcorn (2 Bread)*

2,200-Calorie Menus
Lactose-Restricted

Week 1—Monday

BREAKFAST

1   medium banana (2 Fruit)
1   whole wheat English muffin
    (2 Bread) with
1   tablespoon natural peanut
    butter (1 Meat)

LUNCH

2   cups French Onion Soup (1
    Bread, 1 Vegetable, 2 Fat)
    (198 mg Calcium), see p. 191
1½ cups strawberries (2 Fruit)

SNACK

4   *graham crackers (2 Bread)*
1   *cup grape juice (4 Fruit)*

DINNER

Taco Salad
3   soft tortillas, baked and
    broken in chips (3 Bread)
2   cups shredded lettuce
1   tomato, diced (2 Vegetable)
1   cup pinto beans (2 Meat,
    2 Bread) (90 mg Calcium)
    seasoned with
2   teaspoons chili powder
3   ounces part-skim
    mozzarella cheese, shredded
    (3 Meat) (540 mg Calcium)
3   tablespoons hot sauce

SNACK

2   *cups raw vegetables*
    (2 Vegetable) with
2   *tablespoons low-calorie Ranch*
    dressing (1 Fat)

2,200-Calorie Menus
Lactose-Restricted

Week 1—Tuesday

BREAKFAST

1½ cups oat bran cereal (3 Bread)
1 banana (2 Fruit)

LUNCH

Toasted Ham and Cheese
Sandwich
2 slices whole wheat bread
(2 Bread)
4 ounces lean boiled ham
(4 Meat)
1 ounce low-fat cheese
(1 Meat) (200 mg Calcium)
1 tablespoon margarine (3 Fat)
2 cups celery and carrot sticks
(1 Vegetable)
1 large apple (3 Fruit)

SNACK

1½ cups Very Fruity Frozen Frappé
L.R. (½ Milk, 5 Fruit) (378
mg Calcium), see p. 210
4 graham crackers (2 Bread)

DINNER

2 servings Zucchini Quiche (4
Bread, 6 Vegetable, 4 Meat,
2 Fat) (760 mg Calcium), see
pp. 203–204
½ cup mandarin oranges on
lettuce leaf (1 Fruit)

SNACK

3 cups air-popped popcorn
(1 Bread)

2,200-Calorie Menus
Lactose-Restricted

Week 1—Wednesday

BREAKFAST

1   cup Fruit à la yogurt L.R. (½ Milk, 2½ Fruit) (147 mg Calcium), see p. 204

1   whole wheat English muffin (2 Bread) with

2   teaspoons margarine (2 Fat)

LUNCH

Tuna Sandwich

2   slices whole wheat bread (2 Bread)

1   cup water-packed tuna (4 Meat)

1   teaspoon mayonnaise (1 Fat)

Lettuce plus 3 tomato slices (1 Vegetable)

1   large pear (3 Fruit)

SNACK

1   cup calcium-fortified orange juice (2 Fruit) (266 mg Calcium), see p. 262

DINNER

1½ servings Lasagna (3 Meat, 4½ Bread, 1½ Vegetable, 3 Fat) (459 mg Calcium), see pp. 197–198

1   cup cooked turnip greens (2 Vegetable) (252 mg Calcium)

2   slices Italian bread (2 Bread) with

1   teaspoon margarine (1 Fat)

SNACK

36 grapes (3 Fruit)

2   graham crackers (1 Bread)

2,200-Calorie Menus
Lactose-Restricted

Week 1—Thursday

BREAKFAST

1½ cups raspberries (3 Fruit)
1 scrambled egg (1 Meat) with
1 ounce low-fat cheese mixed in while cooking (1 Meat) (200 mg Calcium)
1 slice dry whole wheat toast (1 Bread)

LUNCH

2 cups Cream of Tomato Soup (2 Meat, 6 Vegetable) (438 mg Calcium), see p. 190
6 saltine crackers (1 Bread)
   Lettuce, tomato, and cucumber salad (2 Vegetable) with
1 tablespoon French dressing (1 Fat)

SNACK

1 banana (2 Fruit)

DINNER

5 ounces baked chicken, skinless (5 Meat)
1 large baked potato (3 Bread) with
1 teaspoon margarine (1 Fat)
1 cup cooked collard greens (2 Vegetable) (360 mg Calcium)
1 French roll (1 Bread) with
2 teaspoons margarine (2 Fat)

SNACK

6 cups air-popped popcorn (2 Bread) with
2 tablespoons Parmesan cheese (½ Meat) (140 mg Calcium)
¾ cup grape juice (3 Fruit)

2,200-Calorie Menus
Lactose-Restricted

Week 1—Friday

BREAKFAST

1 grapefruit (2 Fruit)
1 cup calcium-fortified oatmeal (2 Bread) (400 mg Calcium), see p. 262, with
1 tablespoon nonfat powdered milk (52 mg Calcium)
1 teaspoon margarine (1 Fat)

LUNCH

1 plain flour tortilla (1 Bread)
2 Veggie Burritos (3 Bread, 2 Meat, 1 Fat) (438 mg Calcium), see p. 202
2 cups fresh fruit cocktail (4 Fruit) topped with
2 tablespoons plain, nonfat yogurt (⅛ Milk) (52 mg Calcium)

SNACK

8 *pieces melba toast (2 Bread) with*
3 *tablespoons natural peanut butter (3 Meat)*

DINNER

2 cups Salmon Salad (2 Meat, 4 Vegetable) (280 mg Calcium), see p. 194
1 whole wheat roll (1 Bread) with
2 teaspoons margarine (2 Fat)
1 cup unsweetened peach slices (2 Fruit)

SNACK

1 *cup apple cider (3 Fruit)*
50 *small pretzel sticks (2 Bread)*

2,200-Calorie Menus
Lactose-Restricted

Week 1—Saturday

BREAKFAST

½ cantaloupe (2 Fruit)
Cheese and Mushroom Omelet
1 whole egg plus 2 egg whites
(3 Meat)
1 ounce low-fat cheese (1 Meat)
(200 mg Calcium)
½ cup fresh chopped
mushrooms (1 Vegetable)
¼ teaspoon dried oregano
1 teaspoon margarine (1 Fat)
1 ounce lean grilled ham
(1 Meat)
1 slice whole wheat toast
(1 Bread) with
1 teaspoon margarine (1 Fat)

LUNCH

4 Meatless Enchiladas L.R. (2
Meat, 4 Bread, 2 Fat) (538
mg Calcium), see p. 199
1 cup steamed zucchini
(2 Vegetable)
1 large kiwi, sliced (1 Fruit)

SNACK

½ *cup orange sherbet (2 Bread)*
(50 mg Calcium)

DINNER

2 Cheesy Pita Pocket Sandwiches
(2 Bread, 2 Meat, 2 Vegetable,
2 Fat) (422 mg Calcium), see
p. 195
12 dried apricot halves (3 Fruit)

SNACK

1 *cup Hot Peppermint Patty*
¾ cup hot water
1 ounce sugar-free hot cocoa
mix (1 Fruit)
1 to 2 teaspoons peppermint
extract
2 *sugar cookies (1 Bread)*

2,200-Calorie Menus
Lactose-Restricted

Week 1—Sunday

BREAKFAST

1 cup calcium-fortified orange juice (2 Fruit) (267 mg Calcium), see p. 262

2 small whole wheat bran muffins (2 Bread)

LUNCH

English Muffin Pizza

1 whole wheat English muffin, split (2 Bread), topped with

1 to 2 tablespoons spaghetti sauce

4 green pepper slices (1 Vegetable)

2 ounces part-skim mozzarella cheese (2 Meat) (360 mg Calcium)

Broil until cheese is bubbly.

1 medium orange (2 Fruit)

SNACK

1 *cup Fruity Milkshake L.R. (½ Milk, 3 Fruit) (237 mg Calcium), see p. 208*

8 *dried apricot halves (2 Fruit)*

DINNER

6 ounces broiled whitefish (6 Meat) with

2 teaspoons margarine (2 Fat) lemon juice

1½ cups cooked brown rice with parsley (3 Bread)

1 cup cooked mustard greens (2 Vegetable) (200 mg Calcium)

1 cup cooked carrots (2 Vegetable)

1 whole wheat roll (1 Bread) with

2 teaspoons margarine (2 Fat)

SNACK

½ *cup lime sherbet (2 Bread) (50 mg Calcium)*

6 *vanilla wafers (1 Bread)*

2,200-Calorie Menus
Lactose-Restricted

Week 2—Monday

BREAKFAST

1   cup calcium-fortified orange juice (2 Fruit) (267 mg Calcium), see p. 262
1   bagel (2 Bread) with
2   teaspoons margarine (2 Fat)

LUNCH

1   Chef's Salad with an extra 2 ounces of turkey (4 Meat, 3 Vegetable) (236 mg Calcium), see pp. 192–193, with
2   tablespoons Ranch dressing (2 Fat)
8   bread sticks (4 Bread)
1   cup fresh fruit cocktail (2 Fruit)

SNACK

1   *large apple (3 Fruit)*

DINNER

2   servings Chicken Broccoli Casserole (1 Milk, 4 Meat, 2 Vegetable) (516 mg Calcium), see pp. 195–196
    Tossed greens with 1 cup raw carrots, green pepper, and tomato (1 Vegetable) with
2   tablespoons French dressing (2 Fat)
1   whole wheat dinner roll (2 Bread) with
1   teaspoon margarine (1 Fat)

SNACK

1   *cup pineapple juice (3 Fruit)*
6   *cups air-popped popcorn (2 Bread)*

2,200-Calorie Menus
Lactose-Restricted

Week 2—Tuesday

BREAKFAST

½ cantaloupe (2 Fruit)
1   raisin English muffin (2 Bread, 1 Fruit) with
1   teaspoon margarine (1 Fat)

LUNCH

3   servings Crustless Kale Pie (3 Meat, 1½ Milk, 3 Vegetable, 3 Fat) (1,122 mg Calcium), see p. 196
    Lettuce, tomato, and green pepper salad (1 Vegetable) with
2   tablespoons Italian dressing (2 Fat)
1   small bran muffin (1 Bread)
1   medium pear (2 Fruit)

SNACK

8   *Skinny Nachos (1 Bread, 1 Meat) (200 mg Calcium), see pp. 212–213*

DINNER

6   ounces baked filet of sole (6 Meat) with
1   teaspoon margarine (1 Fat)
    Lemon wedge
1   cup cooked broccoli spears (2 Vegetable)
1   cup whipped potatoes (2 Bread) with
1   teaspoon margarine (1 Fat)
1   tablespoon nonfat powdered milk (52 mg Calcium)
2   slices dry whole wheat bread (2 Bread)

SNACK

1   *large apple (3 Fruit)*
2   *small oatmeal cookies (2 Bread)*

2,200-Calorie Menus
Lactose-Restricted

Week 2—Wednesday

BREAKFAST

1   banana (2 Fruit)
1   cup calcium-fortified orange
    juice (2 Fruit) (267 mg
    Calcium), see p. 262
1½ cups oat bran cereal (3 Bread)
    with
1   tablespoon nonfat powdered
    milk (52 mg Calcium)

LUNCH

Turkey Club Sandwich
3   slices whole wheat bread
    (3 Bread)
1   ounce low-fat cheese
    (1 Meat) (200 mg Calcium)
2   ounces sliced turkey (2 Meat)
2   ounces lean boiled ham
    (2 Meat)
2   teaspoons mayonnaise (2 Fat)
    Lettuce and tomato slice
½   cup Rice Pudding (½ Bread, ½
    Milk, ½ Fat) (87 mg
    Calcium), see p. 212

SNACK

1   *cup unsweetened peach slices*
    (2 Fruit)

DINNER

Spaghetti
1½ cups cooked spaghetti
    noodles (3 Bread)
½   cup tomato sauce (1 Bread)
3   1-ounce meatballs (3 Meat)
Tossed greens with 2 cups
raw vegetables (2 Vegetable)
with
1   tablespoon vinaigrette dressing
    (1 Fat)
1   cup cooked squash
    (2 Vegetable)
1   slice Italian bread (1 Bread)
    with
2   teaspoons margarine (2 Fat)

SNACK

Spicy Hot Chocolate
¾ cup hot water
1 ounce sugar-free hot cocoa
  mix (1 Fruit)
⅛ teaspoon cinnamon

2,200-Calorie Menus
Lactose-Restricted

Week 2—Thursday

BREAKFAST

1 cup grapefruit juice (2 Fruit)
2 Cheese Toasts
   2 slices whole wheat toast
     (2 Bread) topped with
   2 ounces low-fat cheese,
     melted (2 Meat) (400 mg
     Calcium)

LUNCH

2 servings Tomato Rarebit with
   extra slice toast, cut
   diagonally (2 Meat, 3 Bread, 2
   Vegetable) (554 mg Calcium),
   see pp. 201–202
2 cups celery and carrot sticks
   (1 Vegetable)

SNACK

1 *cup cranberry juice (4 Fruit)*
24 *animal crackers (3 Bread)*

DINNER

Pita Pocket Sandwich
1 whole wheat pita pocket
   (2 Bread)
1 cup cooked, chopped chicken
   (4 Meat) with
3 teaspoons mayonnaise (3 Fat)
1 tablespoon nonfat powdered
   milk (52 mg Calcium)
   Lettuce, diced tomato,
   and alfalfa sprouts
   (1 Vegetable)
2 cups fresh fruit (4 Fruit)

SNACK

1 *slice angel food cake (1 Bread)*
1 *cup blueberries (2 Fruit)*

2,200-Calorie Menus
Lactose-Restricted

Week 2—Friday

BREAKFAST

1   cup pineapple juice (3 Fruit)
1   Open-Faced Swiss and Pear
     Sandwich (1 Bread, 1 Meat,
     2 Fruit) (216 mg Calcium),
     see p. 205

LUNCH

1   cup Chicken Salad (4 Meat,
     1 Bread, 2 Fat) (85 mg
     Calcium), see p. 193
     stuffed in whole tomato
     (2 Vegetable)
8   pieces melba toast (2 Bread)

SNACK

3   *cups air-popped popcorn*
     (1 Bread)
1   *cup Fruity Milkshake L.R.*
     (½ Milk, 3 Fruit) (237 mg
     Calcium), see p. 208

DINNER

5   ounces poached salmon
     (5 Meat) with
     Lemon wedge
1   cup cooked brown rice
     (2 Bread)
½   cup cooked green beans
     (1 Vegetable)
1   cup cooked spinach
     (2 Vegetable)
1   slice whole wheat bread
     (1 Bread) with
2   teaspoons margarine (2 Fat)

SNACK

6   *ginger snap cookies (1 Bread)*
1   *cup calcium-fortified orange*
     juice (2 Fruit) (267 mg
     Calcium), see p. 262

2,200-Calorie Menus
Lactose-Restricted

Week 2—Saturday

BREAKFAST

1 cup calcium-fortified oatmeal (2 Bread) (400 mg Calcium), see p. 262, with
1 mashed banana (2 Fruit)

LUNCH

1 serving Pizza Olé (2 Bread, 1 Meat, 2 Vegetable, 2 Fat) (348 mg Calcium), see p. 200 Tossed greens with
1 tablespoon French dressing (1 Fat)
12 grapes (1 Fruit)

SNACK

1 cup Orange Frost (1½ Fruit) (27 mg Calcium), see p. 208

DINNER

5 ounces broiled flank steak (5 Meat)
1 large baked potato (3 Bread) with
2 tablespoons plain, nonfat yogurt (⅛ Milk) (52 mg Calcium)
1 teaspoon margarine (1 Fat)
1½ cups cooked mustard greens (3 Vegetable) (300 mg Calcium)

SNACK

8 pieces melba toast (2 Bread)
2 ounces turkey breast (2 Meat)
1 large apple (3 Fruit)

2,200-Calorie Menus
Lactose-Restricted

Week 2—Sunday

BREAKFAST

1 cup calcium-fortified orange juice (2 Fruit) (267 mg Calcium), see p. 262

4 4-inch whole wheat pancakes (2 Bread, 2 Fat) with

1 teaspoon margarine (1 Fat)

2 tablespoons low-sugar syrup (1 Fruit)

1½ cups unsweetened applesauce (3 Fruit)

LUNCH

Cheeseburger

1 whole wheat bun (2 Bread)

3 ounces lean beef patty (3 Meat)

1 ounce low-fat cheese (1 Meat) (200 mg Calcium) Lettuce, tomato slice, and onion slice (1 Vegetable)

1 tablespoon mustard

1 large apple (3 Fruit)

SNACK

1 *strawberry frozen fruit bar (1 Bread)*

DINNER

5 ounces baked fish (5 Meat)

1 cup cooked collard greens (2 Vegetable) (360 mg Calcium)

1 cup cooked asparagus (2 Vegetable)

4 whole new potatoes, boiled (2 Bread), with

2 teaspoons margarine (2 Fat)

2 teaspoons chopped chives

½ teaspoon grated lemon rind

1 whole wheat roll (1 Bread)

SNACK

1 *small slice lemon sponge cake (1 Bread)*

1 *cup herbal tea*

The Tough Bone
Diet Program Recipes

Cheese Cauliflower Chowder

Yields: 4 servings
1 serving (1 cup): Calories = 192
                  Calcium = 459 mg
                  Cholesterol = 11 mg
                  Exchanges = 1 Milk +
                              1 Meat +
                              1 Vegetable

½   cup chopped onion
1¼ cups water
1   10-ounce package frozen cauliflower
1   4-ounce can sliced mushrooms
2   teaspoons instant chicken bouillon granules
½   teaspoon dry mustard
¾   cup skim milk
4   teaspoons cornstarch
8   ounces low-fat cheese, cut into small pieces
2   tablespoons chopped pimiento

In saucepan, cook onion in water until tender. Add cauliflower, *undrained* mushrooms, bouillon, and mustard. Bring to boil; reduce heat; cover and simmer the vegetable mixture about 8 minutes or until the cauliflower is tender.

Combine milk and cornstarch. Stir into hot vegetable mixture. Cook and stir over medium heat until thick and bubbly. Stir in cheese and pimiento. Heat through, stirring to melt cheese.

Cream of Corn Soup

Yields: 6 servings
1 serving (1 cup): Calories = 202
                   Calcium = 300 mg
                   Cholesterol = 3 mg
                   Exchanges = 1 Bread +
                               1 Milk +
                               2 Fat

3   tablespoons minced onion
2   cups frozen corn, thawed
2½   tablespoons margarine
2   tablespoons flour
1   quart low-fat milk
½   teaspoon salt (optional)
½   teaspoon pepper

In saucepan, sauté onion in ½ tablespoon margarine until soft. Put corn through a food processor, add to onion mixture, and cook until it begins to brown. Stir occasionally. Add remaining margarine, and then the flour. Cook slowly for 3 minutes. Add milk, salt, and pepper, and cook until thickened and smooth.

Cream of Tomato Soup

Yields: 4 servings
1 serving (1 cup): Calories = 154
                   Calcium = 219 mg
                   Cholesterol = 24 mg
                   Exchanges = 1 Meat +
                               3 Vegetable

2   1-pound cans whole tomatoes, low sodium
1¼   cups part-skim ricotta cheese
¼   teaspoon Worcestershire sauce
     Tabasco sauce, to taste
     black pepper, to taste

Combine ingredients in the container of an electric blender. Whirl until completely blended. Place in a saucepan and heat for 20 minutes. Adjust seasonings to taste.

French Onion Soup

Yields: 4½ servings

1 serving (1 cup): Calories = 90

Calcium = 99 mg

Cholesterol = 6 mg

Exchanges = ½ Bread +

½ Vegetable +

1 Fat

1 large onion, thinly sliced
1½ teaspoons margarine
2 10½-ounce cans condensed beef broth
1½ cups water
½ teaspoon Worcestershire sauce
1 tablespoon cooking sherry
4 melba rounds
4 tablespoons grated Parmesan cheese

In saucepan, sauté onions in margarine, covered, over low heat until lightly browned. Add beef broth, water, Worcestershire sauce, and sherry. Bring to boil. Pour into oven-proof bowls. Float melba rounds on top of onion soup; sprinkle each with 1 tablespoon Parmesan cheese. Broil 3 to 4 inches from heat until browned.

Seafood Chowder

Yields: 8 servings
1 serving (1 cup): Calories = 149
                   Calcium = 166 mg
                   Cholesterol = 59 mg
                   Exchanges = 1 Milk +
                               1 Meat

2	cups clam juice
1	onion, sliced
8	new potatoes, unpeeled and diced
2	bay leaves
15	whole peppercorns
1	clove garlic, minced
½	pound clams, cleaned
½	pound white fish, cut into chunks
¼	pound shrimp, peeled and deveined
3	cups skim milk
½	bunch (10 ounces) fresh spinach, washed and chopped, or 10-ounce frozen package, cooked, drained, and chopped

In a large saucepan, cook clam juice, onion, potatoes, and seasonings over medium heat for 15 minutes or until potatoes are done. Add seafood and milk; heat until cooked, about 20 minutes. Stir in spinach; heat for 3 minutes. Serve at once.

Chef's Salad

Yields: 2 servings
1 serving (1 salad): Calories = 207
                     Calcium = 236 mg
                     Cholesterol = 27 mg
                     Exchanges = 2 Meat +
                                 3 Vegetable

½	cup sliced radishes
¼	cup sliced green onions
½	cup thinly sliced cauliflowerets
⅛	cup French salad dressing
2	cups salad greens, torn into bite-sized pieces
2	ounces low-fat cheese, cut into julienne strips
2	ounces turkey breast, cut into julienne strips
4	cherry tomatoes, halved

In a large bowl, combine radishes, green onions, and cauliflowerets with French salad dressing; toss. Refrigerate 4 hours, tossing occasionally. Place salad greens in 2 individual salad bowls. Arrange cheese, turkey, and cherry tomatoes atop greens. To serve, drain vegetable mixture; reserve dressing. Spoon ½ of the vegetable mixture atop each salad. Drizzle with reserved dressing if desired.

Chicken Salad

Yields: 2 servings
1 serving (1 cup): Calories = 448
                   Calcium = 85 mg
                   Cholesterol = 99 mg
                   Exchanges = 4 Meat +
                               1 Bread +
                               2 Fat

2   chicken breasts, skinless, boneless
1   medium apple, finely chopped
¼   cup chopped pecans
2   tablespoons mayonnaise
4   tablespoons plain, low-fat yogurt

Simmer chicken breasts for 20 minutes in small amount of water. Cool and chop into small pieces. Combine the remaining ingredients and mix until well blended. Serve on lettuce lined plate.

Confetti Cottage Cheese Salad

Yields: 4 servings
1 serving (1 cup): Calories = 150
                   Calcium = 125 mg
                   Cholesterol = 9 mg
                   Exchanges = 1 Meat +
                               1 Milk

1   16-ounce container low-fat cottage cheese
¼   cup plain, low-fat yogurt
1   cup shredded carrots
¾   cup chopped tomato
¾   cup chopped green pepper
3   tablespoons thinly sliced green onion
1   teaspoon dried oregano

In a medium bowl, combine all ingredients and mix well. Serve chilled.

Salmon Salad

Yields: 4 servings
1 serving (1 cup): Calories = 130
Calcium = 140 mg
Cholesterol = 10 mg
Exchanges = 1 Meat +
2 Vegetable

1	8-ounce can red sockeye salmon, drained
½	cup fresh orange juice, unsweetened
¼	cup fresh lemon juice
1	small green pepper, chopped
1	small cucumber, chopped
1	tomato, peeled, seeded and chopped
½	red onion, pared and minced
3	tablespoons minced green onion
	leaf lettuce
4	lime wedges

In a large bowl, break salmon into bite-size pieces and crush bones. Combine orange and lemon juice and pour over salmon. Set aside.

Combine green pepper, cucumber, tomato, and onions. Add ⅓ of the vegetable mixture to the salmon mixture. Marinate this combination and refrigerate for 2 to 3 hours.

To serve, arrange salmon salad on leaf lettuce. Place reserved vegetables over salmon. Serve with lime wedges.

―――――――――   *Cheesy Pita Pocket Sandwich*   ―――――――――

Yields: 1 serving
1 serving (1 sandwich): Calories = 225
                        Calcium = 211 mg
                        Cholesterol = 23 mg
                        Exchanges = 1 Meat +
                                    1 Bread +
                                    1 Vegetable +
                                    1 Fat

1   whole wheat pita pocket
1   ounce part-skim mozzarella cheese, grated
1   tablespoon chopped tomato
    lettuce, shredded
1   tablespoon chopped green onion
1   teaspoon Italian dressing

Cut pita bread in half crosswise. Fill each half with mozzarella cheese.
Top the cheese with tomato, lettuce, and green onion. Pour Italian
dressing into each half and serve.

―――――――――   *Chicken Broccoli Casserole*   ―――――――――

Yields: 6 servings
1 serving (⅙ of the recipe): Calories = 214
                             Calcium = 256 mg
                             Cholesterol = 52 mg
                             Exchanges = ½ Milk +
                                         2 Meat +
                                         1 Vegetable

2   cups cubed cooked chicken
1   bunch broccoli, cooked and chopped
1   tablespoon margarine
2   tablespoons flour
2   cups low-fat milk
¼   teaspoon salt
¼   teaspoon pepper
½   cup grated Parmesan cheese

Preheat oven to 400°F. Arrange chicken and broccoli in a casserole dish. Make a thin cream sauce: in saucepan, melt margarine, add flour, and stir until bubbly. Gradually add the milk and cook until sauce thickens. Add salt, pepper, and cheese. Pour over chicken and broccoli in the casserole dish. Bake in oven about 15 minutes until brown and bubbly.

Crustless Kale Pie

Yields: 6 servings
1 serving (⅙ pie): Calories = 186
Calcium = 374 mg
Cholesterol = 11 mg
Exchanges = 1 Meat +
½ Milk +
1 Vegetable +
1 Fat

	nonstick cooking spray for pie plate
4	teaspoons diet margarine
2	medium onions, sliced
1	garlic clove, minced
4	cups (two 10-ounce packages) frozen chopped kale, thawed
¾	cup egg substitute
1½	cups evaporated skim milk
3	ounces part-skim mozzarella cheese, shredded
½	teaspoon pepper
½	teaspoon salt

Preheat oven to 350°F. Spray a 10-inch pie plate with nonstick cooking spray. Melt margarine in medium skillet over medium-high heat. Sauté onions and garlic until tender. Remove from heat.

Squeeze thawed kale to remove all excess liquid. Stir kale into onion mixture and combine. Spread evenly in pie plate.

In separate bowl, combine egg substitute, evaporated milk, mozzarella cheese, salt, and pepper. Pour into prepared pie plate, stirring to combine. Bake 30 minutes, until center is almost set. Let cool 10 minutes before serving.

Lasagna

Yields: 6 servings
1 serving (⅙ recipe): Calories = 476
Calcium = 306 mg
Cholesterol = 71 mg
Exchanges = 2 Meat +
3 Bread +
1 Vegetable +
2 Fat

Tomato Sauce

3	tablespoons olive oil
½	cup chopped onion
1	clove garlic, minced
1	small carrot, grated
3	tablespoons chopped green pepper
1	bay leaf
1½	teaspoons dried oregano
1	teaspoon dried thyme
1	teaspoon dried basil
3	tablespoons fresh chopped parsley
3	cups chopped tomatoes
1½	six-ounce cans tomato paste
1	teaspoon salt
½	teaspoon brown sugar
¼	teaspoon pepper

In saucepan, heat oil and sauté garlic and onion in oil until onion is soft. Add carrots, green pepper, bay leaf, and herbs. Stir well, then add tomatoes, tomato paste, and seasonings. Simmer for 30 minutes. Discard bay leaf.

Lasagna

3	cups tomato sauce (recipe above)
¾	pound lasagna noodles
½	cup chopped walnuts
1	medium bunch (2-10 ounces) fresh spinach, chopped, or 2 10-ounce frozen packages, cooked, drained, and chopped
12	thin slices (6 ounces) part-skim mozzarella cheese
¼	cup grated Parmesan cheese
1	cup low-fat cottage cheese

Preheat oven to 350°F. Cook noodles in boiling water according to package directions. Drain. Toast nuts in oven until lightly browned, stirring frequently.

Spread ¾ cup of sauce in bottom of 8 × 8-inch baking dish. Cover with ⅓ of noodles on bottom, then ⅓ of spinach, ¼ of nuts, ¼ cup cottage cheese, 1 tablespoon Parmesan cheese, and 1 layer of mozzarella cheese. Repeat layers twice. Spread the last cup of sauce and the remaining nuts and cheeses on top. Bake for 40 minutes and let stand 10 minutes before cutting.

Meatless Enchiladas

Yields: 4 servings
1 serving (2 enchiladas): Calories = 453
Calcium = 402 mg
Cholesterol = 37 mg
Exchanges = 2 Meat +
3 Bread +
1 Vegetable +
2 Fat

Sauce

1	tablespoon safflower oil
1	tablespoon chili powder
1½	tablespoons flour
1½	cups water
1	teaspoon vinegar
1	teaspoon garlic powder
¾	teaspoon onion powder
¼	teaspoon salt
½	teaspoon dried oregano leaves
½	teaspoon chopped fresh parsley

In a small saucepan, heat oil, chili powder, and flour to make a paste. Add water gradually to make a smooth sauce; add vinegar, garlic powder, onion powder, salt, oregano, and parsley. Bring to a boil. Lower heat; simmer uncovered for about 3 minutes.

Filling

1¼ cups grated part-skim mozzarella cheese
¾   cup refried beans
½   cup low-fat cottage cheese
1   medium onion, finely chopped

8   corn tortillas
1   cup Mock Sour Cream (see recipe below)
4   tablespoons chopped green onions

Mock Sour Cream

1   cup low-fat cottage cheese
2   tablespoons low-fat buttermilk
¾   teaspoon fresh lemon juice

Blend cottage cheese, buttermilk, and lemon juice in blender container or with mixer until smooth. Makes 1 cup.

Preheat oven to 350°F. Reserve ⅓ of the grated cheese for topping. Mix refried beans, remaining cheese, cottage cheese, and onions in a bowl. Warm tortillas in the oven. Place ¼ cup of bean filling down the center of each tortilla. Roll up; place seam side down in shallow baking dish. Pour sauce over filled enchiladas and sprinkle with reserved cheese. Bake 20 minutes or until bubbly. Top with Mock Sour Cream and chopped green onions before serving.

Meatless Enchiladas L.R.

Yields: 4 servings
1 serving (2 enchiladas): Calories = 328
                          Calcium = 269 mg
                          Cholesterol = 11 mg
                          Exchanges = 1 Meat +
                                      2 Bread +
                                      1 Fat

Follow recipe for Meatless Enchiladas (pp. 198–199), but **omit** Mock Sour Cream.

== **Pizza Olé** ==

Yields: 8 servings
1 serving (⅛ pie): Calories = 365
                    Calcium = 348 mg
                    Cholesterol = 30 mg
                    Exchanges = 2 Bread +
                                1 Meat +
                                2 Vegetable +
                                2 Fat

½   cup plus 1 tablespoon enriched corn meal
1½ cups whole wheat flour
1   tablespoon baking powder
½   teaspoon salt (optional)
¾   cup skim milk
¼   cup vegetable oil
1   12-ounce jar taco sauce
1   15½-ounce can Mexican-style chili beans, undrained
1   medium green pepper, cut into thin rings
2   cups (8 ounces) low-fat cheese, shredded

Preheat oven to 450°F. Grease 14-inch round pizza pan. Sprinkle 1 tablespoon corn meal evenly into prepared pan. In a medium bowl, combine remaining ½ cup corn meal, flour, baking powder, and salt. Add milk and oil; stir with fork until mixture forms a ball.

Press dough into prepared pan; shape edge to form rim. Bake 15 minutes. Spread taco sauce evenly over partially baked crust. Top with beans, pepper rings, and cheese; continue baking 10 minutes or until cheese is melted.

== **Roni Cheese Bake** ==

Yields: 6 servings
1 serving (about 1 cup): Calories = 450
                         Calcium = 389 mg
                         Cholesterol = 188 mg
                         Exchanges = 2 Meat +
                                     2 Bread +
                                     2 Vegetable +
                                     2 Fat

1   32-ounce jar meatless spaghetti sauce
⅔   cup water
1   15-ounce container part-skim ricotta cheese
2   eggs, lightly beaten
1   teaspoon crushed oregano leaves
1   teaspoon garlic powder
1   teaspoon dried basil
     nonstick cooking spray for casserole dish
2   cups (8 ounces) uncooked elbow macaroni
1   8-ounce package part-skim mozzarella cheese slices

Preheat oven to 350°F. In a medium bowl, combine spaghetti sauce and water. In another bowl, combine ricotta cheese, eggs, oregano, garlic powder, and basil. Spray a $13 \times 9 \times 2$-inch casserole dish with nonstick spray and spoon ⅓ of the sauce into the dish. Top with 1 cup of the uncooked elbow macaroni, ½ of the ricotta cheese mixture, ½ of the mozzarella cheese, and ⅓ of the tomato sauce. Repeat layers using remaining macaroni, ricotta cheese mixture, and tomato sauce. Cover with aluminum foil. Bake 45 minutes. Uncover. Top with remaining mozzarella cheese. Bake 15 minutes longer. Let stand 10 minutes before cutting.

Tomato Rarebit

Yields: 6 servings
1 serving (⅓ cup): Calories = 165
                 Calcium = 277 mg
                 Cholesterol = 9 mg
                 Exchanges = 1 Meat +
                            1 Bread +
                            1 Vegetable

¼   cup finely chopped onion
2   tablespoons finely chopped green pepper
1   teaspoon diet margarine
1   10¾-ounce can tomato soup, condensed
2   cups (8 ounces) low-fat cheese, shredded
¼   teaspoon dry mustard
¼   teaspoon Worcestershire sauce
6   slices toast, cut diagonally

In a saucepan, cook onion and green pepper in margarine until tender. Set aside. Heat soup in the top of a double boiler. Add cheese to soup and cook over boiling water, stirring constantly until cheese is melted and mixture is smooth. Stir in mustard, Worcestershire sauce, onion, and green pepper. Serve over toast pieces.

—————————————— *Veggie Burritos* ——————————————

Yields: 2 servings
1 serving (2 burritos): Calories = 470
                        Calcium = 438 mg
                        Cholesterol = 22 mg
                        Exchanges = 3 Bread +
                                    2 Meat +
                                    1 Fat

    2   teaspoons olive oil
    ½   onion, chopped
    2   stalks fresh broccoli, chopped
    8   ounces tofu (firm type), cut into ¼-inch cubes
    4   flour tortillas
    2   ounces Monterey Jack cheese, shredded
    1   small tomato, chopped
    4   tablespoons picante sauce

Preheat oven to 300°F. Heat olive oil in a large skillet and sauté onion until translucent. Add broccoli and tofu. Cook until broccoli turns bright green and tofu is thoroughly heated. Set aside.

Place tortillas on cookie sheet. Evenly distribute one-quarter of shredded cheese on each tortilla. Place in oven just until cheese is melted; remove from oven.

Put about 2 to 3 tablespoons of broccoli/tofu mixture in a strip 2 inches wide down the middle of each tortilla. Add 1 tablespoon of chopped tomatoes. Return to oven for 5 to 10 minutes or until thoroughly heated. Remove and add 1 to 3 teaspoons of picante sauce (depending on personal taste) to each tortilla. Roll the sides in and serve immediately.

Zucchini Quiche

Yields: 4 servings

1 serving (¼ pie): Calories = 386
Calcium = 380 mg
Cholesterol = 44 mg
Exchanges = 2 Bread +
3 Vegetable +
3 Meat +
1 Fat

Crust

1	tablespoon active dry yeast
½	cup warm water
½	cup whole wheat flour
¾	cup all-purpose flour
¼	teaspoon salt

Dissolve yeast in water. Stir in flour and salt. Knead dough on floured board for 5 minutes until smooth and elastic. Let rise for 45 minutes.

Filling

1	tablespoon margarine
4	cups thinly sliced, unpeeled zucchini
1	cup coarsely chopped onion
3	tablespoons chopped fresh parsley
¼	teaspoon salt
½	teaspoon pepper
½	teaspoon garlic powder
½	teaspoon dried basil leaves
½	teaspoon dried oregano leaves
3	egg whites
2	cups grated part-skim mozzarella cheese
2½	teaspoons brown mustard

Preheat oven to 375°F. Heat margarine in a large skillet and add zucchini and onion; cook until tender, about 10 minutes. Stir in parsley and seasonings. Set aside. In a large bowl, blend egg whites and cheese. Stir into vegetable mixture.

Transfer raised dough to an ungreased 10-inch pie pan. Press over bottom and up sides to form crust. Spread mustard over crust. Pour vegetable mixture evenly over crust. Bake for 25 to 35 minutes or until knife inserted near center comes out clean. If crust becomes too brown, cover with foil during last 10 minutes of baking. Let quiche stand 10 minutes before serving.

Fruit à la Yogurt

Yields: 2 servings
1 serving (1 cup): Calories = 208
                     Calcium = 250 mg
                     Cholesterol = 7 mg
                     Exchanges = 1 Milk +
                                 2 Fruit

1   banana
1   orange
½   cup strawberries
1   cup plain, low-fat yogurt
1   tablespoon honey
1   teaspoon grated orange peel

Cut fruit into bite-size pieces, combine, and place in 2 fruit cups. Set aside. In a small bowl, combine yogurt, honey, and orange peel until well blended. Divide mixture in half and spoon on top of fruit. Serve chilled.

Fruit à la Yogurt L.R.

Yields: 2 servings
1 serving (1 cup): Calories = 172
                     Calcium = 147 mg
                     Cholesterol = 3 mg
                     Exchanges = ½ Milk +
                                 2½ Fruit

Follow recipe for Fruit à la Yogurt (above), but use only ½ **cup** yogurt.

—————— *Open-Faced Swiss and Pear Sandwiches* ——————

Yields: 4 servings
1 serving (1 sandwich): Calories = 156
                        Calcium = 216 mg
                        Cholesterol = 6 mg
                        Exchanges = 1 Bread +
                                    1 Meat +
                                    2 Fruit

   4   slices whole wheat bread
   4   1-ounce slices low-fat Swiss cheese
   2   medium pears, pared, cored, sliced
   ½   teaspoon cinnamon

Preheat oven to broil. Toast bread. Place a cheese slice on each piece
of toast. Arrange sliced pears on cheese. Sprinkle cinnamon on pears.
Broil 10 minutes or until lightly browned. Serve hot.

—————— *Sunrise Pancake Stack* ——————

Yields: 6 servings
1 serving (1 wedge): Calories = 236
                     Calcium = 216 mg
                     Cholesterol = 19 mg
                     Exchanges = 2 Bread +
                                 1 Meat +
                                 ½ Fat

   1½ cups whole wheat flour
   2   teaspoons baking powder
   1   teaspoon grated orange peel
   1   egg white
   2½ tablespoons honey
   ¼   cup skim milk
   ¾   cup fresh orange juice
   1   tablespoon safflower oil
       nonstick cooking spray for griddle
   1½ cups part-skim ricotta cheese

In a medium bowl, combine flour, baking powder, and orange peel. In a
separate bowl, combine egg white, honey, milk, orange juice, and oil.
Stir the wet ingredients into the dry ingredients just enough to moisten.

Cook four large pancakes on a griddle sprayed with nonstick spray. Spread ½ cup ricotta cheese between each pancake. Cut into wedges and serve with low-sugar syrup.

─────────────────── ## *Yogurt and Fruit Parfait* ───────────────────

Yields: 1 serving
1 serving (1 cup): Calories = 160
               Calcium = 415 mg
               Cholesterol = 18 mg
               Exchanges = 1 Milk +
                             2 Fruit

- 8 ounces plain, non-fat yogurt
- ¾ cup strawberries
- ¼ cup blueberries

Spoon ¼ of the yogurt into a parfait dish. Top with ½ of the strawberries, followed with another layer of ¼ yogurt. Top with the blueberries, followed with another layer of ¼ yogurt. Top with remaining strawberries and yogurt. Save one strawberry as garnish for the top. Serve chilled.

─────────────────── ## *Dilly Sauce* ───────────────────

Yields: 3 servings
1 serving (½ cup): Calories = 84
               Calcium = 175 mg
               Cholesterol = 4 mg
               Exchanges = 1 Milk +
                             ½ Fat

- 1 tablespoon diet margarine
- 1 tablespoon minced onion
- 1 tablespoon cornstarch
- ¼ teaspoon salt
- ½ teaspoon dried dill weed
- ⅛ teaspoon black pepper
- 1 cup skim milk
- ½ cup plain, low-fat yogurt

In a small saucepan, melt margarine. Add onion and sauté until tender. In a small bowl, combine cornstarch, salt, dill, black pepper, and milk.

Stir into saucepan. Bring to a boil. Cook and stir over medium heat until thickened, about 1 minute. Remove from heat. Stir in yogurt. Serve over fish.

Fruited Cocoa

Yields: 4 servings
1 serving (1 cup): Calories = 153
Calcium = 257 mg
Cholesterol = 65 mg
Exchanges = 1 Milk +
1 Meat

1	tablespoon fresh lemon juice
1	cup fresh orange juice
1	egg
6	tablespoons sweetened cocoa mix
1½	cups skim milk
2	tablespoons nonfat powdered milk

In a blender container, combine lemon juice and orange juice. Add egg, cocoa, milk, and powdered milk, blending after each addition. Garnish with a twist of orange. Serve chilled.

Fruity Milkshake

Yields: 1 serving
1 serving (1 cup): Calories = 150
Calcium = 202 mg
Cholesterol = 10 mg
Exchanges = ½ Milk +
2 Fruit

½	cup skim milk
1	tablespoon nonfat powdered milk
½	cup frozen unsweetened strawberries
½	banana
½	cup ice cubes

In a blender container, combine ingredients with ice and blend until frothy.

Fruity Milkshake L.R.

Yields: 1 serving
1 serving (1 cup): Calories = 160
                   Calcium = 237 mg
                   Cholesterol = 1 mg
                   Exchanges = ½ Milk +
                                    3 Fruit

Follow recipe for Fruity Milkshake (p. 207), but use ½ **cup calcium fortified orange juice** instead of ½ cup skim milk.

Orange Frost

Yields: 8 servings
1 serving (1 cup): Calories = 45
                   Calcium = 27 mg
                   Cholesterol = 0 mg
                   Exchanges = 1½ Fruit

1½ cups orange sherbet
1   6-ounce can frozen calcium-fortified orange juice concentrate, undiluted
4   ice cubes
1   cup ice water
3   12-ounce cans Diet Slice, chilled

In a blender container, combine all the ingredients except Diet Slice. Cover and blend until smooth. Pour into 8 glasses. Pour Diet Slice into sides of glasses. Stir gently.

Peachy Fruit Shake

Yields: 2 servings
1 serving (1 cup): Calories = 120
                   Calcium = 285 mg
                   Cholesterol = 8 mg
                   Exchanges = 1 Milk +
                                    1 Fruit

1   cup plain, low-fat yogurt
½   cup skim milk
½   cup water-packed peach halves
1   tablespoon honey

In a blender container, combine all ingredients. Cover and blend until smooth. Pour into 2 large glasses. Serve immediately.

=============================== **Pinana Frost** ===============================

Yields: 2 servings
1 serving (1 cup): Calories = 100
                   Calcium = 167 mg
                   Cholesterol = 3 mg
                   Exchanges = ½ Milk +
                               1½ Fruit

1   cup skim milk
1   cup sliced banana
3   tablespoons frozen pineapple juice concentrate, undiluted
¼   teaspoon vanilla extract

In a blender container, combine all ingredients. Cover and blend until smooth. Serve immediately.

=============================== **Strawberry Delight** ===============================

Yields: 1 serving
1 serving (1 cup): Calories = 165
                   Calcium = 315 mg
                   Cholesterol = 30 mg
                   Exchanges = 1 Milk +
                               2 Fruit

1   cup skim milk
½   cup sliced strawberries
1   tablespoon sugar
¼   teaspoon vanilla extract

In a blender container, combine milk, strawberries, sugar, and vanilla. Cover and blend on high speed until strawberries are pureed. Garnish with whole strawberry.

Very Fruity Frozen Frappé

Yields: 1 serving
1 serving (1½ cups): Calories = 266
                    Calcium = 288 mg
                    Cholesterol = 1 mg
                    Exchanges = 2 Fruit +
                                1½ Milk +
                                1 Fat

1   cup plain, low-fat yogurt
1   banana, frozen*
1 to 2 tablespoons frozen fruit juice concentrate, undiluted
⅛   teaspoon vanilla extract

In a blender container, combine all ingredients. Cover and blend on high speed until smooth. Serve immediately.

*To freeze ripe bananas, remove the peel, cut into quarters, and seal in an airtight freezer container.

Very Fruity Frozen Frappé L.R.

Yields: 1 serving
1 serving (1½ cups): Calories = 241
                    Calcium = 378 mg
                    Exchanges = ½ Milk +
                                5 Fruit

1   banana, frozen*
1   cup calcium-fortified orange juice
1   tablespoon nonfat powdered milk
10 ice cubes

Put all ingredients in a blender container and blend on high speed until smooth. Serve immediately.

*To freeze ripe bananas, remove the peel, cut into quarters, and seal in an airtight freezer container.

========================== *Calico Cracker Spread* ==========================

Yields: 7 servings (1¾ cups)
1 serving (4 tablespoons): Calories = 64
                            Calcium = 132 mg
                            Cholesterol = 3 mg
                            Exchanges = ½ Meat +
                                        ½ Vegetable

½	cup plain, low-fat yogurt
1	cup part-skim ricotta cheese
⅛	cup chopped green pepper
⅛	cup chopped red pepper
¼	cup sliced green onion
½	cup shredded carrots
⅛	teaspoon black pepper

In a mixing bowl, combine all ingredients. Refrigerate. Serve with your favorite crackers.

========================== *Nibbler's Surprise* ==========================

Yields: 4 servings
1 serving (½ cup): Calories = 209
                    Calcium = 270 mg
                    Cholesterol = 33 mg
                    Exchanges = ½ Milk +
                                ½ Meat +
                                2 Fat

1½	cups plain, low-fat yogurt
1	cup shredded part-skim mozzarella cheese
¼	cup wheat germ
¼	cup finely chopped toasted almonds
2	tablespoons chopped green onion
	paprika, to garnish

Combine all ingredients in a bowl and stir well to blend. Refrigerate. Serve with fresh vegetables.

Rice Pudding

Yields: 6 servings
1 serving (½ cup): Calories = 99
　　　　　　　　　Calcium = 87 mg
　　　　　　　　　Cholesterol = 85 mg
　　　　　　　　　Exchanges = ½ Bread +
　　　　　　　　　　　　　　　½ Milk +
　　　　　　　　　　　　　　　½ Fat

½　cup cooked rice
¼　cup sugar
2　eggs, beaten*
½　teaspoon vanilla extract
¼ to ½ teaspoon almond extract
⅛　teaspoon nutmeg
　　Dash salt
1½ cups skim milk, scalded

Preheat oven to 350°F. In 1½-quart ungreased casserole dish, combine rice, sugar, eggs, vanilla and almond extracts, nutmeg, and salt. Gradually stir in milk until well combined. Place casserole dish in 13 × 9-inch baking pan; fill pan with 1 inch hot water. Bake for 55 to 65 minutes or until knife inserted near center comes out clean. Stir pudding after 30 minutes of baking. Serve warm or cold.

*Can substitute ½ cup egg substitute.

Skinny Nachos

Yields: 1 serving
1 serving (8 pieces): Calories = 140
　　　　　　　　　　Calcium = 200 mg
　　　　　　　　　　Cholesterol = 16 mg
　　　　　　　　　　Exchanges = 1 Bread +
　　　　　　　　　　　　　　　　1 Meat

1　soft corn tortilla
　　Seasoning (i.e., Bakon's Cheddar Cheese; cayenne pepper, or your favorite)
1　ounce part-skim mozzarella cheese, shredded

Preheat oven to 350°F. Cut corn tortilla into 8 triangular "pie" slices. Add seasonings of choice to chips. Bake on cookie sheet for 15 minutes. Sprinkle cheese over crispy chips and broil until cheese is bubbly.

Yogurt Frozen Treat

Yields: 12 servings
1 serving (1 treat): Calories = 68
                     Calcium = 75 mg
                     Cholesterol = 2 mg
                     Exchanges = ½ Milk +
                                 ¼ Fruit

2   10-ounce cartons frozen strawberries, thawed
1   tablespoon unflavored gelatin
2   8-ounce cartons plain, low-fat yogurt
12 3-ounce paper cups

Drain strawberries. Place drained liquid in a saucepan and sprinkle with gelatin. Cook over low heat, stirring constantly, until gelatin dissolves. Mix strawberries, yogurt, and gelatin mixture in a blender container until smooth. Place paper cups on a tray or a baking pan. Fill with blended mixture and cover cups with a sheet of aluminum foil. Freeze until firm.

TEN

Do Calcium
Supplements Work?

Recent reports in the press have raised an important question that has been nagging away at the millions of people who are concerned about osteoporosis: "Do calcium supplements really work in preventing bone loss?"

Let me respond to this question first by relating a true story about Sarah, a 60-year-old woman who came in for a medical examination because of severe lower-back pains. These pains had begun about five years before, but a variety of doctors had been unable to find the source of the pain.

Sarah had been quite athletic, and she had pursued a productive professional career up until her midfifties. But by the time she reached 60, she had become so debilitated by back and hip pains that she had to quit work and spend most of her time in a wheelchair at home. Predictably, she became quite depressed about her physical condition, and she had concluded that there was no answer to her physical problems—until she consulted an expert in osteoporosis.

This specialist and his staff, in investigating Sarah's medical history, found that she had gone through a normal menopause at age 50. A couple of years after that, she had begun to take estrogen replacement treatments. Also, she had no history of osteoporosis in her family, she had a moderate-size bone structure, she was a nonsmoker, and she did not drink alcohol excessively.

In short, Sarah seemed a very unlikely candidate for osteoporosis at her age—except for one thing: She had a relatively low calcium intake in her diet. She consumed only about 350 to 400 mg. of calcium a day, and she took no calcium supplements.

The bone specialist did a radiologic (X ray) examination, which revealed severe osteopenia, or bone loss, in the vertebrae, but no fractures. However, the X rays of the hips showed healed fractures of the neck of one thighbone (femur) and a new fracture of the other femur.

Upon biochemical testing of her urine, the specialist determined that Sarah probably had a problem with conserving calcium in her body. She also appeared to have an extremely deficient capacity to absorb calcium.

Finally, the physician did bone-density studies that confirmed the existence of moderately severe osteoporosis. Specifically, a single-photon instrument showed that the density of her radius, or forearm bone, was only about 60 percent of what it should have been for a normal woman her age. Furthermore, a dual-photon test revealed that the density of her lower spine was only 80 percent of what would have been expected for someone of her age, weight, and height.

Sarah was immediately placed on treatment that involved the medication Calderol to overcome her problem with absorbing calcium. She was also given a highly absorbable calcium supplement, a form of calcium citrate, which nearly quadrupled her calcium intake to about 1,500 mg. daily.

Sarah began to show improvement very quickly. Within the first four months, she reported an increase in her strength and a lessening of her back pain. By the end of six months, Sarah was out of her wheelchair, and her pain had almost completely disappeared.

Bone-density studies conducted one year after the initial tests revealed that the calcium-based treatment was doing a great job. The calcium malabsorption problem had been corrected, and the additional calcium in her system had resulted in a 6 percent increase in the bone density of her radius, and a 4 percent increase in the density of her spine.

By the end of this first year of treatment, Sarah had returned to work, and she had also begun to participate in the leisure-time athletics she loved so well. When she came in for her most recent bone-density study after being on the calcium treatment for four years, her bone density had stabilized at 15 percent higher in her radius and 9 percent higher in her spine.

Now, her physician feels that Sarah is no longer at risk for further fractures. As long as she continues indefinitely on her current therapy, he expects her to be able to pursue a normal lifestyle. In short, calcium supplements were decisive in transforming this woman's life. So if you ask me, "Do calcium supplements help?" I'll respond without hesitation, "Sure, they help—if you use them wisely!"

But even with such success stories, a number of objections are still being raised to certain uses of calcium supplements. Let's take some time now to consider them.

Is There a Case Against Calcium Supplements?

The *Harvard Medical School Health Letter* told its readers in April 1987 that "it is hard to escape the conclusion that calcium has been oversold as a weapon against osteoporosis." In particular, the writer of this report had in mind two recent studies that have questioned whether calcium supplements, when they are taken alone, are really effective in fighting bone loss.

The first of the studies was conducted in Denmark by Dr. Bente Riis and his colleagues and reported in the January 22, 1987, issue of the *New England Journal of Medicine.* During a two-year study, Riis and his team examined the effect of calcium supplementation on bone loss just after menopause in 43 women.

The women were assigned to three separate groups:

1. The first group received estrogen combined with progesterone.

2. The second group received 2,000 mg. a day of oral calcium in the form of a calcium carbonate supplement.

3. Finally, the third group was given a placebo.

Then, "before" and "after" tests were done on the women's bone-density levels. Specifically, their forearms were measured by single-photon absorptiometry, and their spines and other parts of their bodies were measured by a dual-photon absorptiometry technique.

The final results? On the whole, the estrogen-treated group did the best. Their bone density remained constant, while the women receiving calcium or only a placebo experienced a significant decrease in their bone density. The group that received the calcium supplements had about the same bone loss as the placebo group in the spongy bones of the wrist and spine. But they did a little better than the placebo group in the loss of other bone.

In the second study, Dr. Bruce Ettinger and two colleagues at two medical centers in San Francisco explored the relative merits of treating postmenopausal women with (1) calcium supplements alone, (2) calcium supplements plus a small amount of estrogen, and (3) only a placebo. After dividing the 73 women in their study into these three groups and monitoring their progress for two years, Ettinger and his fellow researchers made the following findings:

• The women who took only a placebo lost an average of 9 percent of the trabecular bone in their spines.

• Those taking only the calcium supplements lost even more of their bone mass—an average of 10.5 percent.

• But the women who took the calcium supplements *and* the small doses of estrogen increased their bone density by an average of 2.3 percent.

"Calcium supplements alone do not protect against the accelerated bone loss that occurs at menopause and that preferentially affects trabecular bone," these investigators concluded.

So what are we to make of all this? Clearly, there is evidence that there may be limits to what calcium supplements can do for us. But exactly what are those limits? And what guidelines should we follow to get the best use out of the many calcium supplements available?

The Rules of
the Supplement Game

A fundamental truth—and an assumption that I make throughout this book—is that *everyone*, no matter what age, background, or risk category, should consume 1,000 to 1,500 mg. of calcium daily. This calcium may be taken either through the diet or through appropriate supplements.

The simple reason for this assumption is that calcium intake is essential for every human being's proper bone development and maintenance. In short, no matter what special considerations certain people or groups may observe in getting the best use of their calcium, the fact remains that if they want full protection against bone loss, they should get calcium in sufficient quantities on a daily basis.

Having stated this basic assumption, I now want to "fine tune" it in light of various recent research findings. To this end, I find it most helpful to think in terms of a number of "rules" of calcium supplement use that are emerging from the various scientific studies.

Rule 1. Calcium supplements, when taken alone, may be more effective in preventing "hard" cortical bone loss than in preventing "soft" trabecular bone loss.

Dr. Charles Pak, in surveying various studies on the use of

calcium supplements, has come to this conclusion: Overall, the density in the cortical bones—such as the shaft of the forearm or the thigh— declines at a reduced rate after calcium supplementation. In contrast, the density of "soft" bone, such as the tissue in the spine, often continues to decline unabated, despite the use of supplements. (See Dr. Pak's "Nutrition and Metabolic Bone Disease," *Nutritional Diseases: Research Directions in Comparative Pathobiology*, Alan R. Liss, Inc., 1986, pp. 215–40.)

Rule 2. Postmenopausal women should consider combining their calcium intake with estrogen replacement therapy.

As you know, when a woman passes through menopause, her body loses most of its ability to produce estrogen. This lack causes a great decrease in her ability to produce the active form of vitamin D, which is necessary for adequate calcium absorption. As a result, postmenopausal women may experience alarming rates of bone loss for several years, especially in their "soft" trabecular bone areas, such as the spine and wrist.

As we've already seen, some studies indicate that calcium supplements taken alone may not help many postmenopausal women ward off bone loss in their spines and other soft-bone areas. But Dr. Bruce Ettinger has found that when supplements are taken with even relatively small doses of estrogen, density of the spine may actually increase.

Also, as we saw in the preceding case, Sarah developed osteoporosis when her calcium intake was low—even when she was taking estrogen. Furthermore, she did much better when she took calcium.

Still, Dr. Ettinger's work hasn't been confirmed. So don't lower your dose of estrogen without first consulting your physician.

In short, it seems wise for many postmenopausal women who are at risk for bone loss to consider, with their physicians' guidance, a two-pronged defense against the threat of osteoporosis: (1) First, be sure you are consuming enough calcium, through supplements or other means, to make proper bone maintenance possible; (2) then, use estrogen replacement therapy to activate the vitamin D in your system and to pave the way for the calcium to be used in bone mineralization.

If you can't take estrogen, remember, as stated in chapter 4, that calcium with a good exercise program might work as well.

Rule 3. Be aware that different types of calcium supplements may be absorbed by your body with varying degrees of efficiency.

The bioavailability of calcium supplements may vary from supplement to supplement, or from individual to individual. Variations may occur if the supplement is taken with food, on an empty stomach, or after a "bowel cleansing" from an enema.

Here are some salient observations on several of the main calcium supplements by Dr. Charles Pak. His thoughts are based both on his own research and on his review of the scientific literature, and his conclusions assume absorption of the calcium under normal health and living conditions.

• *Calcium carbonate.* This salt is the most widely used calcium supplement and is found in such products as Os-Cal. Like most other supplements, calcium carbonate will usually dissolve quite well in the normally acidic environment of the stomach. But it hardly dissolves at all without the help of acid. Thus, the bioavailability of calcium carbonate may be impaired if a person has a relatively low stomach acidity or high stomach alkalinity (designated by the letters *pH*). On the other hand, you can overcome this problem if the supplement is taken with certain foods, such as meat or juice.

This lack of adequate acids may be present in people who have a condition known as "achlorhydria," which involves a lack of hydrochloric acid in the stomach. Individuals with pernicious anemia or cancer of the stomach—and even some people with no other health problems at all—may have this difficulty. In addition, stomach acid secretion may diminish as a person gets older. Finally, calcium carbonate may become less soluble in individuals who are being treated with antacids or with cimetidine.

So, if you're a person who may be unlikely to absorb this supplement, check with your physician to find alternate ways of getting your calcium.

• *Calcium phosphate.* Although this form of calcium is the one usually found in milk and dairy products, it's also possible to get calcium phosphate in supplement form. Many of the same concerns about solubility as we discussed with calcium carbonate apply also to the phosphate. The carbonate type is used by more people, however, because it's generally thought to be more bioavailable than the phosphate.

• *Calcium gluconate.* The calcium in this supplement is readily absorbed by most people. But it's not widely used because the pills are huge and contain only about 9 percent calcium, which is considerably less than many other supplement pills.

• *Calcium citrate.* Studies conducted by Dr. Pak and others indicate that this substance may have optimum bioavailability. In comparing the citrate supplement with both calcium carbonate and calcium phosphate, Dr. Pak found that when taken on an empty stomach, calcium citrate was the most absorbable by the body. Also, calcium citrate is generally more soluble than calcium carbonate and calcium phosphate: some of it can be dissolved even in the absence of gastric acid.

In one study, he gave 14 people, ages 22 to 37 years, 1,000 mg. of oral calcium daily in the form of calcium citrate or calcium carbonate. Then, he estimated the amount of calcium absorbed from each product by measuring the rise in calcium in the urine.

"The rise in urinary calcium was significantly higher following oral administration of calcium citrate than of calcium carbonate," he said. As a result, he concluded that the greater rise in the urinary calcium "reflects higher solubility of calcium citrate and availability of calcium."

Of course, studies comparing the various supplements are continuing, and it will most likely be a while before anything definitive can be said about the over-all advantages of one supplement over another. In the meantime, just assume that calcium carbonate or calcium citrate is preferable unless you have a definite physical condition that militates against a particular supplement—such as problems with low acidity levels in your stomach.

For example, if you have trouble secreting stomach acid and prefer to take calcium supplements on an empty stomach, calcium citrate might be better for you. On the other hand, if you don't want to take your supplement on an empty stomach, the two salts might be similar in their effect.

Rule 4. Don't forget your vitamin D!

Vitamin D is a necessary ingredient in the absorption of calcium from any source, including supplements. But most people don't need any vitamin D supplements. For example, those who are regularly exposed to sunlight usually get plenty of vitamin D. For most people, about half of their vitamin D gets into their bodies through their diets, and the rest comes from the reaction of their skin to the sun's ultraviolet radiation.

On the other hand, older people who don't get outside too often may have some vitamin D deficiencies, and they are prime candidates for a vitamin D supplement. In general, vitamin D supplements should involve daily consumption of no more than 400 to 800 international units (IU). And remember: Some calcium supplements that you buy already contain vitamin D, so be sure to check the labels before you buy any extra.

However, as I've said, most people don't have to worry about such problems. Here's a case in point: The Federal Drug Administration has said that "calcium intakes ranging from 1,000 to 2,500 mg. daily do not result in hypercalcemia in normal individuals."

Clearly, calcium supplements are a multifaceted tool in maintaining good health. First and most important, the majority of people can count on many popular absorbable supplements to provide a good calcium balance in the blood for maximum bone-construction activity. Finally—though there is considerable controversy over this point—calcium may even be helpful for some people in the treatment of high blood pressure.

On balance, then, for most people the benefits of taking calcium supplements will far outweigh any possible negative effects. Calcium supplements should prove to be an extremely valuable tool for you as you strive to build a system of tough bones throughout your body.

ELEVEN

How Can You Be Tested for Osteoporosis?

Osteoporosis is sometimes called a "silent" disease because it's extremely difficult to detect until obvious symptoms, such as broken bones, occur. As a result, it's hard for many people to work up the motivation to take preventive steps on their own, or to seek help from a physician—even when they suspect they have a problem. Usually, most individuals need fairly clear-cut evidence that something is indeed wrong with them before they're willing to take action.

So, is there any way to break through the secrecy and silence that surrounds the devastating work of osteoporosis? Specifically, is there any way to predict the onset of the disease—or to tell whether you have a problem before symptoms appear?

At present, there is no generally approved, accepted, surefire method to ascertain the precise condition of your bones prior to a clear signal such as a fracture. To be sure, some physicians feel strongly that one or more of the diagnostic techniques we'll discuss in this chapter can become a predictive tool. But there's no consensus on this issue—not by a long shot.

To help you get some idea about where you stand with regard to osteoporosis, I formulated the Bone-Loss Risk Factors Evaluation, which you applied to your own situation (see chapter 2). By being able to place yourself in a certain risk category, you have at least gotten some preliminary idea about whether you're in serious danger of getting osteoporosis.

In addition to identifying your risk level, you can undergo some blood and urine tests, such as the ones that indicated calcium absorption problems with Sarah in chapter 10. Also, both animal and human studies have indicated that tests of the urine and blood may reveal certain hormones and proteins that can help predict the onset of osteoporosis.

But much of this research is still in a very early stage. In general, at present, you can't expect your blood or urine to give you definitive answers about the state of your bones. In fact, the calcium levels and other values in your blood and urine may be perfectly normal—yet you may be in the throes of a devastating case of osteoporosis!

So how can you tell if it's likely that you're suffering from osteoporosis? Usually, a person sees his physician because of a pain or an obvious fracture. Usually, the first thing an expert in bone problems will do is evaluate the state of the person's health and the nature of the pain. Then, he'll often do an X ray of the area where the pain is located. This X ray, or "radiologic" exam, will show whether a bone is actually broken. Also, to the trained eye there may be indications of osteoporosis on the X ray, such as telltale patterns in the bones.

But the X ray is only a preliminary step. If these initial exams suggest that osteoporosis may be a potential problem, the specialist will probably turn next to one or more of the three best tools now generally available to evaluate the condition of your bones. These "three big tests" for osteoporosis are single-photon absorptiometry, dual-photon absorptiometry, and quantitative computed tomography (QCT).

But don't let the medical terminology throw you. The basic way these tests work and what they can tell you about the state of your bones are fairly easy to understand.

The Three Big Tests

Single-photon absorptiometry. This diagnostic technique is used primarily to measure the density of "hard" cortical bone in the forearm. To undergo the test, the patient usually sits down and places his arm on a flat surface, such as a large arm of a chair. Then, a machine below the arm shoots a single beam of photons—or a stream of radiant energy from a radioactive iodine source—down through the arm. The bone's degree of resistance to the beam allows the specialist to measure the person's bone density.

But many times, especially with postmenopausal women or anyone experiencing back pains, this single-photon approach just isn't appropriate. Instead, it's advisable to rely on one of the other two "big tests."

Dual-photon absorptiometry. Like the single-photon method, this approach involves the shooting of a beam of photons through one targeted portion of the body to determine bone density. But this time, if the spine is the area of interest, for example, the patient usually lies on her back under the energy source. Then, photon beams at two different energy levels are beamed through the body into the part of the backbone that's being checked.

This approach allows the specialist to take quite accurate measurements of the mineral density of the entire bone area of a section of spine. This technique can also be used to measure density of the hip. Then, he'll compare his patient's bone density in that area with standard figures for a normal person of the same sex and age to see whether osteoporosis has become a problem.

In both types of photon diagnosis, by the way, the amount of radiation that enters the body is relatively low and well within limits that are considered medically safe.

Quantitative CT scans (QCT or "CAT" scans). With this third test, the patient lies on her back, with knees and hips bent. She flattens her lower spine against several tubes containing various minerals that are used in taking the measurements. Then she is moved into a kind of tunnel, where beams of radiation are shot through her body and translated by computer into a bone-density number.

This approach, like the dual-photon method, is especially helpful for postmenopausal women or others with spinal problems because it allows the specialist to focus on the bone density of the vertebrae.

Also, the QCT has an advantage over the dual-photon because with it, the specialist can measure the density in selected parts of the vertebrae—especially the softer trabecular tissue. The dual-photon technique, you'll recall, measures the density of the entire spinal area, and that may include a significant percentage of cortical bone. With the QCT, in contrast, measurements can be taken of *only* the softer trabecular bone in the spine or in other parts of the body. This more precise kind of measurement can be quite helpful as the physician tries to determine the best method of treatment for the patient.

But there are also a number of problems with the QCT. For one thing, the accuracy may be considerably inferior to that of the dual-photon approach because the fat in the bone marrow tends to skew the measurements collected by the QCT beam. Also, the exposure to radiation is considerably higher with QCT than with the other methods.

In the final analysis, the choice of tests will depend on the nature of your problem and on the equipment available at the center where you're being evaluated. In any event, it's important for you, as the patient, to know in general terms what the tests you're being given can and can't do. That way, you'll be in a position to ask your physician intelligent questions and become a more intelligent "consumer" of the medical services you're receiving.

In general, as I've said, these three tests will be used after some symptoms or pains appear. But they usually *won't* be employed beforehand as a predictive device for the general public. There are a number of reasons for not making general, early use of these three diagnostic techniques at this time.

First, the measurements of the density of hard bone by the single-photon method may not be applicable to the density of the spine. Second, the remaining two tests are relatively expensive, and they usually aren't covered by medical insurance when they're used only for preventive purposes, before symptoms appear. Also, it's sometimes difficult to interpret the measurements they provide without other diagnostic tests or without knowing what the person's bone-density values were when he or she was younger.

For these and other reasons, some experts have questioned the predictive value of bone-density measurements to determine the risk of getting bone fractures. So, many physicians feel that using these methods as predictive techniques just isn't warranted.

But not everyone agrees. In fact, a number of the nation's major medical journals—including the *New England Journal of Medicine* and the *Journal of the American Medical Association*—have printed ongoing letters that record the controversy on the predictive value of such techniques as single-photon absorptiometry. In general, the weight of expert opinion suggests that you can't predict density in the trabecular bone of the spine simply by determining the bone density in the forearm or wrist. Instead, if you want to know the bone density in both places, you have to take two separate measurements—and that means a single-photon test of the forearm and probably a dual-photon test of the spine.

For the present, then, the average person will probably have to be satisfied with relying on the "three big tests" for osteoporosis as a means to evaluate symptoms such as pain or fractures. These techniques just aren't appropriate at this point for general use as preliminary predictive tools for osteoporosis.

But note: If you place in the very high risk group on the Bone-Loss Risk Factors Evaluation described in chapter 2, you might want to talk to your physician about measuring your bone density.

Despite the limitations we face at present, the outlook for the future is bright. Scientists in a variety of research centers are currently working on new approaches to testing bone density that could make today's methods look like the Model T. Now, it takes about one hour to check the density of the spine and hip with dual-photon absorptiometry. In the future, however, it may be possible to determine the mass of many bones throughout the entire skeletal structure in just a few minutes.

When some of these new measuring devices are perfected and their price is brought down to a level where an ordinary clinic can make them available to the general public, we'll finally be in a position to predict. We'll know more precisely at earlier and earlier ages who might be at risk for osteoporosis and who isn't.

TWELVE

Why You Should Watch What You Drink

Even a brief glance at the Tough Bone Diet Program in this book will reveal how important I think our drinking habits are. On the positive side, as a means to protect us against bone loss, I can't think of a better natural food than a drink we've emphasized in those menus—skim milk.

But there are also some negative considerations that should cause us to be very careful about what we drink. You can infer as much about healthy beverage guidelines from what we've left out of the Tough Bone menus as you can by what we've included. As far as the risk of osteoporosis is concerned, two of the most important items we've omitted from the menus are alcohol and caffeine.

The Alcohol Issue

What effect can excessive alcohol consumption have on your skeletal structure?

You'll begin to understand the potential problems when you consider what happened to Joe, a muscular, athletic 30-year-old construction worker who never dreamed he might run into a problem with his bones. Joe was known as one of the strongest workers in his company until one day, when he was carrying a medium-weight container, he experienced a moderately sharp pain in the middle of his back.

Because the pain wasn't overwhelming and soon subsided, Joe didn't worry about it at first. But during the next three years he experienced several other pain episodes, which he related to the lifting and pushing he was doing at work. Gradually, the pain became a constant condition, though he found he could still tolerate it and perform his occupational tasks.

Finally, a new, sharper pain struck Joe in a slightly higher part of his back as he was bending over to pick up a shoe. Because the increased severity and duration of the pain interfered with his ability to carry on a normal life, he sought medical help from a specialist in back problems.

During the examination, the physician took X rays of Joe's spine. These pictures showed an old "collapse fracture" of one of the thoracic vertebrae in the middle of his back, and also a new vertebral fracture a little lower on the spine. As the physician, who was an expert in osteoporosis, examined the X rays further, he noticed that the other vertebrae had a "washed out" appearance, indicating considerable deterioration and probable loss in bone density.

With the X rays in hand, the doctor quizzed Joe on his medical history, but he failed to find any existence of past bone disease. Also, Joe's family history didn't suggest any predisposition for bone disease. Furthermore, Joe was getting plenty of calcium in his diet—about 1,200 to 1,500 mg. daily.

But the nutritional assessment of his diet revealed a major difficulty— and a likely candidate for the cause of his bone problems: Joe drank at least fifteen beers and a fifth of vodka each week, with most of the alcohol being consumed on the weekends.

Because heavy consumption of alcohol is known to be a major risk factor for bone-loss disease, including osteoporosis, Joe's physician proceeded with more extensive tests to evaluate his precise condition. Blood tests showed he had normal serum levels for some of the bone-related substances, such as calcium, phosphorus, electrolytes, thyroid hormone, and parathyroid hormone. Tests of his urine also revealed a high-normal calcium level—indicating that he had adequate calcium absorption. In addition, urine tests showed that his "fasting urine" calcium was normal, which suggested that his kidneys were handling the calcium in his body properly.

But then, when the specialist did bone-density studies, the real problems began to emerge. A dual-photon exam revealed that his spinal density was abnormally low—about 80 percent of what would have been expected in a person of his age and size. Specifically, the test showed that the density of his spinal bone was .990 grams per centimeter squared, when the normal reading would have been 1.260.

Clearly, Joe had a serious problem with osteoporosis. With young men like Joe, the most frequent causes of this kind of bone loss are alcoholism and low testosterone (male hormone) levels. Since Joe's testosterone was normal, the doctor concluded that the source of the problem was Joe's heavy drinking. The only treatment he recommended was that Joe greatly reduce or cease his drinking.

When Joe understood the serious condition of his bones and the danger to his health, he immediately stopped consuming all alcohol. Within a year, his back pains had subsided considerably, and further density studies showed a slight increase in his bone mass. Joe still does not drink alcohol, and there is every indication that as time goes on, his condition will continue to improve.

A number of studies have confirmed that experiences such as Joe's have solid grounding in scientific fact. Researchers have shown that alcoholics are particularly prone to losing bone density in the softer trabecular skeletal areas—such as the crest of the hip bone (iliac), the neck of the thighbone (femur), the heel bone (calcaneus), and the vertebrae in the spine.

But how exactly does alcohol cause these bone problems? There are several possible explanations, including the tendency of alcohol to encourage:

- Poor nutritional habits, with low consumptions of calcium and vitamin D

- Defective absorption of calcium and vitamin D as a result of disorders of the pancreas or the liver

- Abnormal metabolism of vitamin D because of cirrhosis of the liver

- Excessive calcium loss in the urine

- A direct negative impact on the absorption of calcium

- An inhibition of the bone-remodeling mechanism—or the work of the "bone-construction crews," as we've been calling them in this book

Dr. Daniel Bikle and other researchers explored this last possibility in a 1985 investigation conducted at the Department of Medicine at the University of California, San Francisco, and the Veterans Administration Medical Center. They evaluated bone disease in 8 white men between the ages of 49 and 61, all of whom had been abusing alcohol for at least ten years.

The measurements taken in this study showed that the average mass of the men's spongy vertebral bone was 58 percent of the normal density, and their average hard, cortical bone was 90 percent of normal. The researchers concluded that the bone loss in these men was the result of "an inhibition of bone remodeling by a mechanism independent of calciotropic hormones." (*Annals of Internal Medicine*, 1985.)

But you don't have to be an alcoholic to be at risk of bone loss from your drinking habits. In another study, done by Dr. Ego Seeman and several colleagues at the Mayo Clinic, investigators found that drinking alcoholic beverages even on a lesser scale can be a risk factor for spinal osteoporosis. In fact, they put drinking on a level with one of the most serious bone destroyers of all—smoking.

The 105 men in this four-year study consumed an average of 3 ounces of alcohol a day. And the impact of their drinking had caused them serious bone-loss problems.

"The risk of spinal osteoporosis with vertebral fracture was significantly greater . . . among persons who drank alcoholic beverages . . . than among those who did not," the scientists said. (*American Journal of Medicine*, vol. 75, December 1983, p. 979.)

So, in practical terms, what can we conclude from these findings? If you're at relatively high risk for osteoporosis or you already have the disease, I strongly suggest that you strictly limit or eliminate your consumption of alcohol. Even for those who seem not to be at risk, alcohol consumption should be kept as low as possible—preferably no more than 1 ounce a day. The impact that alcohol can have on your bones is potentially too devastating to take any chances.

Is There a Problem with Caffeine?

Scientific findings on the impact of caffeine consumption on your bones are quite scanty. Still, a number of physicians feel that the consumption of caffeine-containing beverages, such as coffee, tea, and certain colas, may contribute to bone loss. So they recommend that the use of these drinks be limited by those who are at serious risk for osteoporosis or who already have the disease.

The argument against caffeine goes like this: Drinking a beverage containing caffeine will increase the loss of calcium in the urine. With less calcium in the body for use in bone formation, a negative calcium balance may occur in the blood. The end result could be that the bones will tend to lose more calcium than they take in through the diet, and bone density will decrease.

Some experts also believe that caffeine stimulates the bone-demolition work of the osteoclasts.

As I said, solid scientific verification isn't readily available yet, but a number of physicians feel that caffeine may be a problem. In dealing with their patients, some follow this guideline: An additional 100 mg. of calcium daily is required to compensate for every two cups of coffee you drink.

Whether this is actually true remains to be seen. But until more definite data become available, my advice on caffeine for those at low risk of bone disease is this: Consider limiting your caffeine consumption to no more than two cups of coffee per day. Those at higher risk for osteoporosis should limit their coffee intake to no more than one cup per day, or cut it out entirely.

Now, let's turn to a topic that has much clearer negative implications for the condition of your bones—smoking.

THIRTEEN

Why Smoking Will Put You at Risk

Smoking, especially cigarette smoking, has turned out to be one of the greatest enemies of good health in our era. Cigarette smoking has been directly linked to heart disease, lung cancer, and a variety of other ills—not the least of which is osteoporosis.

How does smoking cause bone loss? The mechanisms are apparently somewhat different for women than for men. In women, cigarette smoke affects the liver by causing it to convert estrogen into a compound that is different from the normal estrogen used by the body in the bone-formation process. As a result, female smokers have less usable estrogen in their systems, and this makes them more susceptible to accelerated bone loss.

Also, certain studies have shown that women who smoke have an earlier menopause than those who don't. And as you know, an early menopause, with the loss of estrogen-making capacity by the ovaries, is a major risk factor for the development of osteoporosis.

In addition to these considerations, women who smoke tend to be leaner than those who refrain from the habit. Leanness, of course, is another important risk factor for bone-loss disease. The lack of body fat on smokers, both female and male, is probably a direct result of their lower intake of food. The thinness may also reflect relatively poor nutritional habits, including low calcium consumption.

As mentioned earlier, one other reason why leanness is a risk factor for osteoporosis is that people with low body fat put less pressure on their bones than do those who are heavier. The extra weight is important because it promotes the development of denser bones.

There's still another factor that links leanness and bone loss: Lean women on average have less estrogen in their bodies than do women who are heavier. The reason for this is that female fat tissue transforms substances that are precursors of estrogen into estrogen itself.

As a result, fatter women have more estrogen in their bodies to prevent bone demolition and to stimulate the production of active vitamin D—a process that is essential for efficient calcium absorption and tougher bones.

Some studies have also reported that tobacco smoking reduces the levels of the male hormone testosterone in men. And low testosterone levels are associated with accelerated loss of bone mass.

There may be a number of other factors that contribute to the tendency of smokers to be at higher risk for osteoporosis. For example, smokers may on the whole exercise less strenuously than nonsmokers because of a diminished lung capacity and poor over-all fitness.

In any case, we do not yet have all the answers to the question about the exact mechanisms by which smoking contributes to osteoporosis. But there's one thing that we do know definitely: Smoking is a major contributor to dangerously high levels of bone loss in many people. Here is some of the hard evidence:

• In a survey of the estrogen profiles of smokers and nonsmokers, Dr. Brian MacMahon and several of his colleagues reported in the *New England Journal of Medicine* (October 21, 1982) that smokers had "substantially and significantly lower levels of all three major estrogens. . . ."

MacMahon also observed that an "increased risk of osteoporosis or osteoporotic fractures has been reported among women who smoke." Then he concluded that because estrogens can protect against fractures, it's "possible that the mechanism whereby smoking increases the risk [of fractures] . . . is through a reduction in endogenous estrogens."

• In a Mayo Clinic study that we've already mentioned in another context, 105 men with spinal osteoporosis were evaluated in light of the risk factors associated with their disease. The researchers found that the "risk of spinal osteoporosis was . . . significantly greater among men who smoked cigarettes than among those who did not."

The average patient with osteoporosis in this study smoked nearly one and a half packs of cigarettes per day and had had the habit for more than thirty-six years.

• In a 1976 study, Dr. Harry W. Daniell of Redding, California, evaluated the bone conditions of a group of 103 women whom he divided into two age groups: 40 to 49 years, and 60 to 69 years. He found that in the older group, the smokers showed more bone loss than the nonsmokers.

• In a study reported in the November 20, 1986, issue of the *New England Journal of Medicine,* Dr. Jon J. Michnovicz of Rockefeller University and his fellow researchers focused on the impact of smoking on estrogens in the body. Among other things, they found that smoking had a negative impact on the liver's role in processing estrogen.

Specifically, they found that in women who smoked at least fifteen cigarettes per day, the smoking caused their livers to produce a significant increase of a relatively useless form of estrogen, which their bodies quickly disposed of.

With less estrogen available, of course, the risk of osteoporosis increases.

• A University of Washington group conducted a study of white women, ages 50 to 74, who had suffered a fracture of the hip or forearm. They reported in 1982 in *Obstetrics and Gynecology* that the "risk of hip fracture was elevated in thin women and in those who smoked cigarettes, particularly among nonusers of estrogen."

Also, they determined that among the estrogen users, neither weight nor smoking affected the risk of forearm fractures—though smoking *did* increase the risk among those who didn't take estrogen.

Clearly, the weight of the evidence is overwhelmingly against smoking. The mechanisms by which smoking contributes to bone loss are still being explored, and as each new study comes out, the explanations get more complex. The relationships between estrogens, fat tissues, and liver functions can certainly be confusing!

But the detailed scientific explanations, as important as they are, shouldn't be allowed to obscure the main message here: *Smoking is bad for your bones!*

FOURTEEN

Osteoporosis in Children— and the Question of Inheritance

True osteoporosis is very rare in children. But certain habits and traits that emerge in childhood may be danger signals that a youngster is one of the 15 to 25 million people at risk for osteoporosis later in life.

A major bone-loss factor that's present in childhood is genetic make-up, and those genes will have a major impact on the risk of developing osteoporosis. The activity of all of our bone cells is orchestrated by many hormones, chemicals, and other substances in the body. Moreover, our cells have a genetic code that determines our ability to put together those "bone-construction crews" that are so essential in the process of bone formation.

The importance of heredity begins with the capacity we're born with to develop a certain bone mass, according to Dr. B. Lawrence Riggs, the Mayo Clinic's expert on osteoporosis. Riggs explains, "The influences of heredity, race and sex on the incidence of osteoporosis can apparently be explained, in part, by their effects on initial bone density." (*New England Journal of Medicine,* June 26, 1986.)

Riggs goes on to note that osteoporosis apparently tends to crop up in family groups because of a "genetically determined variation in initial bone density."

What Riggs is referring to here is a general tendency that some people inherit to develop osteoporosis later in life. None of this is absolutely predetermined, of course. Even if a child has inherited a family propensity toward bone loss, he can usually avoid the disease by observing the basic rules of lifestyle, nutrition, exercise, and preventive medicine that we've been discussing in this book.

I say "usually," by the way, because sometimes—very infrequently—

a child will inherit a gene for a certain type of osteoporosis that makes it almost inevitable that he'll get that specific type of the disease. For example, one rare type of inherited osteoporosis is *osteogenesis imperfecta*. This disease is actually a group of four bone disorders that results in such symptoms during childhood as great skeletal fragility, multiple fractures, scolosis (a curvature of the spine), and sometimes deafness. Another very rare form of inherited osteoporosis is *homocystinuria*, which in childhood may result in a very fragile skeleton, abnormally long and slender fingers and toes, and perhaps mental retardation.

But such inherited diseases, which are passed on by a very specific gene or inherited defect, are much more the exception than the rule. Usually, the role that heredity plays is more general. For most children, as well as adults, a family history of osteoporosis should stand just as a reminder that they *may* have more of a tendency toward development of osteoporosis than most other people. In a sense, they are genetically "programmed" to have lower bone mass or to experience a greater rate of bone loss than the average person. So they should be even more attentive than other people to watching their diets and other health practices that may affect bone loss.

No matter what your family history, however, you should pay close attention to certain practices that may lay the groundwork for either tough or weak bones later in life. The first question to ask yourself to check whether your child is developing habits that will prevent bone loss is this: "Does my child have a good diet?"

A "good" diet is one that will enable the youngster to reach his or her peak bone mass by the critical age range of 25 to 35 years. And that means a diet that contains a minimum calcium intake of 1,000 to 1,500 mg. daily. Furthermore, a proper diet should be well balanced, such as the ones described in detail in chapter 9. In other words, the total calories should be divided into approximately 50 to 70 percent carbohydrates, 10 to 20 percent protein, and 20 to 30 percent fat.

Unfortunately, however, today children at younger and younger ages are going on radical weight-loss diets or embarking on unbalanced, faddish regimens that are tailor-made to prevent them from achieving their peak bone mass.

For example, as I mentioned briefly in chapter 1, some parents in Boston placed their children on a macrobiotic vegetarian diet, with no nutritional supplements. In studying 32 of these children, Dr. Johanna T. Dwyer, of the Tufts Medical School, found that the youngsters often suffered from rickets, a childhood bone disease that is relatively rare in this country.

More commonly, children of all ages will avoid drinking milk or consuming many dairy products, either because they don't like them or they want to lose weight. But the final result may be paving the way to skeletal disaster.

Nutrition researcher John Anderson of the University of North Carolina at Chapel Hill studied more than 500 college-age women by recording their dietary histories and measuring the density of the radius, one of the two bones in their forearms. He found that the women with the worst bone mineral content were also the ones who had stopped drinking milk during adolescence.

Another expert in childhood bone problems, University of Utah pediatrician Gary Chan, studied the condition of 88 boys and girls, ages 3 to 16. He concluded: "As a pediatrician, I'm concerned that poor bone health established in childhood can lead to adult osteoporosis."

More bad news about the outlook for our children's bone health comes from data compiled by the National Center for Health Statistics. In that report, the researchers found that girls ages 15 to 19 consumed only 608 mg. of calcium a day—or about half the RDA of 1,200 for their age group, and considerably less than the 1,500 that I've recommended.

Fortunately, there is some indication that youthful bones can retain greater amounts of calcium than those of adults. Researcher Velimir Matkovic of the University of Washington Medical School studied 31 14-year-old girls to see how well they retained calcium at varying amounts of calcium intake. He discovered that their bones retained about 20 percent of the calcium they consumed, whether they took in only 300 mg. daily or as much as 1,500 mg. Adults, in contrast, usually eliminate more calcium when they are consuming the higher amount.

"Young skeletons appear to have the ability to store extra amounts of calcium instead of excreting it," Matkovic said. "That's not true in later years."

But this ability of youngsters to process calcium is no reason to get complacent. Parents must constantly monitor their children's diets to be sure that minimum amounts of calcium are being consumed. Otherwise, the child may fail to develop the peak bone mass of which he or she is capable—and that will increase the likelihood of osteoporosis later in life.

In addition to providing children with a good diet, I'm a great believer in getting them started with good exercise habits, including some variation on the weight-bearing and calisthenics programs presented in chapters 5 and 6. In children, as well as in adults, giving the skeletal structure a good workout helps build tougher, stronger bones—bones with enough mass that they can become relatively impervious to osteoporosis later in life.

But again, moderation is the key here. There are a number of cases involving young athletes who have overdone it with exercise, and the physical activity has backfired on their bones.

We've already discussed the problem of female runners who put in so many miles and lose so much weight that they stop menstruating. As a result, their estrogen levels fall, their ability to stimulate the production of active vitamin D decreases, and their bone density decreases as well. With such a dangerous sequence in effect, osteoporosis and painful fractures are just around the corner.

Young men can encounter similar problems with bone loss if their running causes their testosterone to drop to dangerously low levels. Or they may become victims of osteoporosis if, in their obsession with exercise, they neglect to eat properly. A young man who loses excessive amounts of weight or fails to take in adequate calcium because of poor nutrition may end up with fractures that are often the first symptoms of osteoporosis.

A similar problem has confronted young ballet dancers who lose weight, have poor nutrition, and experience a delayed beginning of menstruation or periods of amenorrhea. For example, a study of 75 young dancers by Dr. Michelle P. Warren and other researchers was reported in the May 22, 1986, issue of the *New England Journal of Medicine*. These women were members of four professional ballet companies and obviously pushed themselves to the limit of their physical capabilities.

Dr. Warren and her colleagues found that a delay in menstruation, or the cessation of menstruation for long periods of time after it does start, could predispose these young women to scoliosis (curvature of the spine) and stress fractures. Other studies have indicated that scoliosis can be the first harbinger of full-fledged osteoporosis later in life.

Exercise, like good food and plenty of calcium, is absolutely essential for laying the groundwork for tough bones. But too much may have the opposite effect. Our children need balance in their lives as much as adults do. And it's up to parents to provide the kind of wise guidance that will result in the best possible physical foundation for their children's later lives.

FIFTEEN

Osteoporosis:
An Epidemic That Can
Be Controlled

Susan, a small, elegant woman in her early sixties, had been diagnosed as having osteoporosis because compression fractures were discovered in her back. She was beginning to develop the classic dowager's hump and had been experiencing increasing back pain.

When she first came in for treatment, she rated the pain she was feeling at a level of 6 on a scale of 1 to 10, 1 being no pain and 10 being intolerable pain. This scale is one that has commonly been used at the Spine Education Center in Dallas, which provides educational programs for those suffering from osteoporosis and other bone and joint problems related to the back. Susan's pain was especially bad in her lower back and her hip region.

Like many other people who have osteoporosis, Susan couldn't expect to fully reverse the progression of her disease. But during the course of her treatment she did learn a great deal about living comfortably with it.

First of all, in a diet designed to retard the disease, she raised her calcium intake from about 400 mg. per day to about 1,500 per day, through a calcium carbonate supplement. Also, she continued to take estrogen and progesterone, which she had started just after her menopause, more than a decade earlier.

Another important step Susan took was to learn more about "body mechanics"—that is, ways of moving and positioning her body so as to reduce her pain and discomfort. In particular, she learned how to sit, get up, stand, reach, and move about in ways that put less pressure on her spine.

She also began doing special therapeutic exercises designed to relieve some of the pressure on her back and hip. These exercises

extended her spine and built up and stretched the muscles that supported and surrounded her back and hip.

When Susan returned to the therapists only four weeks later, it
was immediately apparent that a dramatic change had taken place. She
still felt some pain in both her lower back and her hip—but now she
rated that pain at only a 2, rather than a 6! Furthermore, she had been
able to increase the physical activities she loved, such as walking on
paths near her country home and playing with her young grandchild.

Her husband, one of the first to notice the positive change in her
activity levels, was overjoyed at her improvement. In fact, he had
already started planning several trips and outings, which he said he had
"kept on hold indefinitely" because of her bone condition.

Obviously, this woman had not experienced a reversal in her basic
bone condition in that short, four-week period. But just as obviously,
something beneficial had happened in her life—and I would have to
attribute her improvement mostly to the way she had learned to live
with her osteoporosis.

Now let's look more closely at some of the guidelines that Susan
and many others have followed to reduce the pain and debilitation of
osteoporosis. Many of these suggestions and techniques are based on
information from the Spine Education Center in Dallas, which has
worked closely with osteoporosis patients at our clinic and at other
medical facilities. For further information, write: Spine Education Center, 6161 Harry Hines Bl., Suite 300, Dallas, Texas 75235.

Living Successfully
with Osteoporosis

Susan—like a number of other osteoporosis patients who have been
fortunate enough to get treatment from trained physical therapists—
learned how to apply new knowledge in several important areas:

- Body mechanics

- Sleep and resting positions

- Recreational and sports activities

- Special therapeutic exercises

- Techniques to reduce back pain

As we examine each of these areas, try to personalize the suggestions to see how you can use them in your own situation. That way,

you'll be in a position to understand the full range of possibilities for living successfully with osteoporosis—and reducing the possibility of fractures and other injuries. Many of these suggestions, by the way, are useful and advisable for *everyone*, and not just those with osteoporosis, back pain, or other symptoms.

Body Mechanics

When you sit:

1. Keep your knees higher than your hips. If that's not possible, lean forward and support your back by resting your arms on a desk surface.

2. Use foot rests—i.e., a telephone book or the rungs of a chair.

3. Don't twist. If an item falls to the floor, get up from the chair to pick it up.

4. When driving a car, place your arm on the back of the seat to support your back if you have to turn around to look behind you.

5. Hold the telephone receiver in your hand—don't cradle it on your shoulder.

6. Move as close as possible to your desk or steering wheel and still maintain a level of comfort. Use a back support as you sit.

7. Don't sit in the same position for more than an hour at a time. If possible, stand up and move around every half hour.

If you operate a word processor, computer, or other device with a cathode ray tube:

1. The screen should be at your eye level or no more than 15 degrees below it. Raise the screen with blocks or phone books if it's too low.

2. Your chair should fit under your desk. Arm rests are helpful for support.

3. Use a pillow, rolled-up towel, or back support if the chair is too deep or uncomfortable.

4. Put your feet on a foot rest, child's stool, phone book, or box to reduce the pressure on your back.

When you stand:

1. Use a wide base of support. Put one foot in front of the other and bend your knees slightly. Pull in your stomach and tuck in your buttocks.

2. Use equipment such as the edge of a table to help you support your body.

3. Whenever possible, put one foot on a ledge, box, or bar. Don't keep the same foot up indefinitely—shift back and forth between feet.

4. Change your body position frequently.

5. Try to stand on a rubber mat or pallet, especially if the floor surface is concrete.

6. Cushioned footwear will give you extra protection.

When you push:

1. Use your legs, not your back.

2. Start the push with your feet in a diagonal position, but don't twist your body as you push.

3. Keep the object you're pushing in front of you.

4. Bend your elbows and stay as close as possible to the object.

When you pull:

1. Pulling is harder than pushing—so be especially careful.

2. Have a firm grip on the object.

3. Keep the object as close to your side as is possible.

4. Don't twist.

5. If a cart you're pulling is lightweight, pull with both hands behind you to keep from twisting.

6. Use a diagonal stance, rather than a parallel stance, when pulling an object. Again, however, be sure not to twist your body.

When you lift:

1. Keep the load directly in front of you.

2. Keep your feet staggered (in a diagonal stance), with one foot alongside the object and the other foot behind the object.

3. Get down on the same level as the object.

4. Placing your knee on the floor will give you leverage.

5. An elbow on the knee may provide additional leverage.

6. *Keep the load close to your body.* This is an extremely important point.

7. Use your legs, not your back.

8. Control your load so that the weight doesn't shift and put dangerous pressure on one side of your body or the other.

9. After you've lifted the load to a carrying position, don't turn quickly in a twisting motion—instead, pivot your entire body.

10. Don't pivot or turn while you're in the process of lifting the object.

11. Only lift a weight that you can handle easily and that fits between your knees.

12. If an object is too heavy, get some help!

When you turn or pivot:

1. Use your entire body. The lower back isn't designed for turning or twisting.

2. Step in the direction that you're turning. Pivot off the foot that's opposite from the stepping foot. So, if you're carrying an object to your right, step first with the right foot into the turn and pivot off the left foot. Or if you're carrying an object to the left, step first with the left foot into the turn and pivot off the right foot.

3. Shift your weight in the direction you're moving.

4. Keep the load you're carrying close to your body.

5. Don't throw the load down or away from you. This movement can cause twisting.

6. If the load is too heavy for you, get some help.

Sleep and Resting Positions

When you sleep or rest, assume positions that put the least amount of stress on your back and joints. For example:

• If you sleep on your back, place a pillow under your head and knees. *Don't* place a pillow only under your head.

• If you sleep on your side, put a pillow under your head *and* a towel roll under your waist (just above your hips), *and* a pillow between your thighs. Or put pillows only under your head and between your legs. But *don't* put a pillow only under your head.

• If you sleep on your stomach, place a pillow only under your stomach. But *don't* put a pillow under your head.

If you simply want to rest your back for a few minutes, the best position, where there is the least amount of stress on your disks, is this:

Lie flat on the floor on your back; raise your legs off the floor at the hips; and place the lower part of your legs (from the knees down) flat on the top of a chair, couch, coffee table, or stack of pillows. Adjust the height of the item you're using as a leg rest so that you feel comfortable.

When should you assume this position? There are at least three occasions: (1) when you feel your back begin to get tight; (2) after lunch for about fifteen minutes; and (3) when you're reading, watching TV, or talking on the phone.

Recreational and Sports Activities

You should always warm up with slow stretching exercises before you do any athletic activity. Those who have back problems—or who want to minimize the possibility of back injury—may want to keep these tips in mind:

• *Bicycling.* Adjust the seat so you don't have to stretch your legs to reach the pedals. Raise the handlebars so you don't have to bend over so far. Allow your arms to support your torso.

• *Tennis, racquetball, squash, and other racket sports.* Play with someone who will allow you to take it easy. Keep your knees bent when you serve. Stay on your toes as you move about. This way you'll be more likely to pivot your body, rather than twist it, as you turn from side to side.

• *Golf.* Reduce any twisting motion in your back by turning your toes outward and pulling your heels closer together as you swing. Reduce your backswing to three-fourths of your normal motion. Shift your weight as you swing.

• *Bowling.* Bend your knees, and don't twist your body. Support yourself by placing a hand on your knee whenever possible. Warm up the side of your body you don't use by swinging the ball back and forth with that hand. This way, you'll reduce the stress produced by sports activities that exercise only one side of the body.

• *Softball and baseball.* As with all other sports, begin by doing slow stretching exercises. When you bat, pivot on the balls of your feet. Wear knee pads to field grounders. In this way, you'll be more likely to squat down rather than bend at the hips.

Basic Exercises for Those with Severe Back Pain or Osteoporosis

In chapters 5 and 6 I recommended extensive exercise programs designed to build up your bone density and to help maintain bone mass throughout life. Sometimes, however, the pain may be too great for you to stick with these programs.

As an alternative, there are some less strenuous exercises, which therapists have found can help relieve pain and also promote some degree of muscle-toning and flexibility. Keep these general rules in mind for each exercise:

1. Do each exercise carefully and slowly.

2. Start with 5 repetitions of each exercise, and work up to 10 repetitions.

3. Perform the exercises twice a day, every day.

4. If an exercise is painful after 5 or fewer repetitions, omit that exercise from your routine.

Following are the exercises:

• *The pelvic tilt.* Lie on your back on the floor with your knees bent so that your feet are flat on the floor. Place one hand under the small of your back and press your lower back against that hand. You should feel your stomach muscles tightening as you flatten and straighten your back against the floor.

• *The sitting chest-stretch.* Sit in a chair with your feet propped up, and hold your arms at your sides with your elbows bent. Try to touch your elbows together behind your back. You should feel a stretching sensation in your chest and shoulder area. Return to the starting position.

• *The side stretch.* While sitting or standing, reach your arms up above your head and lace your fingers together. Keeping your arms above your head, bend your body at your waist, moving first to the left and then to the right.

• *Knee-to-chest stretch.* Also known as the "Williams exercise," this movement involves first lying on your back on the floor with your knees bent and your feet flat on the floor. Then, bring your left knee up to your chest and "hug" it to your body. Hold this position for a count of 30. Next, bring your right knee up to your chest and "hug" it to your body. Hold this position for a count of 30. Finally, bring both knees up to the chest and "hug" them together for a count of 30. This entire cycle of three "hugs" constitutes 1 repetition.

• *Hip extension.* Holding on to the back of a chair, stand and slowly raise one leg straight out behind you. Keep your back and your knees straight. You should feel the muscles of your buttocks and the back of your thigh tighten up. Hold for a count of 3 and then repeat with the other leg.

• *Hamstring stretches.* A number of types of exercises can help you increase the flexibility of your hamstring muscles (those on the backs of your thighs). For example, you can sit on the floor with your legs outstretched and then lean forward and reach your hands out toward one foot and then the other.

Or you can lie on your back on the floor with your knees bent and your feet flat on the floor. Then, raise one leg into the air, grip the back of the raised leg, and begin to push the foot toward the ceiling until you feel a stretching sensation in the back of the raised leg.

Or you might stand on one foot and place the other foot in front of you on a chair or other raised area. Then bend forward until you feel a stretching sensation in the back of the elevated leg.

Other motions that are often recommended by physical therapists to promote flexibility and "looseness" include rolling your head from side to side and shrugging your shoulders.

These techniques can help those who already suffer from some of the symptoms of osteoporosis and may also help those without symptoms to live safer lives, free of back pain, fractures, or other consequences of brittle bones. But in the last analysis, each person has to learn to take care of his skeletal structure in his or her own special, individual way.

As we've seen throughout this book, there are several different levels of concern about bone problems—levels that may require some-what different strategies at various age levels. For example:

• Younger people should try to build up their peak bone mass so that they reduce the dangers they may face later from natural bone loss.

• Middle-aged people need to develop approaches to exercise, nutrition, hormone treatment, and other preventive techniques that will enable them to maintain as much bone density as possible.

• Older people should focus their attention both on maintaining their bone mass and on preventing those fractures and other bone injuries that can impair their mobility and even lead to death.

• Those who already are suffering from osteoporosis should explore ways to maintain the bone density they already have. Furthermore, they should learn to minimize their pain and maximize their ability to lead normal lives. It's certainly possible to live successfully with osteoporosis—*if* you just take a little time to think through your situation, develop a sound therapeutic strategy, and then apply that strategy to your daily life.

To be sure, osteoporosis is a terrible enemy to our health and even to our very lives. But there's no reason to give up just because you're in a high-risk category or even because you already have symptoms of the disease. You can triumph over this silent scourge to health—if you resolve that prevention and control of osteoporosis are truly viable possibilities in your life.

Selected References

Chapter 1:
The Lifelong Battle in Your Bones

Aitken, J.M. "Osteoporosis of Pregnancy." *The Lancet,* July 6, 1985, p. 42.

"A Lot of Hoopla Over Plain Old Calcium." *Fortune,* May 26, 1986.

"An Aching Back Does Not Have to Signal a Permanent End to All Vigorous Activity." *The New York Times,* October 17, 1987.

"The Big Bucks in Knees and Elbows." *The New York Times,* February 1, 1987.

Buchner, David M., and Eric B. Larson. "Falls and Fractures in Patients with Alzheimer-Type Dementia." *Journal of the American Medical Association,* vol. 257, no. 11, March 20, 1987, p. 1492.

"Calcium and Women: An Update." *New York Daily News,* January 11, 1987.

Carpenter, Thomas O., et al. "Lysinuric Protein Intolerance Presenting as Childhood Osteoporosis." *New England Journal of Medicine,* vol. 312, no. 5, January 31, 1985, pp. 290–94.

Cooper, Kenneth H. and Millie. *The New Aerobics for Women,* chapter 17, "Aerobics as Prevention and Treatment for Osteoporosis." New York: Bantam Books, 1988.

"Diagnosing Vertebral Wedge Deformities." *Journal of the American Medical Association,* vol. 254, no. 18, November 8, 1985, p. 2560.

Fonseca, V., et al. "Osteopenia in Women with Anorexia Nervosa." *New England Journal of Medicine,* vol. 313, no. 5, August 1, 1985, pp. 326–27.

Kaplan, Frederick S., M.D. "Osteoporosis." *Clinical Symposia,* CIBA Pharmaceutical Company, CIBA-GEIGY Corporation, vol. 35, no. 5, 1983.

"Low Calcium Tied to High Blood Pressure." *The New York Times,* July 13, 1982.

Melton, L. Joseph, III, et al. "Osteoporosis and the Risk of Hip Fracture." *American Journal of Epidemiology,* vol. 124, no. 2, 1986, pp. 254–61.

"No Bones 'Bout Calcium's Benefit." *New York Daily News,* February 16, 1986.

"Of Caffeine, Calcium." *Insight,* September 22, 1986.

"Osteoporosis." National Dairy Board, Arlington, Virginia, 1985.

"Osteoporosis Can Be Prevented!" Special advertising supplement, *Health & Fitness '87.*

"Osteoporosis: Debilitating Bone Condition Can Be Prevented." *The New York Times,* January 11, 1984.

"Osteoporosis: Is It In Your Future?" An informational guide from Marion Laboratories, 1984, Marion Laboratories, Inc., Kansas City, Missouri, pp. 9–16.

"Osteoporosis Screening Isn't Reliable, Say Docs." *New York Daily News,* September 1, 1986.

"Osteoporosis. Why Detect Early Osteoporosis?" Endocrine Associates of Dallas P.A., Osteoporosis Center, Dallas, Texas.

"The Osteoporotic Syndromes." *Cecil Textbook of Medicine,* Fifteenth Edition, W.B. Saunders Company: Upper Montclair, New Jersey, 1975, pp. 2242–46.

"Panel Suggests Methods to Avoid Bone Disorder." *The Wall Street Journal,* April 5, 1984.

"Prevention Is the Key to Chronic Back Pain." *The New York Times,* July 10, 1985.

"Reap the Benefits of Good Posture." *New York Daily News,* August 23, 1987.

"A Remedy That Shores Up Those Old, Tired Bones." *Business Week,* November 24, 1986, p. 113.

"Research Suggests Calcium Supplements Fail to Ward Off Bone Disease in Women." *The Wall Street Journal,* July 29, 1986.

Schwartz, Tony. "Ah, My Non-Aching Back." *New York,* March 16, 1987, pp. 44–50.

Shangold, Mona M. "Do Women Require Special Guidelines?" *Sports Medicine Bulletin,* vol. 22, no. 2, 1987, p. 6.

Smith, Everett L., Jr., and John R. Cameron. "Spontaneous Fracture Index, Female Caucasian." Chart, University of Wisconsin, Bone Mineral Laboratory.

"Study Recommends Brief Rest for Back Pain." *The New York Times,* October 26, 1986.

"A Swig of Calcium?" *New York Daily News,* November 30, 1986.

"Theory on Calcium and Bone Loss Is Disputed." *The New York Times,* January 22, 1987.

"Those Ever-Popular Dietary Supplements: Are They Helpful, Harmless or Harmful?" *The New York Times,* February 11, 1987.

"Treating Bone Diseases with Electricity." *The New York Times,* July 29, 1987.

"Try Some Good Old Exercise." *New York Daily News,* January 17, 1987.

"Understanding Back Pain: Recognizing the Symptoms and Relieving the Agony." *The New York Times,* October 7, 1987.

"The Wasting Away of Women's Bones." *New York Daily News,* March 23, 1984.

Chapter 2:
Are You at Risk for Serious Bone Loss?

Alderman, Beth W., et al. "Reproductive History and Postmenopausal Risk of Hip and Forearm Fracture." *American Journal of Epidemiology,* vol. 124, no. 2, 1986, pp. 262–67.

Aloia, John F., et al. "Risk Factors for Postmenopausal Osteoporosis." *American Journal of Medicine,* vol. 78, January 1985, pp. 95–100.

Daniell, Harry W. "Osteoporosis of the Slender Smoker." *Archives of Internal Medicine,* vol. 136, March 1976, pp. 298–304.

Doepel, Laurie K. "Looking at Menopause's Role in Osteoporosis." *Journal of the American Medical Association,* vol. 254, no. 17, November 1, 1985, pp. 2379–80.

Hahn, Theodore J., et al. "Altered Mineral Metabolism in Glucocorticoid-Induced Osteopenia." *Journal of Clinical Investigation,* vol. 64, August 1979, pp. 655–65.

Melton, L. Joseph, III, et al. "Osteoporosis and the Risk of Hip Fracture." *American Journal of Epidemiology,* vol. 124, no. 2, 1986, pp. 254–61.

"Risk Factors in Postmenopausal Osteoporosis." *The Lancet,* June 15, 1985, pp. 1370–72.

Seeman, Ego, et al. "Risk Factors for Spinal Osteoporosis in Men." *American Journal of Medicine,* vol. 75, December 1983, pp. 977–83.

"Skeletons Record the Burdens of Work." *The New York Times,* October 27, 1987.

Zimran, Ari, et al. "Histomorphometric Evaluation of Reversible Heparin-Induced Osteoporosis in Pregnancy." *Archives of Internal Medicine,* vol. 146, February 1986, pp. 386–88.

Chapter 3:
The Principle of Peak Bone Mass

"The Challenge of Osteoporosis." Editorial, *Archives of Physical Medicine and Rehabilitation*, March 1981, pp. 135–37.

Cummings, Steven R. "Epidemiology of Osteoporotic Fractures: Selected Topics." *Report of the Seventh Ross Conference on Medical Research*, Ross Laboratories, Columbus, Ohio, pp. 3–8.

Fardon, David F. *Osteoporosis: Your Head Start on the Prevention and Treatment of Brittle Bones*. New York: Macmillan, 1985.

Johnston, C. Conrad, Jr. "Method of Osteoporosis." *Current Therapy*. Edited by Howard F. Conn, M.D., W.B. Saunders Company: Upper Montclair, New Jersey, 1975, pp. 458–60.

Notelovitz, Morris, and Marsha Ware. *Stand Tall! The Informed Woman's Guide to Preventing Osteoporosis*. Gainesville, Florida: Triad Publishing, 1982.

"The Osteoporotic Syndromes." *Cecil Textbook of Medicine*, Fifteenth Edition, W.B. Saunders Company: Upper Montclair, New Jersey, 1975, pp. 2242–46.

Riggs, B. Lawrence, and L. Joseph Melton III. "Involutional Osteoporosis." *New England Journal of Medicine*, vol. 314, no. 26, June 26, 1986, pp. 1676–184.

Riggs, R.L., et al. "Changes in Bone Mineral Density of the Proximal Femur and Spine with Aging." *Journal of Clinical Investigation*, vol. 70, October 1982, pp. 716–23.

Silber, Tomas J. "Osteoporosis in Anorexia Nervosa." *New England Journal of Medicine*, vol. 312, no. 15, April 11, 1985, pp. 990–91.

Stevenson, John C., and Iain MacIntyre. "Prevention of Postmenopausal Osteoporosis." *The Lancet*, August 10, 1985, pp. 334–35.

Chapter 4:
Exercise: The First Answer to Osteoporosis

Aloia, John F. "Exercise and Skeletal Health." *Journal of the American Geriatric Society*, vol. XXIX, no. 3, 1981, pp. 104–07.

————. "Prevention of Involutional Bone Loss by Exercise." *Annals of Internal Medicine*, vol. 89, no. 3, September 1978, pp 356–58.

Block, Jon E., et al. "Does Exercise Prevent Osteoporosis?" *Journal of the American Medical Association*, vol. 257, no. 22, June 12, 1987, pp. 3115–17.

Cauley, Jane A., et al. "Comparison of Methods to Measure Physical

Activity in Postmenopausal Women." *American Journal of Clinical Nutrition*, vol. 45, 1987, pp. 14–22.

Kriska, Andrea M., et al. "A Randomized Exercise Trial in Older Women: Increased Activity Over Two Years and the Factors Associated with Compliance." *Medicine and Science in Sports and Exercise*, vol. 18, no. 5, 1985, pp. 557–62.

Krolner, Bjorn, et al. "Physical Exercise as Prophylaxis Against Involutional Vertebral Bone Loss: A Controlled Trial." *Clinical Science*, vol. 64, 1983, pp. 541–46.

Lane, Nancy E., et al. "Long-Distance Running, Bone Density, and Osteoarthritis." *Journal of the American Medical Association*, vol. 255, no. 9, March 7, 1986, pp. 1147–51.

Lindberg, Jill S., et al. "Increased Vertebral Bone Mineral in Response to Reduced Exercise in Amenorrheic Runners." *Western Journal of Medicine*, vol. 146, no. 1, January 1987, pp. 218–19.

"Long Swims, Strong Bones." *American Health*, June 1987, p. 42.

"Medical Researchers Issue New Warnings on Heavy Exercise." *The Wall Street Journal*, February 3, 1984.

Nelson, Miriam E., et al. "Diet and Bone Status in Amenorrheic Runners." *American Journal of Clinical Nutrition*, vol. 43, June 1986, pp. 910–16.

"Osteoporosis Prophylaxis in a Postmastectomy Patient." Questions and Answers section, *Journal of the American Medical Association*, vol. 248, no. 9, September 3, 1982, pp. 1108–09.

Rigotti, Nancy A., et al. "Osteopenia and Bone Fractures in a Man with Anorexia Nervosa and Hypogonadism." *Journal of the American Medical Association*, vol. 256, no. 3, July 18, 1986, pp. 385–88.

"Running—Good for Your Bones." *Running & FitNews*, vol. 4, no. 7, July 1986, pp. 1–7.

Smith, Everett, Jr., et al. "Physical Activity and Calcium Modalities for Bone Mineral Increase in Aged Women." *Medicine and Science in Sports and Exercise*, vol. 13, no. 1, 1981, pp. 60–64.

Chapter 7:
The Promise of Estrogen Replacement

"Correspondence—Fractures and Estrogen." *New England Journal of Medicine*, vol. 304, no. 13, March 26, 1981, pp. 787–88.

"Correspondence—Treatment of Osteoporosis." *New England Journal of Medicine*, vol. 312, no. 10, March 7, 1985, p. 647.

"Data Back Estrogen Therapy." *The New York Times,* April 30, 1987.

"Dozens of Factors Critical in Bone Loss Among Elderly." *The New York Times,* February 17, 1987.

"Estrogen and Osteoporosis." *Group Practice News,* April–May 1987.

"Estrogen Is Advised as Help for Heart." *New York Daily News,* April 30, 1987.

"Estrogens for Osteoporosis." *FDA Drug Bulletin,* vol. 16, no. 1, June 1986, pp. 5–6.

Goldin, Barry R., et al. "Estrogen Excretion Patterns and Plasma Levels in Vegetarian and Omnivorous Women." *New England Journal of Medicine,* vol. 307, no. 25, December 16, 1982, pp. 1542–47.

Heaney, Robert P., et al. "Menopausal Changes in Calcium Balance Performance." *Journal of Laboratory Clinical Medicine,* December 1978, pp. 953–63.

"A Lack of Estrogens, Not of Calcium, Is the Leading Cause of Osteoporosis in Women." *The New York Times,* February 25, 1987.

MacMahon, Brian, et al. "Cigarette Smoking and Urinary Estrogens." *New England Journal of Medicine,* vol. 307, no. 17, Oct. 21, 1982, pp. 1062–65.

"New Comforts for Old Bones." *Newsweek,* September 17, 1984, p. 79.

"Osteoporosis: Current Concepts." *Report of the Seventh Ross Conference on Medical Research.* Ross Laboratories, Columbus, Ohio, pp. 5–8.

Riggs, B. Lawrence, and L. Joseph Melton III. "Involutional Osteoporosis." *New England Journal of Medicine,* vol. 314, no. 26, June 26, 1986, pp. 1676–86.

Chapter 8:
The New Secret Weapons
of Drug and Hormone Therapy

Anderson, C., et al. "Preliminary Observations of a Form of Coherence Therapy for Osteoporosis." *Calcified Tissue International,* 1984, pp. 341–43.

Coindre, Jean-Michel, et al. "Bone Loss in Hypothyroidism with Hormone Replacement." *Archives of Internal Medicine,* vol. 146, January 1986, pp. 48–53.

Frey, Harald. "Fluoride in the Treatment of Osteoporosis." Editorial, *Acta Medica Scandinavica,* vol. 220, 1986, pp. 193–94.

Frost, H.M. "Treatment of Osteoporosis by Manipulation of Coherent Bone Cell Populations." *Clinical Orthopaedics and Related Research,* no. 143, September 1979, pp. 227–44.

Johnston, C. Conrad, Jr. "Method of Osteoporosis." *Current Therapy.* Edited by Howard F. Conn, M.D., W.B. Saunders Company: Upper Montclair, New Jersey, 1975, pp. 458–60.

"Newfound Hormone Regulates Calcium." *Insight,* August 24, 1987, p. 48.

Pak, Charles Y.C., et al. "Attainment of Therapeutic Fluoride Levels in Serum Without Major Side Effects Using a Slow-Release Preparation of Sodium Fluoride in Postmenopausal Osteoporosis." *Journal of Bone and Mineral Research,* vol. 1, no. 6, 1986, pp. 563–71.

————. "A Safe and Effective Treatment of Primary Osteoporosis by Intermittent Application of Slow-Release Sodium Fluoride: Augmentation of Vertebral Bone Mass and Inhibition of Fractures." Center on Mineral Metabolism and Clinical Research, Department of Internal Medicine, and Division of Orthopedic Surgery, Department of Surgery, University of Texas Health Science Center at Dallas, Texas, pp. 1–26.

Rasmussen, H., et al. "Effect of Combined Therapy with Phosphate and Calcitonin on Bone Volume in Osteoporosis." *Metabolic Bone Disease and Related Research,* vol. 2, 1980, pp. 107–11.

Riggs, B. Lawrence, et al. "Effect of the Fluoride/Calcium Regimen on Vertebral Fracture Occurrence in Postmenopausal Osteoporosis." *New England Journal of Medicine,* vol. 306, no. 8, February 25, 1982, pp. 446–50.

Riggs, B. Lawrence, and L. Joseph Melton III. "Involutional Osteoporosis." *New England Journal of Medicine,* vol. 314, no. 26, June 26, 1986, pp. 1676–84.

Simonen, Olli, and Ossi Laitinen. "Does Fluoridation of Drinking-Water Prevent Bone Fragility and Osteoporosis?" *The Lancet,* August 24, 1985, pp. 432–33.

Slovik, David M., et al. "Restoration of Spinal Bone in Osteoporotic Men by Treatment with Human Parathyroid Hormone (1-34) and 1,25-Dihydroxyvitamin D." *Journal of Bone and Mineral Research,* vol. 1, no. 4, 1986, pp. 377–81.

"Those Needy Bones Can Put on Mass." *Insight,* July 13, 1987, p. 53.

Williams, Ann R., et al. "Effect of Weight, Smoking, and Estrogen Use on the Risk of Hip and Forearm Fractures in Postmenopausal

Women." *Obstetrics and Gynecology,* vol. 60, no. 6, December 1982, pp. 695–99.

Chapter 9:
The Tough Bone Diet Program

"Bone Up on Calcium!" Guideline based on data in *Agriculture Handbooks,* nos. 8 and 456.

"Calcium Update." *Dairy Council Digest,* vol. 58, no. 3, May–June 1987, pp. 13–18.

Freudenheim, Jo L., et al. "Relationship Between Usual Nutrient Intake and Bone-mineral Content of Women 35–65 Years of Age: Longitudinal and Cross-sectional Analysis 1–4." *American Journal of Clinical Nutrition,* vol. 44, 1986, pp. 1863–76.

Goldin, Barry R., et al. "Estrogen Excretion Patterns and Plasma Levels in Vegetarian and Omnivorous Women." *New England Journal of Medicine,* vol. 307, no. 25, December 16, 1982, pp. 1542–47.

"High Calcium Diet Plan." Carnation Healthcare Services, Los Angeles, California.

"Moderation Saves Bones." *American Health,* July 1987, p. 134.

Nelson, Miriam E., et al. "Diet and Bone Status in Amenorrheic Runners." *American Journal of Clinical Nutrition,* vol. 43, June 1986, pp. 910–16.

"Nutritional Assessment . . . Looking for Clues." *Nutrition Times,* vol. 1, no. 3, August 1986, pp. 1–8.

"Osteoporosis." *Health Waves,* vol. 1, no. 4, fall 1985, pp. 6–11.

"Osteoporosis: Is It in Your Future?" Informational Guide from Marion Laboratories, Kansas City, Missouri, March 1985, pp. 1–16.

"Over 206 Reasons to Recommend Dairy Calcium." Advertisement, 1987, National Dairy Board, PSM 4/87.

Pak, Charles Y. C., et al. "Nutrition and Metabolic Bone Disease." *Nutritional Diseases: Research Directions in Comparative Pathobiology,* Alan R. Liss, Inc., 1986, pp. 215–40.

Pak, Charles Y. C. "Nutrition and Metabolic Bone Disease with Special Emphasis on the Role of Calcium." Medical Grand Rounds, Southwestern Medical School, University of Texas Health Science Center at Dallas, March 6, 1986, pp. 1–22.

Raeburn, Paul. "The Stone-Age Diet." *American Health,* July 1987, pp. 70–76.

Sutnick, Mona R. "Nutrition: Calcium, Cholesterol, and Calories."

Medical Clinics of North America, vol. 71, no. 1, January 1987, pp. 123–34.

"Very-Low-Calorie Diets and Cardiac Dysfunction." *Nutrition & the M.D.: A Continuing Education Service for Physicians & Nutritionists,* vol. 13, no. 6, June 1987, p. 1.

Chapter 10:
Do Calcium Supplements Work?

Aurbach, G.D. "Parathyroid Hormone and Calcitonin." *Cecil Textbook of Medicine,* Fifteenth Edition, W.B. Saunders Company: Upper Montclair, New Jersey, 1975, pp. 2213–14.

"Buying Guide: Calcium Supplements." University of California, Berkeley, *Wellness Letter,* November 1986.

"Calcium Alone May Not Stop Brittle Bones." *USA Today,* July 31, 1986, p. 1.

"Calcium, Estrogens, and Postmenopausal Osteoporosis." *Internal Medicine Alert,* vol. 9, no. 3, February 13, 1987, pp. 9–12.

"Calcium: Oversold." *Harvard Medical School Health Letter,* Department of Continuing Education, Harvard Medical School, Boston, Massachusetts, April 1987, pp. 1–2.

"Calcium Update." *Dairy Council Digest,* vol. 58, no. 3, May–June 1987, pp. 13–18.

"Dietary Calcium and Blood Pressure." *Running & FitNews,* vol. 5, no. 7, July 1987, p. 1.

"Dietary Calcium and Colonic Cancer." *New England Journal of Medicine,* vol. 314, no. 21, May 22, 1986, pp. 1388–89.

Ettinger, Bruce, et al. "Postmenopausal Bone Loss Is Prevented by Treatment with Low-Dosage Estrogen with Calcium." *Annals of Internal Medicine,* vol. 106, no. 1, January 1987, pp. 40–45.

Harvey, J.A., et al. "Dose Dependency of Calcium Absorption: A Comparison of Calcium Carbonate and Calcium Citrate." *Journal of Bone and Mineral Research.* Accepted for publication, 1988.

Heaney, Robert P., et al. "Calcium Nutrition and Bone Health in the Elderly." *American Journal of Clinical Nutrition,* vol. 36, November 1982, pp. 986–1013.

Heaney, Robert P. "Calcium Therapy in Osteoporosis." *Bone Loss: A Clinical Update on Osteoporosis.* New York: Biomedical Information Corporation, vol. 1, no. 4, 1979, pp. 1–4.

———. "Premenopausal Prophylactic Calcium Supplementation." Questions and Answers, *Journal of the American Medical Association*, vol. 245, no. 13, April 3, 1981, p. 1362.

Johnston, C. Conrad, Jr. "Osteoporosis." *Current Therapy*. Edited by Howard F. Conn, M.D., W.B. Saunders Company: Upper Montclair, New Jersey, 1975, pp. 458–60.

Lindberg, Jill S., et al. "Increased Vertebral Bone Mineral in Response to Reduced Exercise in Amenorrheic Runner." *New England Journal of Medicine*, vol. 146, no. 1, January 1987, p. 39.

Pak, Charles Y. C. "Nutrition and Metabolic Bone Disease with Special Emphasis on the Role of Calcium." Medical Grand Rounds, Southwestern Medical School, University of Texas Health Science Center at Dallas, March 6, 1986, pp. 1–22.

"Prevention and Treatment of Postmenopausal Osteoporosis." *The Medical Letter on Drugs and Therapeutics*, vol. 29 (issue 746), August 14, 1987, pp. 75–77.

Prevention Report ("Abstracts"). Public Health Service, U.S. Department of Health and Human Services, Switzer Building, Room 2132, June 1987.

Riggs, B. Lawrence. "Session IV—Calcium." Draft, pp. 1–4.

Riis, Bente, et al. "Does Calcium Supplementation Prevent Postmenopausal Bone Loss?" *New England Journal of Medicine*, vol. 316, no. 4, January 22, 1987, pp. 173–78.

Smith, Everett L., Jr., et al. "Physical Activity and Calcium Modalities for Bone Mineral Increase in Aged Women." *Medicine and Science in Sports and Exercise*, vol. 13, no. 1, 1981, pp. 60–64.

"Straight Talk About Calcium and Your Body Language." Free supplement, Associated Milk Producers, Arlington, Texas, 1985.

Sutnick, Mona R. "Nutrition: Calcium, Cholesterol, and Calories." *The Postmenopausal Woman*, vol. 71, no. 1, January 1987, pp. 123–34.

Tiegs, Robert D., et al. "Calcitonin Secretion in Postmenopausal Osteoporosis." *New England Journal of Medicine*, vol. 312, no. 17, April 25, 1985, pp. 1097–1100.

Chapter 11:
How Can You Be Tested for Osteoporosis?

Abbasi, Rafat, and Gary D. Hodgen. "Predicting the Predisposition to Osteoporosis." *Journal of the American Medical Association*, vol. 255, no. 12, March 28, 1986, pp. 1600–1604.

"Bone Mineral Screening for Osteoporosis." Correspondence, *New*

England Journal of Medicine, vol. 317, no. 5, July 30, 1987, pp. 315–16.

"Densitometry of the Peripheral Skeleton to Detect Osteopenia." Letters to the Editor, *Journal of the American Medical Association*, vol. 255, no. 16, April 25, 1986, pp. 2162–63.

Genant, Harry K., et al. "Diagnosis and Assessment of Osteoporosis Using Quantitative CT." *Applied Radiology*, August 1987, pp. 55–61.

Hall, Ferris M., et al. "Sounding Board: Bone Mineral Screening for Osteoporosis." *New England Journal of Medicine*, vol. 316, no. 4, June 22, 1987, pp. 212–14.

"Involutional Osteoporosis." Correspondence, *New England Journal of Medicine*, vol. 316, no. 4, January 22, 1987, pp. 215–17.

Lane, J.M., et al. "Osteoporosis: Current Diagnosis and Treatment." *Geriatrics*, vol. 39, no. 4, April 1984, pp. 40–47.

Mazess, Richard B., and J.R. Cameron. "Densitometry of Appendicular Bone in Osteoporosis." Letters to the Editor, *Journal of the American Medical Association*, vol. 254, no. 14, October 11, 1985, p. 1906.

"The Osteoporosis Fracture Threshold." *Southern Medical Journal*, March 1987.

Podenphant, Jan, et al. "Serum Bone GLA Protein and Other Biochemical Estimates of Bone Turnover in Early Postmenopausal Women during Prophylactic Treatment for Osteoporosis." *Acta Medica Scandinavica*, vol. 218, 1985, pp. 329–33.

"Screening for Osteoporosis." *Internal Medicine Alert, A Semi-monthly Survey of Current Development in Internal Medicine*, vol. 8, no. 13, July 15, 1986, pp. 49–51.

Chapter 12:
Why You Should Watch What You Drink

Bikle, Daniel D., et al. "Bone Disease in Alcohol Abuse." *Annals of Internal Medicine*, vol. 103, no. 1, 1985, pp. 42–48.

Turner, Russell T., et al. "Demonstration That Ethanol Inhibits Bone Matrix Synthesis and Mineralization in the Rat." *Journal of Bone and Mineral Research*, vol. 2, no. 1, 1987, pp. 61–66.

Chapter 13:
Why Smoking Will Put You at Risk

"Cigarette Smoking and Bone Loss During Hormone Replacement

After Menopause." Correspondence, *New England Journal of Medicine*, vol. 314, no. 13, March 27, 1986, p. 854.

Daniell, Harry W. "Osteoporosis of the Slender Smoker." *Archives of Internal Medicine*, vol. 136, March 1976, pp. 298–304.

MacMahon, Brian, et al. "Cigarette Smoking and Urinary Estrogens." *New England Journal of Medicine*, vol. 307, no. 17, October 21, 1982, pp. 1062–65.

Michnovicz, Jon J., et al. "Increased 2-Hydroxylation of Estradiol as a Possible Mechanism for the Anti-Estrogenic Effect of Cigarette Smoking." *New England Journal of Medicine*, vol. 315, no. 21, November 20, 1986, pp. 1305–08.

Williams, Ann R., et al. "Effect of Weight, Smoking, and Estrogen Use on the Risk of Hip and Forearm Fractures in Postmenopausal Women." *Obstetrics and Gynecology*, vol. 60, no. 6, December 1982, pp. 695–99.

Chapter 14:
Osteoporosis in Children—
and the Question of Inheritance

Abbasi, Rafat, and Gary D. Hodgen. "Predicting the Predisposition to Osteoporosis." *Journal of the American Medical Association*, vol. 255, no. 12, March 28, 1986, p. 1600.

Dent, C.E., and M. Friedman. "Idiopathic Juvenile Osteoporosis." *Quarterly Journal of Medicine*, new series XXXIV, no. 134, April 1965, pp. 177–210.

"For Children, A Vegetarian Diet May Not Be Harmful, But Must Be Carefully Planned." *The New York Times*, March 23, 1987.

"For Women Who Haven't Gotten the Message Yet: Thin Isn't Necessarily In." *The New York Times*, March 18, 1987.

Horowitz, Michael, et al. "Lactose and Calcium Absorption in Postmenopausal Osteoporosis." *Archives of Internal Medicine*, vol. 147, March 1987, p. 534.

"The Littlest Dieters." *Newsweek*, July 27, 1987, p. 48.

"Nutrition News," *American Health*, July 1987, pp. 134–35.

Warren, Michelle P., et al. "Scoliosis and Fractures in Young Ballet Dancers." *New England Journal of Medicine*, vol. 314, no. 21, May 22, 1986, pp. 1348–53.

Winter, Robert B. "Adolescent Idiopathic Scoliosis." Editorial, *New England Journal of Medicine*, vol. 314, no. 21, May 22, 1986, pp. 1379–80.

Appendix I

Calcium-Rich Foods

Food Group	Amount	Calcium (mg)	Calories	Lactose (gm)
Primary Calcium Sources				
Dairy Group				
Skim milk	8 ounces	300	90	12
2% low-fat milk	8 ounces	300	120	12
1% low-fat milk	8 ounces	300	100	12
Whole milk	8 ounces	290	150	11
Buttermilk	8 ounces	285	100	11
Chocolate milk, whole milk	8 ounces	285	210	12
Nonfat powdered milk	1 tablespoon	52	27	4
Low-fat yogurt, plain	1 cup	415	160	15
Low-fat yogurt, fruited	1 cup	345	230	15
Ricotta cheese, part skim	½ cup	340	170	4
Swiss cheese	1 ounce	270	110	.6
Provolone cheese	1 ounce	214	100	.6
Monterey cheese	1 ounce	212	110	.6
Cheddar cheese	1 ounce	204	115	.6
Gouda cheese	1 ounce	200	100	.6
Colby cheese	1 ounce	195	112	.7
Mozzarella cheese, part-skim	1 ounce	180	70	.8
American cheese	1 ounce	175	110	.5
Mozzarella cheese, whole milk	1 ounce	150	80	.8
Cottage cheese, 2% low-fat	½ cup	80	100	8
Ice milk, soft	½ cup	140	110	5
Ice cream, vanilla, soft	½ cup	90	135	4.5
Ice cream, hardened	½ cup	90	92	5

Food Group	Amount	Calcium (mg)	Calories	Lactose (gm)
Secondary Calcium Sources				
Meat Group				
Sardines (with bones) canned in oil, drained	3 ounces	370	175	0
Salmon (with bones), canned	3 ounces	170	120	0
Oysters, raw	7–9 (½ cup)	115	80	0
Tofu, processed with calcium sulfate	3 ounces	108	60	0
Shrimp, canned	3 ounces	100	100	0
Beans, dried, cooked	1 cup	90	280	0
Fruit/Vegetable Group				
Collards, raw	½ cup	180	30	0
Kale, raw	½ cup	150	30	0
Bok choy	½ cup	125	30	0
Turnip greens, raw	½ cup	125	30	0
Mustard greens	½ cup	100	30	0
Broccoli	½ cup	100	30	0

Appendix II

Calcium-Fortified Products

Food Product	Amount	Calcium (mg)	Calories
Hi-Calcium Vitamin A & D Borden's 2% Fat Milk, (Borden, Inc.)	8 ounces	700	120
Alba Sugar-Free Hot Cocoa Mix	1 envelope	300	60
Alba '77 High Calcium Shake	1 envelope	300	70
Plus Calcium Citrus Hill Orange Juice (Procter and Gamble)	6 ounces	200	90
Minute Maid Orange Juice "Calcium Fortified 100% Orange Juice" (Coca-Cola Foods)	6 ounces	300	90
Gold Medal Flour—All Purpose (General Mills, Inc.)	4 ounces (approximately 1 cup)	200	380
Wholewheat Total Cereal (General Mills, Inc.)	1 ounce (approximately 1 cup)	200	110
Total Corn Flakes (General Mills, Inc.)	1 ounce (approximately 1 cup)	200	110
Total Instant Oatmeal (General Mills, Inc.)	1 ounce	200	90
Hollywood Bread (National Bakers Services, Inc.)	1 slice	150	40
Yoplait Breakfast Lowfat Yogurt (Yoplait USA, Inc.)	6 ounces	500	220

Appendix III

Recipe Analysis
Per Serving

Recipes	Amount	Cal-ories	Cal-cium (mg)	Lac-tose (gm)	Choles-terol (mg)	Exchanges
Cheese Cauliflower Chowder	1 cup	192	459	6.2	11	1 Meat 1 Milk 1 Vegetable
Cream of Corn Soup	1 cup	202	300	8	3	1 Bread 1 Milk 2 Fat
Cream of Tomato Soup	1 cup	154	219	2.5	24	1 Meat 3 Vegetable
French Onion Soup	1 cup	90	99	.4	6	½ Bread 1 Fat ½ Vegetable
Seafood Chowder	1 cup	149	166	4.5	59	1 Milk 1 Meat
Chef's Salad	1 salad	207	236	2.1	27	2 Meat 3 Vegetable
Chicken Salad	1 cup	448	85	4	99	4 Meat 1 Bread 2 Fat
Confetti Cottage Cheese Salad	1 cup	150	125	5	9	1 Meat 1 Milk
Salmon Salad	1 cup	130	140	0	10	1 Meat 2 Vegetable
Cheesy Pita Pocket Sandwich	1 sandwich	225	211	.8	23	1 Bread 1 Meat 1 Vegetable 1 Fat
Chicken Broccoli Casserole	⅙ recipe	214	258	4.5	52	½ Milk 2 Meat 1 Vegetable
Crustless Kale Pie	⅙ pie	186	374	3.4	11	1 Meat ½ Milk 1 Vegetable 1 Fat
Lasagna	⅙ recipe	476	306	2.4	71	2 Meat 2 Fat 1 Vegetable 3 Bread
Meatless Enchiladas	2 enchiladas	453	402	4.4	37	2 Meat 3 Bread 1 Vegetable 2 Fat
Meatless Enchiladas L.R.	2 enchiladas	328	269	3	11	1 Meat 2 Bread 1 Fat

Recipes	Amount	Calories	Calcium (mg)	Lactose (gm)	Cholesterol (mg)	Exchanges
Pizza Olé	⅛ pie	365	348	3.1	30	2 Bread 1 Meat 2 Vegetable 2 Fat
Roni Cheese Bake	1 cup	450	389	3.7	188	2 Meat 2 Bread 2 Vegetable 2 Fat
Tomato Rarebit	⅓ cup	165	277	2.8	9	1 Meat 1 Bread 1 Vegetable
Veggie Burrito	2 burritos	470	438	.7	22	3 Bread 2 Meat 1 Fat
Zucchini Quiche	¼ pie	386	380	1.6	44	2 Bread 1 Fat 3 Vegetable 2 Meat
Fruit à la Yogurt	1 cup	208	250	7.5	7	1 Milk 2 Fruit
Fruit à la Yogurt L.R.	1 cup	172	147	7	3	½ Milk 2½ Fruit
Open-Faced Swiss and Pear Sandwich	1 sandwich	156	216	.6	6	1 Bread 1 Meat 2 Fruit
Sunrise Pancake Stack	1 wedge	236	216	2.5	19	2 Bread 1 Meat ½ Fat
Yogurt and Fruit Parfait	1 cup	160	415	15	18	1 Milk 2 Fruit
Dilly Sauce	½ cup	84	175	6.5	4	1 Milk ½ Fat
Fruited Cocoa	1 cup	153	257	4.5	65	1 Milk 1 Meat
Fruity Milkshake	1 cup	150	202	10	4	½ Milk 2 Fruit
Fruity Milkshake L.R.	1 cup	160	237	4	1	½ Milk 3 Fruit
Orange Frost	1 cup	45	27	.75	0	1½ Fruit
Peachy Fruit Shake	1 cup	120	285	10.5	8	1 Milk 1 Fruit
Pinana Frost	1 cup	100	167	6	3	½ Milk 1½ Fruit
Strawberry Delight	1 cup	165	315	12	5	1 Milk 2 Fruit
Very Fruity Frozen Frappé	1½ cups	266	288	15	30	2 Fruit 1 Fat 1½ Milk
Very Fruity Frozen Frappé L.R.	1½ cups	241	378	4	1	½ Milk 5 Fruit
Calico Cracker Spread	4 tablespoons	64	132	2.2	3	½ Meat ½ Vegetable
Nibbler's Surprise	½ cup	209	270	6.4	33	½ Milk 2 Fat ½ Meat
Rice Pudding	½ cup	99	87	3	85	½ Bread ½ Milk ½ Fat
Skinny Nachos	8 pieces	140	200	.8	16	1 Bread 1 Meat
Yogurt Frozen Treat	1 treat	68	75	2.5	2	½ Milk ¼ Fruit

Appendix IV

Computer Analysis of Sample Menus

Day	Calories	Protein (gm)	Fat (gm)	Carbohydrate (gm)	Calcium (mg)	Cholesterol (mg)
WEEK 1	**1,500-Calorie High-Calcium**					
Monday	1576	71	44	224	1614	50
Tuesday	1558	68	46	218	1528	107
Wednesday	1543	87	43	202	1267	133
Thursday	1632	80	48	220	1183	378
Friday	1582	80	46	212	1695	80
Saturday	1635	74	51	220	1491	338
Sunday	1620	80	36	244	1812	152
Average	1593	77 (19%)	45 (25%)	220 (56%)	1513	177
WEEK 2	**1,500-Calorie High-Calcium**					
Monday	1770	79	66	215	1496	146
Tuesday	1345	69	41	175	1607	250
Wednesday	1575	90	47	198	1394	289
Thursday	1537	92	33	218	1340	141
Friday	1400	79	30	201	1125	78
Saturday	1531	90	47	187	1514	175
Sunday	1486	72	46	196	1215	131
Average	1520	82 (22%)	44 (26%)	199 (52%)	1384	173
WEEK 1	**2,200-Calorie High-Calcium**					
Monday	2476	117	64	358	1486	409
Tuesday	2378	105	70	332	2264	173
Wednesday	2207	116	67	285	1578	221
Thursday	2222	100	54	334	2224	69
Friday	2452	132	72	319	2759	125
Saturday	1988	95	72	240	1662	356
Sunday	2366	121	70	313	2114	206
Average	2299	112 (19%)	67 (26%)	313 (54%)	2012	222

Day	Calories	Protein (gm)	Fat (gm)	Carbohydrate (gm)	Calcium (mg)	Cholesterol (mg)
WEEK 2 2,200-Calorie High-Calcium						
Monday	2037	100	61	272	1944	147
Tuesday	2296	129	76	274	2100	528
Wednesday	2037	116	45	292	1518	204
Thursday	2292	115	52	341	1436	129
Friday	2513	119	97	291	2369	218
Saturday	2113	114	61	277	1394	206
Sunday	2222	107	78	273	1592	227
Average	2215	113 (20%)	67 (27%)	288 (52%)	1765	237
WEEK 1 1,500-Calorie Lactose-Restricted						
Monday	1427	86	42	176	852	205
Tuesday	1530	57	38	240	1011	103
Wednesday	1643	85	46	220	1212	399
Thursday	1595	55	55	220	1013	35
Friday	1622	66	38	254	1045	72
Saturday	1573	65	57	200	1140	309
Sunday	1486	73	42	204	1209	116
Average	1554	70 (18%)	45 (26%)	216 (56%)	1213	177
WEEK 2 1,500-Calorie Lactose-Restricted						
Monday	1567	78	47	208	752	156
Tuesday	1471	63	43	208	1716	66
Wednesday	1547	78	43	212	1190	230
Thursday	1537	82	33	228	851	138
Friday	1633	64	57	216	1439	135
Saturday	1536	84	56	174	1129	210
Sunday	1565	66	53	206	772	107
Average	1549	74 (19%)	47 (27%)	207 (53%)	1121	149
WEEK 1 2,200-Calorie Lactose-Restricted						
Monday	2230	87	46	367	1483	111
Tuesday	2174	87	58	326	962	137
Wednesday	2143	110	59	293	1647	242
Thursday	2271	120	67	297	1383	480
Friday	2262	79	70	329	2384	45
Saturday	2160	91	80	269	1455	343
Sunday	2223	109	59	314	1734	180
Average	2215	98 (18%)	63 (26%)	314 (56%)	1578	220

Day	Calories	Protein (gm)	Fat (gm)	Carbohydrate (gm)	Calcium (mg)	Cholesterol (mg)
WEEK 2	**2,200-Calorie Lactose-Restricted**					
Monday	2188	82	72	298	958	34
Tuesday	2117	102	81	245	1948	110
Wednesday	2156	107	68	279	995	313
Thursday	2123	108	47	317	1430	288
Friday	2259	110	67	304	1200	192
Saturday	2205	97	89	254	1069	209
Sunday	2267	119	71	288	1484	300
Average	2191	104 (19%)	71 (29%)	284 (52%)	1298	207